FIRST LOVE

MARIA DIBATTISTA

# *first love*

## THE AFFECTIONS OF

## MODERN FICTION

THE UNIVERSITY OF CHICAGO PRESS

*Chicago and London*

MARIA DIBATTISTA, professor of English and comparative literature at Princeton University, is the author of *Virginia Woolf's Major Novels: The Fables of Anon*.

This publication has been supported by a grant from the National Endowment for the Humanities, an independent federal agency.

The University of Chicago Press, Chicago 60637
The University of Chicago Press, Ltd., London
© 1991 by The University of Chicago
All rights reserved. Published 1991
Printed in the United States of America
00 99 98 97 96 95 94 93 92 91   5 4 3 2 1

Library of Congress Cataloging-in-Publication Data

DiBattista, Maria, 1947–
   First love : the affections of modern fiction / Maria DiBattista.
      p.   cm.
   Includes bibliographical references and index.
   ISBN 0-226-14498-4 (acid-free paper)
   1. English fiction—20th century—History and criticism.   2. Love
in literature.   3. Hardy, Thomas, 1840–1928—Criticism and
interpretation.   4. Lawrence, D. H. (David Herbert), 1885–1930—
Criticism and interpretation.   5. Joyce, James, 1882–1941—
Criticism and interpretation.   6. Beckett, Samuel, 1906–   —
Fictional works.   7. Modernism (Literature)—Great Britain.
8. First loves in literature.   I. Title.
PR888.L69D5   1991
823'.91209354—dc20                                                    90-46356
                                                                            CIP

⊚ The paper used in this publication meets the minimum requirements of the American National Standard for Information Sciences—Permanence of Paper for Printed Library Materials, ANSI Z39.48-1984.

*For my sons*
*Daniel and Matthew*

# CONTENTS

# ACKNOWLEDGMENTS

T
HOUGH I CAN only give brief mention to the friends and colleagues who discussed *First Love* with me over the many years of its writing—Margaret Doody, Paul Fry, David Quint, Esther Schor, P. Adams Sitney, Eric Santner, and Froma Zeitlin—my debt to them is inestimable. Their conversation, advice, and encouragement helped make this work a less lonely and, I hope, more interesting one. I am grateful to Sam Hynes and Uli Knoepflmacher, who read the book in its early and middle stages and offered honest and timely suggestions that helped me bring the work to completion. Particular thanks go to Robert Polhemus and George Levine for their careful criticism of the completed manuscript and suggestions for improvement, all of which I have tried to follow. No one could ask for a more sympathetic reader nor a more generous friend than David Bromwich. My intellectual debt to him extends beyond this work, but I would like to thank him here for the specific suggestions and general support he offered throughout the writing of this book. Two special friends, Suzanne Nash and Brigitte Peucker, could always be relied upon to listen patiently to my thoughts, to belittle my doubts, and to lift my spirits. I am also indebted to Laura Cowan, Lisa Ekstrom, and Wendy Zierler for their assistance in researching *First Love,* and for taking the initiative in seeking out new works and unforeseen connections that later shaped my thinking. I have been extremely fortunate to have had Salena Fuller Krug as a manuscript editor. Her comments and corrections were exacting, astute and unfailingly intelligent. And to Alan Thomas, my editor, special thanks are due for waiting patiently for the manuscript and never losing faith in this project. Finally, my sons, Daniel and Matthew, were more goodnatured than anyone had a right to expect in putting up with their often harried and frequently distracted mother. I dedicate this work to them, in gratitude for suspending their judgment on First Love, at least until the day they will experience it for themselves. Then, I trust, life will teach them better than this book ever could.

Princeton, 1990

# THE "ADVENTURE" OF
# FIRST LOVE

*. . . la première (quel mot terrible!)*
Stendhal, *Le Rouge et le Noir*

EVERYONE, if the testimony of literature, the confidences of friends, and the lore of personal experience are to be believed, remembers his or her first love. That this memory of love vividly endures, while others may fade, seems connected to our recognizing in it all the qualities peculiar to a first as opposed to any successive love. The first, as Stendhal, inimitable chronicler of love, remarks, is charged with a terrible but charismatic authority. It is one of those primal words that summon the great antitheses of life from their lurking places in the interstices of uneventful, habitual life: dread and desire, rapture and despair, chance and necessity, blind contingency and blinding grace. The First comprehends all the risk as well as all the wonder of an unprecedented, yet often long anticipated, encounter with the mysterious powers and imperious feelings that create and command Reality.

It is my argument that First Love represents one of the primal forms of that modern adventure which the great Victorian realists called "beginning the world." Indeed it is my claim that the essential nature of the adventure as the advent of some new feeling, force, or individual capable of revolutionizing the old, customary orders of life is epitomized in the radical narratives of First Love. These narratives condense two terrible meanings of the First: chronological priority and emotional or spiritual precedence. Chronological priority implicates us in all the mysteries of how the undifferentiated sequence of days—the "natural continuity" of life that submerges all conscious awareness of discontinuous development and inner transformations—can assume the fateful shape of a narrative. The emotional or spiritual precedence of the First involves us in the deeper problem of estimating the value of experience, of assigning order and conferring precedence to the sundry loves and keener sublimities that compose human life.

I have called First Love an "adventure," adopting the usage proposed by Georg Simmel in his luminous essay, "The Adventurer." "Something becomes an adventure," writes Simmel, "only by virtue of two conditions: that it itself is a specific organization of some significant meaning with a beginning and an end;

and that, despite its accidental nature, its extraterritoriality with respect to the continuity of life, it nevertheless connects with the character and identity of the bearer of that life—that it does so in the widest sense, transcending, by a mysterious necessity, life's more narrowly rational aspects."[1] The form and the meaning of an adventure are reciprocally determined by its specific organization as *narrative*. What makes First Love at once a paradigmatic and unique adventure is that its significant meaning entails an appreciation of beginning itself— what it means for something or someone to come first. In developing this meaning, First Love discloses the inner nature of the adventurer in his initial encounter with all those powers and potencies of the world that may either abet or vanquish his heroic exertions to create his incomparable, that is, singular, fate.

Simmel's insight that a mysterious necessity conducts the adventurer to a realm of existence that transcends the rational limits of life has been neglected by much recent criticism of the novel, which generally portrays the great subjective forces that shape the destiny of the novelistic "character" as exhibiting the general laws governing desire,[2] but never the fatefulness specific to a concrete love or definite affection. My study regards first affections, these primary and primal feelings, as the mysterious necessity that dictates the obsessive themes and original forms which give to modern fiction its distinct and problematic identity. The adventure of First Love marks the initial and dramatic conjunction of the two great forces that define human life: the objective, material determinants of individual existence (the "accidents" of birth and class placement, the play of chance and the rule of social conventions), and the subjective powers and potencies (desire, dream, the creative will) whose unique combinations constitute an inward necessity. As Simmel explains:

> For by adventure we always mean a third something, neither the sheer, abrupt event whose meaning—a mere given—simply remains outside us nor the consistent sequence of life in which every element supplements every other toward an inclusively integrated meaning. The adventure is no mere hodgepodge of these two, but rather that incomparable experience which can be interpreted only as a particular encompassing of the accidentally external by the internally necessary.[3]

First Love constitutes the "incomparable experience" in which the random contingencies and the specific historical conditions of human life are seized by subjective necessity as the very material and inspiration for a life-narrative. Simmel himself not only recognized the natural affinity between the love affair and the adventure, but emphasized their paradigmatic identity: "A love affair contains in clear association the two elements which the form of the adventure characteristically conjoins: conquering force and unextortable concession, winning by one's own abilities and dependence on the luck which something incalculable outside ourselves bestows on us."[4] As we shall soon see, First Love constitutes the decisive occasion when inner determinations are converted into fateful acts and their necessary consequences. Yet we shall also come to understand that not all First Loves merit such narrative unfolding. For it is not erotic content alone, but, as Simmel insists, *the form of experiencing,*[5] that marks the "specific nature and charm" of the adventure in love. Without this entrancing, life-shaping form, there is no narrative; only, perhaps, that life-fragment which intermittently sparks a fond or melancholy remembrance. In such instances, First Love assumes the partial form of youthful anecdote or inconsequential episode, possessed of all the charm but none of the terrible force of the fateful event that alone determines even as it discloses an inviolable identity.

If I were pressed to isolate a paradigmatic "novelistic" occasion when First Love emerges as a legitimate *problem* for a nascent modern consciousness, I would invoke the moment Emma Woodhouse, that restless fictionalizer, discovers the mysterious necessity that has reigned, unacknowledged and till now unknown, in the unvisited depths of her own heart: "Till now that she was threatened with its loss, Emma had never known how much of her happiness depended on being *first* with Mr. Knightley, first in interest and affection.— Satisfied that it was so, and feeling it her due, she had enjoyed it without reflection; and only in the dread of being supplanted, found how inexpressibly important it had been."[6] For Emma, the status of being first is everywhere consistent with itself. Affection concurs with interest; chronological, social, and emotional priority coincide rather than conflict with each other. This knowledge is what centers her (some might feel *confines* her) in Hartfield, that domain of domestic affections which is entirely congruent with her inner urgings toward self-assertion and social command. Neither distance nor division disturbs the emotional solidarities of Austen's symbolic geography, which figures the spheres of affective life (the "heart's field") and social existence (Highbury) as concentric, rather than eccentric, circles. Emma will end the novel in secure possession of Hartfield (indeed she will never vacate it) and of social eminence in Highbury. The novel's opening description of its heroine as handsome, clever, and rich anticipates this remarkable grace of consolidations. Indeed we might say that both the measure and the proof of Emma's graced existence is that she did not know her heart constituted a riddle until she had solved its mystery.

But though Emma becomes aware of the riddle of the first only when she has found its answer, she cannot completely dispel the "dread" that accompanies her nascent awareness of the mystery posed by first affections—the dread of finding oneself at once emotionally bereft and historically belated. The dread of being supplanted and the fear of loss are symptoms of a larger anxiety, one specific to modernity. It is a dread that the inexpressible but essential truth of her feeling might have languished and disappeared in silence. The expression of feeling is not a grace to be bestowed, but a task to be performed, a matter of self-obligation rather than of erotic or social entitlement.

Emma's dread thus generates a series of vexing social questions and metaphysical perplexities: "Was it new for any thing in this world to be unequal, inconsistent, incongruous—or for chance and circumstance (as second causes) to direct the human fate?" (284). Though the possibility that human existence is not providentially ordered, but arbitrarily and unequally arranged, is not a new thought, it appears to be so to a consciousness newly awakened to reflect on itself and the grounds of its own happiness. In such self-reflections, the mystery of human fate is posed in a specific form—the riddle of the first. This riddle can be formulated only according to the modern perspective of belatedness. It is from this emotional perspective, whose vanishing point defines the horizon of human fate, that we can determine the extent to which our destiny is inwardly determined (a function of what we feel is our due; what, that is, we deserve if there be any justice in the apportioning of human destinies) and the extent to which it is outwardly conditioned (by chance and circumstance, the second or contingent causes of human fate).

The riddle that Emma need only acknowledge and decipher at the end of the novel is the living reality of Anne Elliot's existence. Austen's last work, *Persuasion,* dramatizes the inequality, inconsistency, and incongruity of human destinies by giving us a heroine, Anne Elliot, who is deprived of Emma's graced existence. Anne begins the novel at the point Emma had narrowly averted— with the recognition that her first love has been lost to her. She endures, until the final reconciliation, the heart-wrenching conviction that she has been either forgotten or supplanted in Wentworth's affections. Chance and circumstance are figured as the persuasions to which Anne has understandably but regrettably succumbed, understandable because of her youth, regrettable because in submitting to worldly counsel she has forfeited what was her due—being first in someone's interest and affection. Anne is the heroine who suffers the indignities of those who seem doomed to occupy neither first nor even second, but *no* place in the heart of those closest to her: "her word had no weight; her convenience was always to give way;—she was only Anne."[7] In *Persuasion*, First Love must reassert itself, challenging the temporal reality and combating the emotional depression of belatedness, which is figured as Anne initially appearing to us a heroine whose *time for adventure has passed*. Her emotional peril is literally presented to us as the danger of being written out of the Baronetage, the "book" of life jealously and snobbishly esteemed by her father. Her birth is recorded, but is attended by no further entries, no evidence of ongoing, eventful life. Anne's anxiety about what is to be written of her life consorts with her later outburst that "Men have had every advantage of us in telling their own story" (237). Emma is never reluctant to produce her own stories, because self-mastery, a prerogative of her class as much as a disposition of her temperament, is not perceived as a desirable ideal, but as an actual attribute of her life. Moreover, Emma is never dispossessed of her conviction that circumstances are but secondary causes to the primary determinations of her will.

*Persuasion* is a more "modern" text in concerning itself with a self-loss that is not, as in *Emma*, a "gentle sorrow," but a mortifying reduction to the "art of knowing our own nothingness beyond our own circle" (69). To make something out of nothing Anne must recapture the First Love and assume the authorship of her own happiness. For though she is past the age of blushing, Anne, as we witness when she encounters Wentworth after eight years, is not beyond the age of emotion.

> Eight years, almost eight years had passed, since all had been given up. How absurd to be resuming the agitation which such an interval had banished into distance and indistinctness! What might not eight years do? Events of every description, changes, alienations, removals,—all, all must be comprised in it; and oblivions of the past—how natural, how certain too! It included nearly a third part of her own life.
>
> Alas! With all her reasonings, she found that to retentive feelings eight years may be little more than nothing. (85)

Here we behold the mysterious inner necessity of First Love, the imperious desire that can surmount, to the point of abolishing, the irreversible sequence of days that comprises all species of change—from gradual and almost imperceptible alterations to the most dramatic "alienations and removals." The "retentive feelings" of the first time endure against the persuasions of reason, which counsels that diminishment and eventual oblivion is the certain fate of even the most passionate, heartfelt emotions. We shall see how First Love, in insisting on its own temporality, redefines the relation of time to emotion, forges the great counternarrative that transcends, as Simmel remarks, "life's more narrowly rational aspects."

As Austen suggests, the modern "myth" of First Love emerges and persists during a time of profound historical changes and dislocations—those events of every description, alterations, upheavals, alienations, removals, that are "inevitably" at work in transforming the traditional orders of life. If chance and circumstances may be said, as they are by Austen, to be the second causes of human happiness, we might suggest the first causes that alternately oppose and embolden the retentive power of our first and abiding love: the collapse of status society and the radical alterations of an emerging industrial, capitalist order that encourage, when they do not directly promote, erotic and marital alliances beyond one's appointed station in life; the romantic "discovery" of dissociated states of feeling that distance the promptings of the heart from the rational principles traditionally espoused as the ground of all right conduct; the rise of the feminist movement, which unsettled conventional ideas of the sex-relation and reshaped the very ideals of human union, new ideals whose attainment would henceforth constitute human happiness. I have chosen to describe these causes through their direct and displaced effects—in the idols that First Love creates in response to the social persuasions and historical realities that menaced or disparaged the efforts of modern men and women to become the original authors of their own lives. In First Love that effort commences as a recognizably human adventure into the world and, inevitably, into narrative. As Simmel writes: "When the force which owes its success to itself and gives all conquest of love some note of victory and triumph is then combined with the other note of favor by fate, the constellation of the adventure is, as it were, preformed."[8] In First Love, then, we behold the pre- or Ur-Form of the life-adventure in whose terrible admixtures of conquest and grace the mystery of individual destiny is fatefully represented. First Love is that form of experiencing that links two life-initiating events: the divine visitation of Love and the birth of the artistic vocation. These occurrences are held to be contemporaneous and, as we shall see, are venerated as the origin of "modern" narrative itself.

# FIRST LOVE

> deep as love,
> Deep as first love, and wild with all regret;
> O Death in Life, the days that are no more!

> Tennyson, "Tears, Idle Tears,
> from *The Princess*

> *I associate, rightly or wrongly, my marriage with*
> *the death of my father, in time. That other links*
> *exist, on other levels, between these two affairs*
> *is not impossible. I have enough trouble as it is*
> *in trying to say what I think I know.*

> Beckett, "First Love"

# FIRST AFFECTIONS

WHAT GIVES FIRST LOVE its depth? Why is First Love "deep" enough to contain "all regret"? To pose such questions is already to concede to First Love the fabled lore and emotional power of a human tradition. In our own time, First Love has ceased to be a term designating a novelistic theme and has gained the repute of a subgenre, compiled in "anthologies" of First Love narratives.[1] Not all are susceptible to the charismatic power of this tradition. Some, like Tennyson's Princess, are suspicious of it as a nostalgia for the days that *should* be no more. "Let the past be past," she commands. Verbal fiat, however, is powerless to enforce the emotional disconnection from the past or abolish the prestige of the "first time." For it is not just a vanished time, but a more *vivid* time that Tennyson's lyric bewails, the romantic time of an aroused, entranced, and creative consciousness to whose world-transforming perceptions we commonly give the name of love.

Yet in what appears as an afterthought or apposition, a concession, perhaps, to the mellifluousness of the poetic line, Tennyson reveals that it is not any love, but First Love, that constitutes the poetic past he would recapture. If it were love that was lost, tears might flow, but they would not be characterized as intrinsically idle. A new love might replace the old. Only First Love suffers no repetition, cannot be revived in or over time. When First Love dies, it is buried in an anterior time sealed off and jealously guarded by the boundary god whom the romantics recognized under his psychological and spiritual manifestation, Death-in-Life.

Tennyson's romantic melancholia finds an unlikely comradeship in Beckett's beleaguered ratiocinations. For each, First Love is the original time from which all succeeding times take their measure. Each recounts First Love from the perspective of a troubled present, for Tennyson the sad and strange time of an emotional and narrative impasse, for Beckett the time of a hesitant and confused retrospection. Beckett's narrator reminds us that other links may exist between his father's death and his marriage, that on other levels different and competing myths may be fashioned. I would also forbear to attribute to these first affections what First Love generally claims for itself—precedence in the hierarchy of modern feelings about the world. But like Beckett, I regard First Love a paradigmatic of those life-altering moments in time—bounded by death and initiated by Eros—that transform the undifferentiated sequence of days into a fateful narrative. Beckett's apparently free association actually binds an anxiety about the mysterious relation between Eros, which feels itself to be eternal, to our consciousness of time as an irreversible duration.

It is this anxiety, apparent in all the symptomatic ruptures and discontinuities that formally characterize (some might say afflict) modern narrative, that is "mastered" in the telling of First Love. Like all anxiety effects, First Love narratives, whatever their initial and surface tranquillities, attest to a deep perturbation, a "shock" administered to the self and deranging its ordinary time-space perceptions (what Mikhail Bakhtin calls "chronotopes"). Freud's theory of anxiety was developed to explain the dreams which did not fulfill a wish, but reproduced a traumatic accident or event. In the emotional "logic" of such dreams, Freud deduced, the absence of anxiety led to the traumatic event, and the dream-narrative was deployed to create the anxiety necessary to ward off any future catastrophe.

That love should share the same psychic mechanisms and narrative strategies as fear should not surprise us, since love often mirrors fear in investing overmuch in a single life-altering experience. Here, again, Beckett would seem to be the exception that proves the rule. For Beckett, too, will have his "romances." Even within the hushed interiors of Beckettian consciousness, siren-calls from the outer world manage to penetrate the apparently impermeable shield of consciousness, resonating there, in Hamm's haunting phrase, as "something dripping in my head. A heart, a heart in my head."[2] Some force beckons—or compels—Beckett's solipsists out of the theatrical confines of self. It is the force of Eros, the educative boy-god who leads us out into the realm where the Other—or Others—awaits us. Beckett's sexual satires constitute a peculiar emendation of what I will call, adapting Hardy's neologism, *erotoleptic* narrative, a narrative which represents sexual transport as a literal as well as figurative experience of erotic seizure. Such a characterological reading is forecast and corroborated in the astrological chart of Beckett's first full-fledged creation, Murphy: "Intense Love Nature prominent, rarely suspicioning the Nasty, with inclinations to Purity. When Sensuality rules there is danger of Fits."[3] Murphy's star-sign, the Goat, certifies the Dionysian nature of his seizures. His amatory fits (Murphy suffers from heart attacks, as many as twenty a night!) are symptomatic of the comic Cartesianism that underlies Beckett's representation of Eros as a conductor-god.

In his conduction, Eros can shock and stun the mind as well as convulse the body. Consciousness will respond, as Murphy will in the famous chapter 6, by erecting its own defensive shield against the external stimulus which renders it vulnerable. In his essay "On Some Motifs in Baudelaire," Walter Benjamin remarks that the more efficiently consciousness can shield itself against the direct and unmediated reception of stimuli, "the less do these impressions enter experience (*Erfahrung*), tending to remain in the sphere of a certain hour in one's life (*Erlebnis*)." [4] Benjamin's analysis helps us understand the curious, indeed paradoxical, status of the first time. The rapture of First Love, the sudden cry of profane joy which is its most characteristic—and telling—reflex, is the response to a direct and unmediated "entry into experience." In this initial phase, the heightened stimulus (more poetically termed "love") is precisely what confirms that this moment constitutes an Experience, one that ruthlessly and magnificently annihilates everything not itself.

But one cannot narrate this experience without subjecting it to reflection, that is, to retrospection. First Love, to be told, must be remembered. And it is in this act of remembrance, often commemoration, that it attains its true significance as an experience belonging to a certain hour in one's life. It belongs, that is, to the days that are and can be no more. This is the sad and strange significance of the First regarded as a temporal phenomenon. To tease out this meaning still further, let us return once again to Benjamin's discussion of the power of the shock factor to affect our remembrance of things past:

> Perhaps the special achievement of shock defense may be seen in its function of assigning to an incident a precise point in time in consciousness at the cost of the integrity of its contents. This would be a peak achievement of the intellect; it would turn the incident into a moment that has been lived (*Erlebnis*). Without reflection there would be nothing but the sudden start, usually the sensation of fright which, according to Freud, confirms the failure of the shock defense. [5]

First Love, because it is first, begins without aid of reflection. Its affective reflex is the sudden start, the startling access into feeling. Here the failure of the shock defense enhances rather than detracts from experience. Once subjected to the power of narrative reflection, however, this experience becomes an "incident" assigned, some would say banished, to the realm of the already lived. This particular achievement of the intellect, then, is of a mixed emotional nature. It subdues the "shock" of erotic joy, and so extirpates from consciousness its *defenseless* feelings. Yet the psyche is restored to its integrity only through a loss of warmth. As Origen pointed out in his *Peri Archon, On First Principles,* the word *psyche* is derived from *psychros,* 'cold.' [6]

Coldness is not the impression Benjamin meant to convey in his description of the intellectual "achievement" that converts experience (*Erfahrung*) into "a moment that has been lived" (*Erlebnis,* the time that is no more). He refers, of course, to those influxes that startle and frighten rather than enrapture. Yet pleasure, like pain, can generate anxiety, and necessitate similar mechanisms of defense. First Love attests to the power of Eros to penetrate our defenses, to rend our consciousness and fragment its fragile narcissistic unity. But out of this psychic catastrophe—the "Death-in-Life" that is buried at the heart of all First Love narratives—a "New Life" is born, the life of the artist destined to compose out of the scattered body of his dreams and illusions an enduring image of "totality": the world as a site of fateful relations.

Dante's *La Vita Nuova,* one of the models subjected to Beckett's sardonic parody, instructs us that such a fateful relation is rendered intelligible only as a concordance of narrative beginnings with artistic ends. The opening gesture of *La Vita Nuova* is to mark its own textual origin in First Love: "In that part of the book of my memory before the which is little that can be read, there is a rubric saying, Incipit Vita Nova."[7] For Dante, First Love presents consciousness with its initial text, the book of memory recomposed as artistic autobiography. The New Life begins with the vision of a nine-year-old girl who reveals to the poet "the spirit of life" that will henceforth rule his existence: "Ecce deus fotior me, qui veniens dominabitur mihi" ("Here is a deity stronger than I; who, coming, shall rule over me"). This voice issues from within Dante; Love speaks on behalf of an *inner* determination. This emergence of a lyric voice as a self-consciously *new* expression (the "gentil styl nuovo") is the first and most enduring achievement of First Love. The artist's "inner light" is now empowered as the spiritual cause that can produce material effects. Beatrice, who absorbs this inner light and is herself transfigured by it, becomes, through this act of visionary projection, the site of Dante's narrative as well as spiritual beatitudes. Time and emotion, in the inner combinations devised by the poet's new style, precipitate into a living, organic image. Indeed we might say that Beatrice comes to symbolize the beatitude of the First, of that prime number or chronological priority which confers moral and emotional order to the world. Beatrice personifies the divine universal order fashioned and infused by Love. Dante's faith in Love, the Prime Mover of the spiritual and cosmic orders, must be tested and confirmed before he can arrive at the end in which he will find his true beginning.

*La Vita Nuova* presents this ordeal novelistically; hence our interest in this particular First Love narrative, given new prominence in English literary culture by Dante Gabriel Rossetti's translation. Appearing in 1862, Rossetti's translation and attendant commentary provided a striking countertext to the emergent secular and contractual orders of mercantile capitalism. Gertrude Stein, in one of her "first" literary efforts, *Q.E.D.,* demonstrates, among other things, how

Dante "speaks" to the modern lover. In an apparently random moment, her heroine Adele rereads *Vita Nuova:*

> She lost herself completely in the tale of Dante and Beatrice. She read it with absorbed interest for it seemed now divinely illuminated. She rejoiced abundantly in her new understanding and exclaimed triumphantly "At last I begin to see what Dante is talking about and so there is something in my glimpse and it's alright and worth while" and she felt within herself a great content.[8]

This moment of self-containment or self-contentment (versions of the same joyous feeling of being, being, that is, "alright") comprises both an emotional and temporal plenitude. Adele's "new life" is continuous with Dante's tale of love; her "incipit" ("At last I begin to see . . .") traces her nascent self-knowledge to her "new understanding" of the human tradition devoted to interpreting as well as disseminating the cult of First Love. No "new life" can emerge without this moment of recognition in which the original value of First Love is confirmed by the rhetorical as well as thematic appeal to a *tradition* of such life-transforming and life-directing feeling. Stein, aware that First Love is linked to the new style of the vernacular, expresses this original value in her native American idiom. Adele's vision is "alright and worth while."

To forsake that tradition and succumb to the temptations of rival objects is to commit, as Dante confesses, a kind of narrative as well as amatory apostasy. Dante's most severe moral crisis occurs when he is tempted by a *second* divine apparition, the Lady in the Window. (Rossetti speculates that the Lady in the Window may in fact be a discreet allusion to Gemma Donati, the bride Dante took a year following Beatrice's death.) Dante describes how a visible fantasy of Beatrice dressed in crimson and appearing as he first beheld her rescues him from the erotic and narrative apostasy of attributing to the second what belongs, by divine ordinance, to the first: ". . . my memory ran back, according to the order of time, unto all those matters in the which she had borne a part; and my heart began painfully to repent of the desire by which it had so basely let itself be possessed during so many days, contrary to the constancy of reason" (90). The constancy of reason entails both a narrative and an amatory fidelity to the First Love, which alone arranges matters according to the proper order of time. To represent that order wrought by divine Love, Dante will compose a poem without precedence, in which will be written "what hath not before been written about any woman." The conventional comic ending of marriage is suppressed so that Dante may write a divine and not merely human comedy, the epic work which justifies the aesthetics of *La Vita Nuova*. First love, then, is deep, not because it is love, but because it is first. Its *Incipit* designates the beginning and comprehends the end of the artist's birth into the world that will constitute the future object of his singular, ever faithful representations.

Yet every deep discloses a deeper deep. Just as Dante concedes that in the book of memory there remains a zone of unillumined darkness "before the which little can be read," Tennyson's idle tears echo, but can never fully re-articulate Wordsworth's thoughts at the conclusion of the "Intimations Ode," "thoughts that do often lie too deep for tears." These thoughts, which exist thanks to the human heart by which we live, seem to have no name in the vocabulary available to present or "modern" feelings. They are only known to originate in and preserve the integrity of

> . . . those first affections
> Those shadowy recollections,
> Which, be they what they may,
> Are yet the fountain light of all our day,
> Are yet a master light of all our seeing . . .
>
> (lines 149–53)

"Be that what they may"—the source feelings seem to linger beyond our ability to specify their nature or the intrinsic value of their objects. Still, these first affections "uphold us" and foster the visionary power. Wordsworth's "are yet" asserts this myth of recovery and continuance: the fountain light is also a master light of all our seeing.

The "joy" of First Love is one form of this kind of Apollonian intoxication, as Nietzsche characterized it; an intoxication that "alerts above all the eye, so that it acquires power of vision."[9] Kierkegaard, whose *Either/Or* constitutes, alternately, an infinitely comic and finitely moralizing disquisition on First Love, similarly ascribes to First Love "an absolute alertness, an absolute beholding; and not to do it an injustice, this must be insisted upon."[10]

But what is it precisely that First Love beholds? For Kierkegaard, it is the sight of "a single, definite and actual object, which alone has existence for it, everything else being nonexistent." We shall consider in the next chapter the idolatries specific to First Love, which attributes to the beloved a divinity in whose presence everything—and everyone—else appears impalpable or inconsequent. But such idolatry is itself a projection of what we might term a self-beholding, for what First Love initially discloses to the lover is the image of his own longing.

Joyce, to whom the world appeared as microcosm and macrocosm constructed on the void, on incertitude, represents First Love as an erotic myth that unfolds just at that juncture in which the inner and outer life seem to be moving toward a deep and irreparable dissociation. This impending crisis informs *A Portrait of the Artist as a Young Man,* whose young hero, Stephen Dedalus, anticipates his First Love as a transfiguration that would abolish his spiritual uncertainty before the world's baffling materiality, consume all doubts about the unsubstantial nature of his desire, and so justify the strange tumult of his restless heart:

> The noise of children at play annoyed him and their silly voices made him feel, even more keenly than he had felt at Clongowes, that he was different from others. He did not want to play. He wanted to meet in the real world the unsubstantial image which his soul so constantly beheld. He did not know where to seek it or how: but a premonition which led him on told him that this image would, without any overt act of his, encounter him.[11]

Stephen is poised here on the threshold of First Love, awaiting that "magic moment" that will transport him out of the realm of childhood play into the "real world" where, he believes, his soul's unsubstantial images will be materialized. He is in that state of "voluptuous torture" that for Kierkegaard signaled the spiritual readiness of those "possessed by an enthusiasm for the first." Such enthusiasm both inflames and relaxes a consciousness newly awakened to a sense of its own powers. The lover becomes "so glowing, so inflamed, so lovingly ardent, so dreamy and fertile, sunken as low as a cloud surcharged with rain" that he begins to form a "lively conception of what it means that Jupiter in a cloud or in a gentle rain descended upon the loved one." Here First Love assumes the religious form of a supernatural visitation, an impregnation by the divine forces that rule and replenish the world. In this state of complete receptivity, "the gentlest touch is enough to thrill this invisible, widely extended spiritual body through and through."[12]

Stephen's ardent dreaminess, which anticipates its own extinction in an encounter that will divest his spiritual body of "weakness and timidity and inexperience," reflects the passive narcissism of a childhood not yet outgrown. Later, after he composes his first verse, "To E———— C————," he will seek the substantial image of his erotic imaginings in the mirror of his mother's dressingtable (71). However, only a severe and ultimately unaesthetic spirit would read this early stage of Stephen's development as a cold satire on the passive idealism of youth, which awaits but can never create the conditions of its own self-transfiguration. What Stephen yearns to behold in his mother's mirror is an image validating the integrity of his heart's desire, just as in the earlier mirror phase of infancy he had looked to his mother for a reassuring image of his body's integrity. Stephen's radical sense of difference, which compels him to abstain from the "common and insignificant" play of an unreflecting childhood, is motivated by his longing for an absolute and discrete individuality, one not to be shaken by the thoughtless treacheries and transient emotions of the childish world. Thus Joyce reminds us of the necessary egotism of love, of First Love in particular. In the "mirror stage" reenacted in First Love, the Beloved initially serves to reflect the "deep" and inalienable originality of the lover whose passion she solicits.

Kierkegaard goes so far as to propose a sacred mirroring in First Love. Kierkegaard's B, who argues the religious character of First Love, indulges in a philosophical flourish that transposes the sad seriousness of First Love into a lofty eulogy on its spirit-creating power:

> If there is something so important as to be even eternal, all probability that it may be repeated vanishes. Hence, when one has talked with a certain sad seriousness of the first love as of something which could never be repeated, this is no disparagement of love but a lofty eulogy of it as the eternal power. Thus—for the sake of making a little philosophical flourish, not with the pen but with thought—God only once became flesh, and it would be vain to expect this to be repeated. In paganism it could happen oftener, but this was precisely for the reason that it was not a true incarnation. Thus man is born only once, and there is no probability of a repetition. The notion of transmigration of souls fails to appreciate the significance of birth.[13]

First Love, then, is radically committed to honoring the significance of birth. As a myth of beginnings, it extends the promise that the birth of the hero will represent a true incarnation, and in this lies its appeal to the modern mind, anxious that its life and its creations can never be more than diminished forms of mightier originals. First Love illustrates as it symbolizes that *general* prestige of first things which the young reader more than the mature producer of life is likely to credit with eternal power. The dispensation of the novel decrees that eager, curious, anxious youth, and not seasoned age, shall have adventures, those definitive experiences in which genuine advent, the coming into the world of some original being, still seems possible.

Franco Moretti, in his provocative reassessment of the bildungsroman, interprets this advent as a compromise formation that is far from "innocent." With the collapse of status society, argues Moretti, youth ceases to be defined as a biological stage of development and becomes a problematic "time" in which the young undertake "an uncertain exploration of social space":

> It is a necessary exploration: in dismantling the continuity between generations, as is well known, the new and destabilizing forces of capitalism impose a hitherto unknown *mobility*. But it is also a yearned for exploration, since the selfsame process gives rise to unexpected hopes, thereby generating an *interiority* not only fuller than before, but also—as Hegel clearly saw, even though he deplored it—perennially dissatisfied and restless.[14]

For Moretti, mobility and interiority epitomize not only youth, but its symbolic form as the "specific material sign" of the modern epoch. Around this sign accumulate all the contradictory desires of modernity: "freedom and happiness, identity and change, security and metamorphosis." "Our world," asserts Moretti, "calls for their *coexistence,* however difficult; and it therefore also calls for a cultural mechanism capable of representing, exploring and testing that coexistence."[15]

First Love is one such mechanism, one less implicated in the novelistic mystifications of "everyday life" and the regime of "ordinary administration," mystifications which, according to Moretti, lie at the heart and enfold the ideology of the novelistic "compromise": "Ordinary administration: a time of 'lived experience' and individual growth—a time filled with 'opportunities,' but which excludes by definition both the crisis and genesis of a culture."[16] First Love, as a myth of the new life, prides itself in interpreting its moment of amatory crisis precisely as the genesis of a new literary culture and its new style.

The traditional appeal of First Love emanates from its "legendary" power to provide restless youth with the substantial object to satisfy and confirm its inner desire. First Love promises to overcome the division and recessive splitting of consciousness into inner and outer, surface and "deep" feeling. It grants the lover a glimpse of his destiny as it is reflected in the material existence of another. For First Love to actualize this potential union of subject and object, it must be encountered in the fateful determinants of what Kierkegaard identified as the *occasion.* In the occasion, the contingent and the fateful converge, and external event becomes the catalyst for an inner determination:

> When . . . consciousness has so come to itself that it possesses the entire content, then the moment has arrived which contains the possibility of real creation; and yet something is missing; missing is the occasion, which one might say is equally necessary, although in another sense, it is infinitely insignificant. . . . The occasion is always the accidental, and this is the tremendous paradox, that the accidental is just as absolutely necessary as the necessary.[17]

Kierkegaard condenses the paradoxical nature of the occasion into an aphoristic definition: "The occasion is the last category, the essential transitional category, from the sphere of the idea to actuality."[18]

The readiness, then, is not all. Desire must not only envision, but seize, the occasion of its fulfillment. Like the occasion from which it arises, and indeed, like birth itself, First Love enacts a rite of transition from conception to actuality. It attends and assists at what we might call soul-creation. And primarily as a spirit-manifesting event in the life of the novelistic individual will it concern me in these pages.

The aesthetic character of First Love thus consists in its *occasional* nature. Only unaesthetic individuals experience first love as a mere *episode,* interesting but potentially transient in its spiritual effects. But such individuals can never become novelistic "characters" whose "story" can sustain an entire narrative. The difference between an episode and an occasion is revealed in the etymologies of the words. An episode may be regarded as an event which can be complete in itself, adjacent rather than integral to a larger narrative series (*epi-,* "besides," *eisodos,* "an entrance"); an occasion opportunistically initiates a sequence (Latin: *occasio,* "accidental opportunity," "fit time," derived from *occidere,* "to fall"—to fall, that is, providentially).[19]

We can perhaps best observe the ways in which First Love narratives convert the accidental into an inner determination through a negative instance. Stephen, we remember, refuses the summons of the occasion, and it is in this sense that he remains a young man, a prenovelistic individual whose destiny is still all possibility and not yet a concrete potentiality. *A Portrait of the Artist as a Young Man,* then, may be read as the story of a suspended or lapsed soul-creation. Each time Stephen's soul goes forth to experience, his spiritual body, "unfolding itself sin by sin," inevitably collapses back upon itself, "quenching its own lights and fires." Hence the fine irony of his exultant cry at novel's close: "I go to encounter for the millionth time the reality of experience and to forge in the smithy of my soul the uncreated conscience of my race" (253). That "millionth" comprehends a host of squandered "occasions." If Stephen is to create the conscience of his race, it is his mother's reflections, rather than his father's artifice, that will stand him in good stead. It is the mother who sees her son set off in exile and mirrors for him the life-lesson he must master: to learn in his own life "what the heart is and what it feels" (252). It is First Love that might instruct him in the lore of the heart. In *Ulysses,* as we shall see, he will begin his education in earnest.

Stephen, we might say, both overestimates and undervalues the significance of the first. His beginnings are always shadowed by the ghosts of lost or abandoned occasions. His failure to hold and kiss Eileen as she nimbly dances up and down the tram steps, offering herself and urging the "vanities" of her sex, is just such a lost occasion. He prefers, if that is not too willful a verb, to stand listlessly by, "seemingly a tranquil watcher of the scene before him" (70). Yet Joyce comments, tellingly, that Stephen has "yielded a thousand times" to the allure of her image. Stephen rejects this proffered occasion for typically "modern" reasons—because he wants the first love to be without precedence in the world: "He heard what her eyes said to him from beneath their cowl and knew that in some dim past, whether in life or in revery, he had heard their tale before." What offends Stephen's intellectual imagination is that Eileen offers him a first love as a "twice-told" tale. He wants the first to designate both a temporal and a qualitative apriority. Hence he discounts in advance the significance of this occasion, citing his inner certainty that it is the dim past, and not a radiant future, that this occasion will actualize. Stephen has yet to formulate the terms of the Joycean "compromise" which appreciates the significance of metempsychosis, the rebirth of heroes in the literary transmigration of souls. Joycean aesthetics are anti-Kierkegaardian, Greeker than the Greeks, in this respect. For him spiritual metamorphosis is a repetition with a difference. And it is this difference that Stephen has difficulty in perceiving. For Stephen's jealous intimations are of a curious and indeterminate kind. He cannot specify whether in life or in revery he has encountered the tale Eileen invites him to repeat. If it is in life, he has reason to suspect his status as firstcomer. But if it is in revery, then his suspicion merely projects his own self-distrust.

Stephen's indecision, we might then conclude, dramatizes two responses to the summons of First Love: to see too much or too little in the occasion. He is typical of that unfortunate individual of whom Kierkegaard speaks, the individual who would see the fault, not in himself, but in the occasion. Kierkegaard observes that "two ways lie open before the man to whom 'the first' is significant":

Either "the first" contains promise for the future, is the forward thrust, the endless impulse. Such are the fortunate individuals for whom "the first" is simply the present, but the present is for them the constantly unfolding and rejuvenating "first." Or "the first" does not impel the individual; the power which is in "the first" does not become the impelling power in the individual but the repelling power, it becomes that which thrusts away. [20]

It is the lover's attitude toward "the first" that determines whether his heart will be fascinated or repelled, whether it will commit itself, that is, to acts capable of generating and sustaining a narrative. Fortune or misfortune in love is less the result of an objective and inexorable chain of causes than the product of an inner disposition.

That the impelling—or repelling—power emanates from within the novelistic character helps explain why some first loves are "elected" to receive a complete narrative unfolding and others are left to dissipate and disperse themselves in that incomplete and unsatisfactory narrative fragment, the episode. Those "unfortunate individuals" who do not appreciate the aesthetic significance of "the first," who are not moved by love's rare "occasions," will have no story to tell. Though visited by love, they will remain, like Stephen, enmeshed in contingency. Their lives will unfold as series of "episodes" incapable of impelling narrative, and thus of producing meaning, in time. For the episode, while capable of condensing a spiritual into a material movement, does not significantly alter or transform the relation of emotion to time. That is why the episode, in its fitfulness, can inspire interest in the dramatic intersection of time and emotion, world and desire, but can never arouse the hope for a symbolic mediation between subjective impulses and objective forces, which is, I would claim, the *consolatio* offered us in the fully developed forms of narrative art.

Let us then turn to a more "mature" account of First Love, which honors, as the young Stephen cannot or will not, the validity of this distinction between episode and occasion—Turgenev's *First Love*. Turgenev's exquisite novella begins in the tradition of tales told as after-dinner entertainments. Yet it soon assumes a more modern attitude in attesting that not every first love represents a fateful occasion in which, by loving another, the spirit encounters itself. Turgenev's concern is not with anecdotal material, but with the events that shape a character, that create that world-disturbed and -disturbing "subjectivity" we recognize as "modern" and whose appearance appears to have been contemporaneous with the birth of the novel itself. Three intimate friends assemble after all other dinner guests have left. The host proposes that they exchange stories of their first loves. The first two raconteurs fall under the category of Kierkegaard's "unfortunate individuals" for whom first love is recollected as an isolated and transient episode rather than as a spirit-manifesting occasion. One man cannot admit to a first love because he "began with the second." Pressed to elaborate, he explains that when he first courted a girl, he behaved as if he were already experienced in the ways of love. Then he casually remarks, "Actually I fell in love for the first and last time when I was about six, with my nurse, but that was a very long time ago."[21] Had Freud been a dinner guest, he might have elicited this story in all its telling, incriminating details. The second man also lacks a story to tell, or, rather, like the man remembering his early love of his nurse, is unaware that he has a story to tell. He relates that he did not fall in love until he met his present wife. Their courtship proceeded without notable incidents, as their marriage was arranged by their families. His experience of love did not implicate him in the drama of *fatefulness,* being simply the personal consequence of society's material arrangements to guarantee its own future by making marriages.

But the third guest, who eventually replaces the omniscient narrator and moves the tale into the realm of personal reminiscence, cannot *tell* his love because he fears that his telling will be either too dry or too florid to capture the mood unique to First Love. He insists that his story can only be *written,* our first intimation that it is the destiny of First Love and its idols to be implicated in the fate of the textual. The sensuous excitements of First Love, to which Turgenev seems especially sensitive, are literary as well as erotic. His narrator reveals that as a youth he cultivated romantic postures learned from books. Reveries soon replace reading, from which, in the sweet misery of his passion, he turns away. Turgenev thus identifies the consistent proximity of two rival idolatries in the telling of First Love: the passion for love and the romance of learning. Passion gives First Love its illusion of absolute priority, but learning places First Love within the rich and nuanced culture of romance, lends it, that is, the aesthetic and historical depth it will need to convert the potential of the occasion into an actual narrative. Passion, which is ahistorical (when it is not *trans-historical*), enchants the heart with the vision of what Kierkegaard calls an "immediate infinity." Learning, which is historical, subjects the infinite moment of love to the disciplines of time. This double consciousness characterizes modern love, or more precisely, it marks First Love as a modern invention.

In linking the birth of modern consciousness to the experience of First Love, I hope to explore some of the implications of Bakhtin's account of the bildungsroman, the life-narrative which represents "the image of man in the process of becoming."[22] In these narratives "time is introduced into man, enters into his very image, changing in a fundamental way the significance of all aspects of his destiny and life."[23] Bakhtin proposes that such narratives "can be designated in the most general sense as the novel of human *emergence.*" Bakhtin regards the representation of human emergence as the special province of the bildungsroman, while I would further claim that such emergence generally attests to the synthesizing power of love, which seeks to join the developing self to the material order of persons, places, and things.

First Love narrates this hopeful, productive, yet often disillusive contact with the overmastering erotic and social forces that seem to have human happiness in their keeping. From this encounter it retrieves a vision of the world populated with beloved persons and their precious attributes—persons and attributes that assume the status and perform the function of idols. But to put it this way is to risk falsely characterizing my theme as concerned with purely subjective transformations of the world. First Love marks that inaugural occasion in the life of the novelistic individual when eventful happenings begin to emerge as not only consecutive, but meaningful—that is, potentially fateful—in their consecutiveness. In fact, the prestige of First Love is that, by virtue of its being a first and not a second or third love, it marks that decisive occasion when Time enters the image of man and endows it with an emotional content as well as a narrative form. Lukács and Bakhtin, the two theorists most engaged in analyzing the relation of time to the novel's representation of human consciousness, both describe the "burden of becoming" without resorting to an individualizing psychology. Psychology, of course, complicates when it does not rebel outright against time, family and social history, death, the "reality" principle. Psychology conceives of human consciousness as a highly personalized text of human feeling that observes its own narrative laws of displacement, condensation, and transformation. No true novel can afford to slight, much less dispense with, these texts in representing human subjectivity. The novel's specialized province is not only to make us see, but to make us, as George Eliot, that quintessential novelist, insisted, see *feelingly.*

First Love, understood as a myth of creative initiative, can help us interpret the specific emotional disposition as well as the historical mood of the novels of modern life. We might number among its texts Woolf's *Mrs. Dalloway,* Lawrence's *Sons and Lovers,* and Stein's *Q.E.D.,* all novels which announce the new style—in feeling and in expression, indeed of an expressive feeling—that characterizes modernist literature in its first, exhilarating self-manifestations. *Quod erat demonstrandum*—the syllogism for this literary revolution in feeling might be reasoned as follows: the modern sensibility is, in T. S. Eliot's famous pronouncement, dissociated, deeply alienated or removed from the forces of immanent life. A peculiar sensation characterizes this state of dissociation, what Lukács calls, in his *Theory of the Novel,* "the heaviness of life," and which Eliot has unforgettably captured in Prufrock's self-image: "a patient etherized upon a table." In this leaden state, life appears as a "withered, stale existence, too close to the earth and too far from heaven." [24] Ergo, the antidote must be to restore to life and to narrative a spiritual buoyancy, the levity that marks Woolf's First Love narrative, *Mrs. Dalloway:* "What a lark! What a plunge." [25] These are the first sentiments attributed to Clarissa Dalloway on the fateful day in June which will eventually disclose to her the rich meaning of her past.

Clarissa's "exhilaration" is a complex mood, at once lighthearted and intensive, reckless and oddly portentous ("something awful was about to happen"). It both buoys her in the present and plunges her headlong into the past, where she recaptures the emotionally charged scene of her First Love: the scene is Bourton and the emotion "the purity, the integrity, of her feeling for Sally [Seton]." The "integrity" of this first feeling of love is allied, just as Stein's was allied, to the continuity it discloses between past and present. For Clarissa, as for Stein's Adele, this continuity is apprehended in a text subject to personal citation: " 'if it were now to die 'twere now to be most happy.' That was her feeling—Othello's feeling, and she felt it, she was convinced, as Shakespeare meant Othello to feel it, all because she was coming down to dinner in a white frock to meet Sally Seton!" (51). First Love carries its own unshakable *conviction,* the conviction not only of intense feeling, but of what is *meant* by such feeling. The recollection of First Love restores to Clarissa an incredible lightness of being, buoyant and brave enough to defy the gravity of Death. Confident that she is feeling what Othello feels, and therefore assured that her love, however insignificant its occasion, is, as Stein would say, worthwhile and all right, Clarissa can build up, despite all her dark forebodings, her own "chronotope"— "life; London; this moment of June."

In Joyce, we find a somewhat different dynamic at work. Joyce, ever alert to the correspondence between physical and spiritual motion, overestimated the significance of the First precisely on the syllogistic grounds that the soul may have its virginity as well as the body. [26] Joyce described this spiritual dialectic in his notes to *Exiles:*

Love (understood as the desire of good for another) is in fact so unnatural
a phenomenon that it can scarcely repeat itself, the soul being unable to
become virgin again and not having energy enough to cast itself out again

into the ocean of another's soul. It is the repressed consciousness of this inability and lack of spiritual energy which explains Bertha's mental paralysis. (113)

Yet Joyce may be misdiagnosing Bertha's paralysis, mistaking a symptom for an underlying cause, confusing natural with spiritual effects. Bertha's lack of spiritual energy is the result, not the cause, of her repressed consciousness of the soul's inability to become virgin again. Love may be an unnatural phenomenon, but its uncanniness consists largely in its indestructibility. Eros can never be depleted, but only bound, withdrawn from circulation (in the form of a fixation). Affects, Freud has taught us, are never lost to the mind, only displaced or reversed in the course of their vicissitudes. We thus might profitably compare the extreme immobility of Bertha's emotional state to the extreme immobility of the wolves staring attentively in the Wolf Man's anxiety dream. In Freud's interpretation of the Wolf Man's dream, the rigid immobility of the wolves actually reversed and thus screened the memory of a primal scene, the agitated movements of parental intercourse.[27] We might regard Bertha's paralysis as a similar instance of somatic and affective reversal, by which the agitated movements of her soul are projected in the transposed form of spiritual and linguistic paralysis.

Joyce understands this psychic process dramatically, even if he will not acknowledge it discursively, when he gives to Bertha the final human appeal of the play. Bertha's spiritual energy, apparently immobilized, breaks through her repressed demeanor in her—and the play's—final verbal gesture. She implores the doubting Richard to reenact the primal scene of their love: "Forget me and love me again as you did the first time. I want my lover. To meet him, to go to him, to give myself to him. You, Dick. O, my strange wild lover, come back to me again!" (112). This rhetoric may be too overblown to prove convincing. We may object that Richard's "deep, deep wound of doubt" can never be healed by the balm of Bertha's histrionic lyricism. We might even prefer to see in Richard's suspicions the true expression of the modern imagination, one that, like Richard's, does "not wish to know or to believe," but desires to love " in restless living wounding doubt."

But against this conviction and against these preferences, a wiser character, and one who has no doubt of his wife's adultery, counsels another course. For is not Leopold Bloom's half-repressed smile as he returns from his wanderings to his bed in "Ithaca" a bemused recognition of the energetic power of imagination to make the soul virgin again? What would have made Bloom smile, if he had smiled, seems to be a thought too deep for tears: "To reflect that each one who enters imagines himself to be the first to enter whereas he is always the last term of a preceding series even if the first term of a succeeding one, each imagining himself to be first, last, only and alone whereas he is neither first nor last nor only nor alone in a series originating in and repeated to infinity." [28] Here is the infinite comedy of First Love of which Kierkegaard speaks. Like Emmeline, the heroine of Scribe's play, *The First Love,* and the "occasional" subject of Kierkegaard's inquiry, Bloom is "too good a dialectician . . . to be convinced empirically" that he is not, nor ever will be, Molly's first love. Bloom's romantic conscience, like hers, allows him to "soar above every limit imposed on reality." [29] Bloom reconciles all his "antagonistic sentiments" of envy, jealousy, abnegation, and equanimity within this encompassing narrative paradox: we are neither first, last, only, nor alone, yet in First Love we so imagine ourselves to be. In such imaginings, the narrative series—or human species—recovers the spiritual energy necessary to repeat and so reproduce itself in acts of love.

Such paradoxes would appeal powerfully to the artist of modern mind afflicted by a sense of belatedness. The modern artist wants to make things new, but can only make them new again. The prestige of the first time in modern fiction is inversely proportional to the feeling of having been born in too late a time. This is the great quixotic theme of the novels of modern life, the "regret" of belatedness that inspires Don Quixana to give birth to Don Quixote, to insist on a second birth that is the true birth. First love is deep enough to contain this regret, but also ingenious enough to dream of a new self-incarnation.

## EROTIC PRIMOGENITURE

Other irrational claims to precedence, perhaps less conscionable ones, seem to ensue from First Love. The cultural critic Theodor Adorno alerts us to the latent evils lurking in First Love as a justificatory myth of empowering feeling. Adorno reminds us that the complex interplay between individual desire and the historical world of other beings can collapse into a power struggle for exclusive domination once the prestige of the first becomes the criterion of an objective morality. In *Minima Moralia,* Adorno identifies the source of this erotic conflict as "the phenomenon of the prior engagement: a loved person refuses herself to us not through inner antagonisms and inhibitions, too much coldness or repressed warmth, but because a relationship already exists that excludes another. Abstract temporal sequence plays in reality the part one would like to ascribe to the hierarchy of feelings."[30] Adorno remarks that even in the most highly rationalized society, "there could hardly be rules governing the order in which one met people. The irreversibility of time thus constitutes an objective moral criterion which is intimately related to myth."

For Adorno, objective arrangements which are predicated on "the exclusiveness implicit in time" can lead, "by its inherent law," to unforeseen, and devastating, social consequences:

> Nothing is more touching than a loving woman's anxiety lest love and tenderness, her best possessions just because they cannot be possessed, be stolen away by a newcomer, simply because of her newness, itself conferred by the prerogative of the older. But from this touching feeling, without which all warmth and protection would pass away, an irresistible path leads, by way of the little boy's aversion for his younger brother and the fraternity-student's contempt for his 'fag', to the immigration laws that exclude all non-Caucasians from Social-Democratic Australia, and right up to the Fascist eradication of the racial minority, in which, indeed, all warmth and shelter explode into nothingness.[31]

Precedence in love can lead to unprecedented social tyrannies. The hierarchy of feelings is subjected to a monstrous inversion. Where love, warmth, and protection ought to be, there we find hatred, cold contempt, and the explosion of tenderness into the nothingness of mass exterminations. Once the unique status of the first-in-time is established, it can be abstracted into a principle of universal right to which everyone must conform.

First Love, subject to such abstraction, is in danger of confusing the prerogatives of the firstcomer with the entitlements of the firstborn. The order of feelings in time becomes linked, then identified, with the right to possession. The erotic relation, which ought to allow for freedom of choice and decision, degenerates into a property relation, with its established rules for ascertaining possession and determining succession. We might call this phenomenon "erotic primogeniture," which entails the establishing of a legitimate "chain of possession." As Adorno further observes:

> Historically, the notion of time is itself formed on the basis of the order of ownership. But the desire to possess reflects time as a fear of losing, of the irrecoverable. Whatever is, is experienced in relation to its possible nonbeing. This alone makes it fully a possession and, thus petrified, something functional that can be exchanged for other, equivalent possessions.[32]

In this perversion of the traditional prerogatives granted to the "first" love, what is sought is not a specific property, but a desirable sexual or ethnic trait, one that narcissistically reflects or exclusively pertains to us as firstcomers.

This logic, by which the abstract order of sequence replaces the atemporal order of feelings, underlies Adorno's astounding description of the "irresistible path" which leads from a woman's tender feeling to sibling rivalries, laws of exclusion, and Fascist eradication of racial minority. Adorno's social forebodings are concrete extrapolations of Nietzsche's insight into the genealogy of morals: "Not only were all good things, as Nietzsche knew, once bad things: the gentlest, left to follow their own momentum, have a tendency to culminate in unimaginable brutality." Adorno then isolates the fatal moment that brings the whole dialectic into play. It lies, he asserts, "in the exclusive character of what comes first." [33]

One need not agree with Adorno's specific examples of the brutalities that can result from attributing a mythic exclusiveness to first things in order to appreciate the unsettling implications of his remarks for a study of First Love. I propose to collapse Adorno's social description, eliminating at one end consideration of the young boy's sibling rivalry and, at the other, the Fascist eradication of racial minority, so that I may concentrate on First Love as a myth of the middle distance. First Love may be seen, imaginatively, to occupy that place in consciousness where the psychological and the social intersect and commingle, the space where sexual and social ideals are articulated. Here we can discriminate more clearly how the exclusive character of what comes first determines narrative as well as erotic and social order. Here we can see how First Love can transfigure, but also corrupt, the human heart by which we live.

The form this corruption takes in both psychological and social life is "erotic primogeniture," which masks its inner compulsions in the "objective" guise of sexual idealism. Joyce's outburst in a letter to his brother, Stanislaus, however idiosyncratic in the violent disgust of his repudiation, nevertheless captures the mood of the modernist's sexual revolt against the "spiritualization" of the sex-relation: "I am nauseated by their lying drivel about pure men and pure women and spiritual love and love for ever: blatant lying in the face of the truth. I don't know much about the 'saince' of the subject but I presume there are very few mortals in Europe who are not in danger of waking some morning and finding themselves syphilitic." [34] Modern literary culture indeed arises in reaction to the instinct-vitiating proprieties of bourgeois sexual morality. Shaw saw this revolt as constituting the "quintessence of Ibsenism." [35] The assault on moral idealism represented by Schopenhauer's pessimism, Nietzsche's psychologism, and Ibsen's plays also underlies the new "saince" of Freudian researches into the irrational springs of human actions and affections. I have confined my study to male authors because I believe their work to be more susceptible to the narcissistic beguilements of First Love. The self-annunciatory and self-authorizing properties of First Love assume a troubling configuration in the masculine dream of erotic and cultural precedence. Women may entertain the "touching feeling" of exclusiveness, but do not so consistently appropriate it as the postulate for a social mythology or a narrative system.

We can observe this sexual difference most directly in Hardy's troubled retelling of his courtship of Emma Gifford, *A Pair of Blue Eyes,* a novel in which the debacle of sexual idealism is very much at the heart of Hardy's self-scrutiny. Henry Knight, Hardy's idealist-lover, is also a figure of the modern writer-critic. The desire for erotic primogeniture is attributed to him as a genetic trait: "Inbred in him was an invincible objection to be any but the first comer in a woman's heart." [36] Elfride, the heroine, risks all to test his sexual ideology when she falls in love with him. She questions his preference in hair (he values dark-haired beauties; her hair is light) and color of eyes (he prefers dark; hers, of course, are blue). That Knight eventually falls in love with Elfride, a woman who fails to conform to his aesthetic of female beauty, in part explains Proust's special fascination with this novel. Knight is an ancestor to Charles Swann, the aesthete who falls for a woman who is not his type.

Such ironies typically attend First Love and can portend nothing but catastrophe. Elfride, who has had earlier love affairs, chides Knight: "Am I such a— mere characterless toy—as to have no attrac—tion in me, apart from—freshness?" (344). Hers is a protest against an erotic *childishness* that demands the fresh, renounces the "stale," because it misunderstands the very quality of innocence, being itself so untutored. Knight, deaf to her eloquent defense, lapses into a lover's visionary dreariness on finding that "his idol was second hand": "But there had passed away a glory, and the dream was not as it had been of yore" (345). I am not sure that anyone but Hardy would so dare to ironize and eroticize Wordsworthian dejection in his effort to depict the psychological state of a man whose disappointment in the pursuit of an "inbred" ideal brings him to "the verge of cynicism." For Hardy, of course, "the rough dispelling of any bright illusion" is not an unprecedented but a predictable event in human development. Such rude awakenings are one among many of the "little ironies" life holds in store for dreamy idealists.

Yet one more irony lurks in this fable of precedence. It is wrought by the feminine sufferance transparent in Elfride's own "masculinity fiction": "O, could *I* but be the man and *you* the woman, I would not leave you for such a little fault as mine!" (362). Elfride's reproach takes the form of an imaginative role-reversal. Could the distressed damsel become the knight, she would not misuse the codes of courtesy so, and invoke the cause of honor to justify desertion. Molly Bloom's soliloquy can and should be understood within this tradition of feminine expostulation and reply.

Such female remonstrations identify a primary dialectic that prevails in the course, never smooth, of First Love. The exclusive nature of what comes first can make First Love complicit with certain forms of inadvertent sexual treachery. Idols, even of the lover's own making, can as easily blast as promote the heart's affection. Adorno humanely reminds us that it is "True affection which alone speaks specifically to the other, and becomes attached to beloved features and not the idol of personality, the reflected image of possession." [37] In the following chapter, I will be analyzing the idols of modern fiction precisely in these terms: their capacity to promote or to impede, engage or repel the mind's essentially *novelistic* capacity to identify with the way others actually are, live, and feel. Erotic primogeniture, in trying to ensure the legitimacy and exclusiveness of its idols, can initiate the elimination of all specific tendernesses, loyalties, charities, thus threatening the integrity of the novel as a form that protects the "other," that articulates divergent, not monological points of view, that speaks *to* as well as about the idolized one.

Let me further suggest that the novel preserves its integrity in the face of such fierce, sublime, primarily *lyrical* idolatries through its own inner, bookish disciplines. I use the term "discipline" in the sense Ruskin proposed in his lecture on idolatry—as signifying "the desire of equity and wholesome restraint, in all acts and works of life." [38] I would identify three of these disciplines (that is, figures of equity embodying attitudes of wholesome restraint):

1. Narrative Numbers: the disposition or order of feelings, persons, and events in time. This articulates a generic discipline of equitable distribution.

2. Generational Echo, or Belatedness: the self-conscious concealment of what is derived or imitated, until it can present itself in the guise of a fully developed myth. Joyce's pun on *ecco!* and *echo* encapsulates the creative repetition I have in mind when I speak of this figure, but, in a more general way, so does Thomas Mann's general understanding of myth as a self-consciously *exact* ritual that reanimates a primordial original. I consider the full implications of Mann's concept of myth in my chapter on *The Rainbow,* where the idea of the echo is assimilated in Lawrence's use of what I call "relaxed quotation."

3. Sadness, or the Impotence of Irony: the "mood" of modern recountings,

which acknowledges the ambiguous destiny of its loves, but would still put them just beyond the reach, though still within sight, of that corrosive irony perfected in Flaubertian realism.

These narrative disciplines help stabilize the emotional crisis of First Love. They place its story of emergent human feeling beyond the direct reach of history, the arena of ideological contention and social conflict. Such a strategy is developed to suspend, rather than foolishly ignore, the social and historical "explanations" (to use Gertrude Stein's word) by which realistic novels attempt to comprehend the world. At the same time, the romantic conscience of these works, their imaginary identification with the revolutionary literature of "first affections," is never permitted, as in undiluted romantic narrative (the first half of *Wuthering Heights,* for instance), to enact a sublime abolition of differences. The disciplines of First Love acknowledge divisive ruptures in time (days are no sooner lived than they are no more); they ascertain distances between human agents—the distances enforced by the politics of sex, class, and power, and, ultimately, by the unknown and appalling gods who rule the world. Yet, as we shall see, it is because of rather than in spite of these disciplines that some original feeling or new perception can arrest and at times alter the course of the world, if only for a moment and if only between the pages of a book.

## NARRATIVE NUMBERS

The exclusive character of what comes first obviously affects the order of novelistic representations. It does so by influencing the distribution of what I will call, echoing the formal vocabulary of poetry, narrative numbers. Narrative numbers perform the same structural work as metrical numbers—they determine the order, duration, and distribution of episodes whose significance might otherwise become dissipated in the discursiveness of description or untendentious chronicle. Yeats provides us with a historical perspective on the formal perplexity intrinsic to any representation of the "modernist" occasion, an occasion that typically elicits the essential pathos of all that feels itself to be bereft or belated, yet still entitled to the experience of great and *first* things. Writing in 1898, Yeats proposed that the fin de siècle artist was afflicted by a profound world-weariness, which was intensified by scientific and declamatory modes of thought that stressed the external at the expense of the inward life. Yet because Yeats believed "that the arts lie dreaming of things to come," he comprehended the twilight of the idols through an image of Keatsian pathos: the "autumn of the body" that knows "nothing but the fading and flowering of the world."[39] Out of this ripeness might issue a new order of spiritual understanding: "We are, it may be, at a crowning crisis of the world, at the moment when man is about to ascend, with the wealth he has been so long gathering upon his shoulders, the stairway he has been descending from the first days."[40] Yeats imagines this new ascent as a trajectory of return to the first days of spontaneous spiritual expression.

Narrative numbers, which reflect the particular biases of ascendant feelings, can thus be enlisted to regulate the heartbeat of the autumnal body, sated and absorbed in the process of self-recollection. In trying to reconstruct those generative memories, I will be paying particular attention to the inaugural occasion in the story of First Love: the first glimpse, meeting, or tryst. These initial encounters call into play the very idea of fatefulness, an idea with which the young are almost as much enamored as they are with the body of the beloved. As Kierkegaard appreciated, an "element of truth" is preserved in the tradition of "love at first sight." Such moments, he asserts, exemplify "the double propensity" of everything eternal "of presupposing itself back into all eternity and forward into all eternity": "This is the element of truth in what the poets have often sung so beautifully, to the effect that lovers even at first sight feel as if they already had loved one another for a long while."[41] Love at first sight radically reorganizes and reinterprets human time. In the "immediate infinity" of this moment, lovers seem to possess the full plenitude of past and future time. For Kierkegaard, this feeling of eternity corresponds to and participates in the mystery of the Incarnation, the sublime union of immortal and mortal life. The modern narratives of First Love, however much they may share this feeling of eternity, do not pursue Kierkegaard's religious representations. The modern novel prefers to countenance secular "occasions" of self-transfiguration. It appropriates this "poetic" feeling of eternity to dissolve all inherited, systematic, or inert feelings and thoughts rather than to point the way to ultimate transcendence. Love at first sight in the novel is the moment that organizes, but cannot redeem or abolish, human time.

Thus a large-spirited irony inevitably lurks on the edges of the first and fateful encounter. In such meetings the future, at once an object of personal anxiety and the field of social contention, seems to be projected and already anticipated as an accomplished destiny, subject to no further narrative unfoldings and complications. Miss Counihan is the first Beckettian heroine to attest to the inherent redundancy of all human meetings: "Who ever met," she inquires, "if it comes to that, that met not at first sight?":

"There is only one meeting and parting," said Wylie. "The act of love."

"Fancy that!" said Miss Counihan.

"Then each with and from himself," said Wylie, "as well as with and from the other."

"With and from him and herself," said Neary, "have a little conduction, Wylie. Remember a lady is present."[42]

Miss Counihan, the lady in question, is an omnivorous reader of romances. She regards love at first sight as a useful fiction that disguises the essential equivalence (and promiscuity) of all human exchanges. Wylie would rescue the spirit of human encounter—meeting and parting—by restricting its meaning to the act of love, the act that involves a reciprocal exchange (of each and from each). But his view is expressed in an abstract language that is suspiciously narcissistic, even homoerotic (because grammatically self-mirroring), as Neary, an interested party in this sexual rondo, is quick to point out. Wylie's view is shrewd, as befits his name, but it lacks conduction and so will the opinion of critics who dismiss the presence of ladies as incidental to the stark ritualism of Beckettian meetings. Indeed, Beckett's fictions, read as love stories, can be seen to be about this vital conduction of heat and other *life-indicating* properties in otherwise frigid or moribund bodies. Eros, I repeat, is a conductor-god.

Joyce's retrospective narration seems motivated by this perception. *Ulysses* overcomes its world-weariness when the autumnal body of Molly Bloom, in a harvest of memories, recalls her first kiss under the Moorish Wall. Such memories linger, Joyce insinuates, because they appease the human longing for a renewable, satisfying experience in which the future may be welcomed as a repetition with a difference, an aesthetic space in which foretellings, shadows of coming events, may find their ideal field for erotic dalliance. History, which records, as often as not, the sports of time and chance, is for Joyce the realm of depletion, paralysis, resentment, the place where things rage out of control and where they fall apart. In *Ulysses,* the amatory adventure begins (or recommences) with that siren song that is Joyce's most magical emblem for the enchantment of beginnings: "When first I saw thy form endearing." The Joycean novel would give full expression to this endearing form and, indeed, take it as its own. It is the form that comprehends "Love's bitter mystery," the reality sought by Yeats's Fergus and Joyce's Stephen Dedalus, who has never known First Love except as an epiphanic possibility. First Love gives coherence to Love's mystification, which is necessary if we are to learn, or relearn, not merely to accept but to love the world.

## GENERATIONAL ECHO, OR BELATEDNESS

To love is not to exonerate the world. To appreciate the complex and worldly realism that characterizes First Love narratives, one may turn to Turgenev, author of the poignant *First Love* (1860) and *Spring Torrents* (1871). In *Spring Torrents* Turgenev claims, "First love is exactly like a revolution: the regular and established order of life is in an instant smashed to fragments; youth stands at the barricade, its bright banner raised high in the air, and sends its ecstatic greetings to the future, whatever it may hold—death or a new life, no matter." [43] First Love thus subjects the world to judgment or vindication. Turgenev adopts the rhetoric of a revolutionary age intoxicated by its smashing of the old order and its idols. First Love demands a *new* future whatever its content, even if it has *no content,* even, that is, if it inaugurates the reign of Death-in-Life. What is "on trial" in these narratives is not so much the lover's innocence but the guilt of the world, the harsh Necessity whose law it executes. [44]

Turgenev's *First Love* represents this conflict as generational. The novella recounts how the son vies with the father for power and pride of place. The narrator's cold, distant, but intermittently fervid father communicates this masculine ideal as the substance of his legacy: "To belong to oneself, that is the whole thing in life . . . Know how to want, and you'll be free, and you'll be master too" (49). Male self-mastery is explicitly associated with the power to desire, to know how, not only what, to want.

The plot of *First Love* is thus revealed to be composed of atavistic, oedipal elements which Turgenev, through the narrator, interprets as intimately involved with the psychological and social ideal of male self-mastery. Indeed the climactic revelation scene is played out as a phantasmagoria of the phallic: the son seeks to ambush his unknown rival in the moonlit garden that serves for a trysting place, only to discover, like Oedipus, that his rival is his father. His final vision of his first love, Zinaida, reasserts this theme of paternal mastery in a more sadistic image: he spies his father striking her with his riding crop, branding her with the mark of painful yet irresistible passion. Zinaida's "scar" confirms the virginal boy's suspicions of sexual violence and the "wound" of sexuality that makes women bleed.

These oedipal surveillances of the "primal scene" do not leave the son contemptuous of the father, but admiring of him. Turgenev not only anticipates Freud, but invites him into his narrative when he has his narrator confess: "My wound healed slowly, but towards my father I actually bore no ill feeling. On the contrary, he somehow seemed even to have grown in my eyes. Let psychologists explain this contradiction if they can" (111). To accommodate this "modern" contradiction, Turgenev devises a modernistic conclusion. The son retreats from "the garden," now forever ruined, into social spaces and social time, into, that is, the duration of history. The fate of the principal characters is not dramatized but narrated—the son returns to his studies in St. Petersburg; the father dies of a stroke eight months later; Zinaida dies four years later in childbed, just days before the narrator decides, after various postponements, to see her once more. Nothing survives these historical liquidations and affective losses but a mood. It is this mood which constitutes, I believe, the emotional substance of First Love. These are the narrator's parting and summarizing reflections as he assesses the emotional legacy of his First Love:

> What has come of it all—of all that I had hoped for? And now when the shades of evening are beginning to close in upon my life, what have I left that is fresher, dearer to me, than the memories of that brief storm that came and went so swiftly one morning in the spring?
>
> But I do myself an injustice. Even then, in those lighthearted days of youth, I did not close my eyes to the mournful voice which called to me, to the solemn sound which came to me from beyond the grave. (123)

Turgenev captures, in this grave reprise, the *elegiac* tone endemic to modern feeling—that mournful tone of a sadness that persists beyond the life-chilling breath of irony. Here the buoyant mood of First Love does not contradict, but secretly conspires with, a vision of our destined end. Eros initiates, but Thanatos limits, the course of true love. It is as if First Love is proleptically eager to advance its narrative into the enclosed spaces of elegy, cherishing its days precisely because they are fated to be the "days that are no more." It is in this sense that First Love is in love with death and all the "heavy-hearted" sounds that solemnly call to us from beyond the grave. Death guarantees that First Love will have no successors. First Love is a modern invention precisely to the extent that it articulates not a naive but a sentimental life-myth of our first affections.

## SADNESS, OR THE IMPOTENCE OF IRONY

Literature, Yeats wonderfully claimed, "differs from explanatory and scientific writing in being wrought about a mood, or a community of moods, as the body is wrought about an invisible soul."[45] For Kierkegaard, too, the aesthetic enters into and organizes the personality as mood:

The aesthetic view takes account of the personality in its relation to the environment, and the expression for this relation in its repercussion upon the individual is pleasure. But the aesthetic expression for pleasure in its relation to the individual is mood. In mood the personality is present but only dimly present. For he who lives aesthetically seeks as far as possible to be absorbed in mood, he seeks to hide himself entirely in it, so that there remains nothing in him which cannot be inflected into it; for such a remainder has always a disturbing effect, it is a continuity which would hold him back. The more the personality disappears in the twilight of mood, so much the more is the individual in the moment, and this, again, is the most adequate expression for the aesthetic existence: it is in the moment.[46]

Aesthetic existence may in some sense be said to commence with the First Love, which has the power to transform the moment—the temporal content of the aesthetic—into the momentous.

Yet we might also note that personality does not so much disappear in the "moment" of First Love as dissolve into its characteristic "twilight" mood—sadness. Turgenev's narrator reminds us that sadness is what does *justice* to First Love, which otherwise might be dismissed, perhaps indicted, for squandering all the hopes of youth in a "brief storm that came and went so swiftly." Sadness is the mood that, as its root sense declares, comes of satiety with the world of experience; hence the emotional as well as formal pertinence of Turgenev's frame device, an after-dinner recollection. Joyce, who appreciated the power of "mood" in literary art, worried in his notes for *Exiles* that the "greatest danger in the writing of this play is tenderness of speech or of *mood*" (emphasis mine, to underline the value of Yeats's remarks on literary moods). Joyce insisted that Bertha's love for her child "must, of course, be accentuated by the *position of sadness* in which she finds herself" (126). I take this position of sadness to be the narrative mood in which the fictions of modernity station themselves. There is, I believe, a purposeful contrast in Joyce's insistence on Bloom's sadness as a *wiser* life-mood than Stephen's brooding, derelict melancholia.

The signs of this novelistic *tristesse* are legion in modern fiction, from Ford Madox Ford's "saddest story," *The Good Soldier,* to the moody communities who rally around Pynchon's Tristero. The specific sexual import of novelistic *tristesse* is told in the sadness of Gretta Conroy as she remembers Michael Furey, her first love. Gretta's memory of the boy who died for love of her is the culminating epiphanic event of "The Dead," the story whose end signals the beginning of Joyce's modernist revolution. Gabriel, as latecomer, mockingly regards the sad dreaminess of his wife's memory as an effeminate effusion of the Celtic imagination, whose mythological lore and language Joyce himself forswore for more virile, Hellenic attitudes. Yet as Florence Walzl has shown in her fine analysis of the names given to Gretta's two loves, Michael and Gabriel, the story's conflicting emotions are resolved by archetypal, not nationalistic, allegiances. Walzl notes that in the angelic hierarchies, Michael takes precedence over Gabriel, "a relationship which is probably exemplified in the ascendancy of Michael over Gabriel in Gretta's consciousness."[47] Michael is "the warrior angel of the Last Judgment, depicted in art holding scales and associated with the settling of accounts." He is empowered to rescue the souls of the faithful at the hour of their death. Walzl sees this as a deliberate ambiguity in Joyce's portrayal, where I would stress the ascendancy of Michael Furey, who, at the hour of judgment and the narrative settling of accounts, rescues the story, if not Gabriel, from a spirit-deadening, life-chilling irony.

As a figure of First Love, Michael remains unscathed by the cold insinuations of Gabriel's ironic interrogations:

> —What was he? asked Gabriel, still ironically.
> —He was in the gasworks, she said.
> Gabriel felt humiliated by the failure of his irony and by the evocation of this figure from the dead, this boy from the gasworks.

Gretta's literal reply unmans Gabriel and reveals a spiritual limit that irony can neither penetrate nor dematerialize. His jealous skepticism, like Richard's wounding doubt, recoils upon him, leaving him with a "shameful consciousness of his own person." The shame here is both a sexual abashedness at his own (here literally) "untimely" lust and a recognition of the impotence of irony in the presence of a first and eternal Love. It is the spirit of irony, Gabriel's spirit, that swoons and faintly falls, like the descent of its last end, in the story's final lines.

Thus it is a mistake, I feel, to see in this ending the birth of Joyce the master ironist. A stranger and sadder affect emerges in Gabriel's final and unresentful vision of his wife: "His curious eyes rested long upon her face and on her hair: and, as he thought of what she must have been then, in that time of her first girlish beauty, a strange friendly pity for her entered his soul. He did not like to say even to himself that her face was no longer beautiful, but he knew that it was no longer the face for which Michael Furey had braved death." Gabriel's vision of human temporality, what Dante determined to be the order of time perceived by the constancy of reason, is expressed through a complex rhetoric of times and moods. The time of Gretta's girlish beauty and fatal love—the accomplished past—arouses in Gabriel a generous consciousness of Gretta's face as no longer beautiful enough to inspire the passion that braves death. Irony, with its cold views and frigid distances, remains, like an irritated interlocutor, on the periphery of such a complex and complete feeling for the days and the beauty and the bravery that are no more.

The affecting style of modern narrative, then, is wrought just beyond the horizon defined by the disjunctive and skeptical perspectivism of irony narration. To forge that style is the implicit end of First Love narratives, as Woolf's *Mrs. Dalloway,* Lawrence's *Sons and Lovers,* and Joyce's *Ulysses* attest. The hero or heroine of these narratives is a mystified, "quixotic" latecomer who conquers, it must be admitted, nothing—perhaps does not need to, in a concrete, historical sense. What he or she defeats is the ironic attitude toward the world. Lukács held that irony was "the normative mentality of the novel" and the constitutive structure of the "ideology of modernism." [48] Modernism, he proposed, reifies the distance separating subjective experience and sensation from the objective realm of deeds and events. Yet it must also be said that irony can bridge but cannot fill that space.[49] First Love proposes a counterrhetoric of subjectivity and temporality. It is a rhetoric outwardly limited, but not inwardly determined, by irony. In marking this boundary beyond which irony may not pass, the boundary demarcated by Gretta's stubborn and dreamy immersion in the recollection of her First Love, the "modern" acknowledges its inner debt to Romanticism and the cult of the heart. First love mediates between the Romantic, egotistical sublimity that sees in its affections *first* causes and immortal intimations and the realist's patient enunciation of those material forces that rule the world. Hence its indispensability for the creation of a modern literature, intent on forging myths that will reconcile the generic as well a the emotional contradictions between the reality and the pleasure principles.

## WHY THESE IDOL-MAKERS

Why this one and not another may be the first and finally unanswerable question about first love, or in fact, any love. But I am not willing to concede, as Molly does at the end of *Ulysses,* as well these writers as any others. The authors and the fictions I examine are representative works of beginning, high, and late modernism before it is overwhelmed by the playful, if moody, ironies of a literature we identify (perhaps to acknowledge our own mood of temporal dislocation) as "postmodern." Hardy is an exemplary and necessary figure with which to begin this study of modern love. Auden, in his moving appreciation of Hardy, writes of his undisplaceable position in the history of English modernism, a place which is largely, but never exclusively, a question of "dates":

> Hardy had been born in an agricultural community virtually untouched by industrialism and urban values, and when he died its disintegration was almost completed. The conflict between science and Faith which worried Tennyson, worried him but he had to live longer and so go beyond Tennyson's compromise. The pessimism of Schopenhauer, the determinism of Spinoza were not of course final solutions, but they were a necessary and progressive step in development for certain people placed in a certain situation.
>
> It is not a question of historical date only. Baudelaire and Rimbaud faced conditions in Paris which provincial England did not have to face until after the Great War. That is why they now seem so modern. But no society or individual can skip a stage in their development, though they may shorten it. Whatever its character, the provincial England of 1907, when I was born, was Tennysonian in outlook; whatever its outlook the England of 1925 when I went up to Oxford was The Waste Land in character. I cannot imagine that any other single writer could have carried me through from the one to the other.[50]

I cannot imagine any other writer who could have carried me through from the creation to the demise of the myth of First Love. As a chronicler of human life, Hardy has genuine concerns not just with *novelistic* infractions: lapses in decorum, failures of propriety, or vulgarities in feeling. His mythic subject is that spiritual chagrin which has little to do with the embarrassments of ill-breeding. His tragic agents are Promethean lawbreakers—they violate taboos. My mythical reading of Hardy will concentrate on the first and last tragedies, where these taboos are openly defied and then strictly defended. The first major tragedy, *Return of the Native,* like the first extant fiction, *Desperate Remedies,* describes the violence bred by mother-son love, the oedipal instance of the incest taboo that is our classic model for tragic emotion. The mythical plot of the last tragedy, *Jude the Obscure,* entails repeated assaults on the other major cultural taboo related to my theme, the taboo of virginity (which is also the taboo evoked and flouted in the subtitle of *Tess of the D'Urbervilles*—"A Pure Woman").

In Hardy we encounter, or re-encounter, the primary identification that defines our study of modern idolatry: the first love is mother love, subjective and objective genitive. The formulation is Joyce's, but the formula is by now a commonplace of modern psychology. In the readings that follow, I will rely on Freud and Melanie Klein to trace First Love back to its origin in that dim but emotionally sustaining past—the primal world of infancy. While Freud is the first to demonstrate, as empirical and psychological fact, that First Love is mother love, it is Klein who will describe, at times unforgettably, the ambivalence that inevitably attends this primary identification. For Klein this ambivalence is staged as a psychic battle between two opposing "idols": one, the ministering Good Mother, who nourishes and satisfies; the other, the persecutory Bad Mother, who frustrates and denies. The outcome of their contention determines, according to Klein, the prototype of all our subsequent happy and unhappy loves. To link the child's demands to the erotic quests of modern fiction is not to reduce the fictions of infantile fantasies, but to describe the world of modern novels as it actually seems to me to be: a world of primal urges and sublimated behaviors.

Perhaps no one was more directly in contact with this world of primal feelings than D. H. Lawrence. Consequently, perhaps no other modern writer gives us such lacerating descriptions of their perverse displacements. Lawrence's first great modern novel, *Sons and Lovers,* diagnosed a soul-sickness that Lawrence claimed was legion, the tragedy of "thousands of young men in England . . . it was Ruskin's, and men like him." It was the sickness growing out of the first, reciprocal love of mothers and sons. This love urges the sons into life, yet denies them their manhood: "But when they come to manhood, they can't love, because their mother is the strongest power in their lives, and holds them." [51]

It was not until the great novels of the middle period that First Love was reconceived by Lawrence not in oedipal but in biblical terms, thus liberating him to announce his prophetic theme: the emergence of man and woman alive, individual, self-responsible, creating their own destiny. In the late works this myth continued to inspire Lawrence with something like a sad hope. In *Lady Chatterley's Lover,* Connie Chatterley, who confuses sexual initiation with the experience of First Love, observes the end of her maidenhood in the "roused intimacy of those vivid and soul-enlightened discussions" of the "sex thing": "It marked the end of a chapter. It had a thrill of its own too: a queer vibrating thrill inside the body, a final spasm of self-assertion, like the last word, exciting, and very like the row of asterisks that can be put to show the end of a paragraph, and a break in the theme." [52] Lawrence, an angelic Lawrence, as I shall

somewhat perversely proclaim him, is the messenger come to resume—or repair—the broken theme in his great gospels of modern love, *The Rainbow* and
*Women in Love*.

That the last tale of Joyce's *Dubliners* "The Dead," culminates in a return of
First Love suggests how the Joycean *ricorso,* the structural element of his fictions, whatever the "style" of their telling, is allied to the myth I am enunciat-
ing. My reading of "The Dead" predicates this relationship, which I will elaborate in my analysis of Joyce's "endearing form" in *Ulysses.* And "Beckett's
Affections" attempts to uncover the emotional vastation that motivates what I
deem the exhibitionistic impulse of his irony. Beckett Agonistes is often presented as a purely ironic being, methodically overseeing his own ritual dismemberment or *sparagmos.* I will observe Beckett, the elegist of Murphy, unable to
disassemble the "levers of the tired heart," Beckett the amanuensis of Molloy,
on his way back to Mother, Beckett the banished and bereft son of "First Love."

Whatever their temperamental and stylistic differences, the modernists
who enlist First Love as an engendering myth of their fictions have all been well
schooled in the romantic vein. Kierkegaard comments on what we might expect
of such discipleship:

> The result of an education by novels and romances can be two-fold.
> Either the individual sinks deeper and deeper into illusion, or he emerges
> from it and loses faith in the illusion, but gains a belief in mystification. In
> illusion the individual is hidden from himself; in mystification, he is hid-
> den from others, but both cases are results of a romantic training.[53]

My authors are all the schoolboys of schoolboys, as Stephen Dedalus might say.
Their literature everywhere attests to the disciplines and affective enthusiasms
of their romantic training, from which they have emerged stripped of their faith
in illusion, but not of their belief in mystification. No longer readers, they
become writers, the producers rather than receivers of romantic effects. Each
one has a heart that dilates differently to the tendernesses and fears inspired by
First Love, yet each joins company, as omniscient narrators do, to keep watch
over a more common, pitied, and loved humanity. The idols of modern fiction
give form to this feeling, too deep for tears, which insists on telling itself, as if
for the first time.

TWO

# THE MODERN
# IDOLS

I N *LE LYS DANS LA VALLÉE,* Balzac memorializes first love as a life-absorbing idolatry:

> In the first woman we love we love everything about her; her children are ours, her house is ours, her interests are our interests, her unhappiness is our great unhappiness. We love her dress, her furniture. We are more distressed to hear her crops are damaged than we are when we are losing our own money . . . in other women, later, we look for them to enrich our worn out feelings with the feelings of youth.[1]

Balzac's own first love, Mme de Berny, was dying as he wrote these words, so his sentiments have the peculiar force of a commemorative rather than idly nostalgic retrospection. He attributes to First Love the power to evoke a humanly habitable world—its manner of dress, its furnishings, its domestic economies. Later loves, Balzac tells us, are more genuine instances of narcissistic dalliances, in which it is one's own feelings and not the complex facts of existence that are cultivated to yield the ambiguous bounties of love.

First Love is not a theme for dreamy introverts, unconversant with and uninterested in the world. The affective environment in which First Love unfolds is the vivid here and now, the realm of palpable presences and consequential events. In its "novelistic" extroversions, First Love gives birth to the romance of *reality.* Balzac's own social realism may originate in these jealous devotions of First Love, passionately interested in the world in which the Beloved live and moves.

In the sublime economy proposed by First Love, self-interest and the interest of the Beloved are seen to coincide. Such mutuality vouches for the moral productivity of the artist's world-conquering dream by translating him, as Stephen Dedalus speculates, out of the realm of possibilities into the world of actualities. The formula Stephen devises to articulate this second birth may be said to epitomize the relation between the experience of First Love and the "modern" apprehension of the beginning of the (narratable) life story: "He found in the world without as actual what was in his world within as possible" (175). This formula is advanced through Stephen's reading of Shakespeare's life, which begins by reconsidering the significance of Shakespeare's marriage to Ann Hathaway. Challenging the tradition that Shakespeare's first love was a "mistake," Stephen maintains that for the man of genius all "errors are volitional and the portals of discovery." In submitting to the sexual blandishments of "the ugliest doxy in all Warwickshire," Shakespeare is choosing to act and be acted upon. Stephen projects his own temperamental passivity in describing the dynamics of this encounter: "He chose badly? He was chosen it seems to me." Stephen regards this fateful encounter as the true beginning of Shakespeare's artistic destiny, citing *Venus and Adonis* as the inaugural text of his election to the "new life": "The greyeyed goddess who bends over the boy Adonis, stooping to conquer, as prologue to the swelling act, is a boldfaced Stratford wench who tumbles in a cornfield a lover younger than herself" (157).

We will consider, somewhat later and at greater length, Stephen's self-interested reading of Shakespeare's First Love. What immediately should arrest us in Stephen's argument is his acute sensitivity to the material debts that underwrite our erotic and social commerce with the world. He cannot even commence his revisionary telling of Shakespeare's artistic biography without first inwardly recognizing that his own identity is designated, even as it is shadowed, by the fact of debtorship. His theory that Shakespeare has no truant memory forces him to acknowledge his own debt—and hence the continuity of his former actions with his present character—to his "fellow poet," A. E.: "A. E. I. O. U." (156). Although Stephen apparently has no present plans for *discharging* this debt, he at least understands that he must pay his way to become a "lord of language." To renege on or conveniently "forget" one's debts, as Stephen is tempted to do, is to abandon the vocation of the lover-artist and assume the identity of his parodic double—the sentimentalist. The telegram he speeds to Mulligan as prologue to his act of sundering is the (misquoted) line from *The Ordeal of Richard Feverel,* "A sentimentalist is he who would enjoy [reality] without incurring the immense debtorship for a thing done" (164).

Tellingly, Stephen omits the word "reality" in his citation, thus suggesting that for him enjoyment constitutes an end in itself, regardless of its objects. But enjoyment—indeed possession!—of reality is the goal of the artistic and life quest. One must, however, pay for enjoying reality. As a spoiled priest of the imagination, Stephen suppresses the word "reality," because he fears that the material images—or idols in their general sense—fashioned by the imaginative mind compromise even as they express the spirit's dream of an unfettered freedom. The didactic and ethical inclinations of the novel (which can conflict with its "realist" mandate to document psychological and social effects impartially) share and endorse this spiritual attitude. One of the moral purposes of the novel is to instruct us in the ways in which we are not free, yet still responsible for the particular form our servitude—often another name for our loving—might take. Of course, Stephen can only know the world as a series of bad or looming debts. For him First Love remains the one and only IOU he is eager to acquire. "And my turn? When?" (157).

For Stephen, First Love is the sexual and artistic initiation of the creator as a *miglior fabbro,* the fabulous artificer who remakes the world to reflect the lineaments of his gratified or frustrated desire. His images, products of his material as well as spiritual commerce with the world, have the function and attain the status of idols. They attest to the profound sociability that accompanies and qualifies Joyce's deep imaginative investment in the myth of the artist as the isolated, proud Luciferian rebel, the creator as god-supplanter. For the idol maker, as Ruskin asserts in his magnificent lecture on idolatry, is primarily motivated by the desire for "the companionship of images." Whether that desire is demonic or right is, as Ruskin further remarks, a "grave question," one we must address before assessing the idols fashioned by the artists of First Love.

For Ruskin, the problem of idolatry is framed by two questions: "What—having the gift of imagery—should we by preference endeavor to image?" This question, however, is "subordinate to the deeper one—why we should wish to image anything at all." He observes that though we create idols for different purposes—"to play with them, or love them, or fear them, or worship them"—the same life-furthering intention may be seen to be at work. "The great mimetic instinct underlies all such purpose," Ruskin claims, an instinct that "is zooplastic—life-shaping—alike in the reverent and the impious."[2] The idolizing instinct attends and empowers the mimetic instinct. It is the instinct for realism and realization, which in turn originates in "the desire for the manifestation, description, and companionship of unknown powers; and for possession of a bodily substance . . . instead of an abstract idea."[3] However, the idolater's longing to possess reality in its concrete substance rather than its abstract or formless essence is susceptible to corruption, moral errancy, or vulgar dilettantism. "You must have," admonishes Ruskin, "not only the idolizing instinct, but an ἦϑος which chooses the right thing to idolize!" For the creative power "to discover the nature of justification" requires the presence of a "third passion," the passion for Discipline, defined as "the desire of equity and wholesome restraint":

> Now when a nation with mimetic instinct and imaginative longing is also thus occupied earnestly in the discovery of Ethic law, that effort gradually brings precision and truth into all its manual acts; and the physical progress of sculpture, as in the Greek, so in the Tuscan, school, consists in

gradually *limiting* what was before indefinite, in *verifying* what was inaccurate, and in *humanizing* what was monstrous.[4]

Ruskin's discussion concerns the art of sculpture, which he conceives as "the art of fiction in solid substance." I want to apply his insights to the specific narrative idolatry that is the subject of my study, the idolatry that so troubled Adorno, by which *the first* as a chronological term is invested with a spiritual priority. Ruskin's criteria provide us with a standard for evaluating these idolatrous narratives of the first time. They permit the more positive interpretation of First Love as the instructive occasion (in the Kierkegaardian sense) during which the inaccurate perceptions of the youthful or narcissistic imagination, which contemplates itself as an indeterminate outline, begins to verify its own moral boundaries. First Love, that is, also may be seen as engaged in the discovery of an Ethic Law that would humanize whatever might be indefinite, even monstrous, in imaginative longing. The idols fashioned by First Love thus reflect the lover's ethical character as much as the creative turbulence of his emotional state.

Ruskin, for example, distinguishes between an ignoble idolatry "which consists in the attribution of a spiritual power to a material thing" and a "noble and truth-seeking" idolatry, which he sees comprehended in the "general term of Imagination:—that is to say, the invention of material symbols which may lead us to contemplate the character and nature of gods, spirits, or abstract virtues and powers, without in the least implying the actual presence of such Beings among us, or even their possession, in reality, of the forms we attribute to them."[5]

Ruskin's distinction between ignoble and noble material symbols will permit me to enforce another important distinction that pertains to the idols of First Love, one that will eventually help us to understand and assess how these idols minister to spiritual self-possession. The difference that concerns me here is the difference between an idol and a fetish. The fetish lacks the conceptual dignity and affective range of an idol. The fetish is an animistic or psychological commodity that functions primarily as an amulet to ward off evil or subjugate malevolent forces. By virtue of both its form and its function, the fetish is seen to placate those invisible powers that threaten the fragile, menaced ego. The idol, on the contrary, enjoys a mythological existence and indeed testifies to an imaginative and transformative rather than strictly libidinal and reactive relation toward the object world. The novel is disposed to idolatry precisely to the extent that it perceives the world aesthetically as the domain of "interesting" people and the objects that symbolize their reality-enhancing, spirit-manifest-ing powers. The religious mind disputes this view and proposes the world as an ethical arena for spiritual self-determination. Ruskin attempts to transcend this dichotomy between moral beings and interesting persons. For him the impor-tant and crucial distinction is between idols that minister to the Spirit, and so to Life, and those which ignobly serve the Letter, and so administer Death. Ruskin identifies two forms of "deadly idolatry which are now all but universal in England":

> The first of these is the worship of the Eidolon, or Fantasm of Wealth . . .
> which is briefly to be defined as the servile apprehension of an active
> power in Money, and the submission to it as the God of our life.
> The second elementary cause of the loss of our nobly imaginative
> faculty, is the worship of the Letter, instead of the Spirit, in what we
> chiefly accept as the ordinance and teaching of Deity; and the apprehen-
> sion of a healing sacredness in the act of reading the Book whose primal
> commands we refuse to obey.[6]

The idols of First Love are created, as we shall see, by those imaginative beings responsive to the claims of the Spirit over the tyranny of the Letter. Indeed, in First Love we may observe how the theological imperative to wed the Letter to the Spirit acts as a powerful inner determination. The idolatries of First Love are of cultural interest because they refigure the modern myth of originality as a struggle to determine priority and so establish a scale, if not a hierarchy, of value, one not predicated on the authority of a transcendental Ethical signifier (Ruskin's deity and the book of primal commands He authors and authorizes). They are of consuming psychological interest because they dramatize the fantasies of consciousness in its first encounter with the world of the Other. In these idolatries, we can assess the distinctive attractions and haz-ards of the mind's life-shaping instinct; we can begin to appreciate in what ways idols are life-advancing, and so understand what is forfeited by renouncing them.

I want to begin my assessments by adapting the nomenclature advanced by Francis Bacon's *New Organon*, a work expressing a modern skepticism about the reality of the mind's creations, particularly those which minister to its self-love or self-interest. Bacon speaks generally of an idol as a figment of thought. Idols are delusive images of truth that can be dismissed by the rational correction of error and the purgation of baseless or ignoble superstitions. But it is Bacon's analysis of the idols in their specific kinds that proves exceedingly useful in characterizing the nature and function of the idols peculiar to First Love. The universal idols he considered under their provenance as Idols of the Tribe: they "have their foundation in human nature itself and in the tribe or race of men."[7] Bacon compares the human understanding to a false mirror, "which, receiving rays irregularly, distorts and discolours the nature of things by mingling its own nature with it." The Idols of the Tribe, then, owe their existence and take their particular conformation from the general nature and workings of the human understanding. The Idols of the Cave, on the other hand, are created out of a particular disposition or temperament and so reflect a more determined, often a more ingenious, subjectivity. Idols of the Market Place denote the verbal illusionism in which words either are assigned to realities that do not exist (Bacon cites Fortune and Prime Mover as examples of such unverifiable phantasms) or designate realities irregularly defined. Finally, Bacon identifies as a separate but related species of phantasm the Idols of the Theater, which are the products of systems. They are "plainly impressed and received into the mind from the playbooks of philosophical systems and the perverted rules of demonstration."[8] These idols cannot be refuted, for to do so is to enter into the dialectical abyss of their own erring imaginative systems. The countercharm to such infatuating idols is equilibrium of mind, under which the understanding of the world might finally commence. *New Organon* was to educate or lead man out of the wilderness into the promised land of rationalist understanding—the kingdom of man. If the idols would be renounced and "put away with a fixed and solemn understanding," then the understanding would be "thoroughly freed and cleansed; the entrance into the kingdom of man, founded on the sciences, being not much other than the entrance into the kingdom of heaven, whereinto none may enter except as a little child."[9]

*New Organon* is a modern text dating to 1620. Its conception of the new learning encompasses both a rational course of intellectual instruction and scientific inquiry and a metaphor for the duty of consciousness to itself: to work its own liberation from its self-benighting, self-enslaving idolatries. This is also the work undertaken by Nietzsche in his proposed "revaluation of all values." *The Twilight of the Idols* was his "grand declaration of war" against the idols that oust the "realities" of existence. But Nietzsche also plotted another strategy to recover his "high spirits":

> Another form of recovery, in certain cases even more suited to me is to *sound out idols* . . . There are more idols in the world than there are realities: that is *my* "evil eye" for this world, that is also *my* "evil ear". . . . For

once to pose questions here with a *hammer* and perhaps to receive for
answer that famous hollow sound which speaks of inflated bowels—what
a delight for one who has ears behind his ears—for an old psychologist
and pied piper like me, in presence of whom precisely that which would
like to stay silent *has to become audible. . . .* [10]

Nietzsche, the idol smasher, describes a diseased modernity engorged by its
idolatry and emitting, like Beckettian moribunds, the malodorous wind of
bloated bowels. Christianity is the spiritually infectious agent, and Dionysian
*ecstasis* the prescribed emetic.

Nietzsche's *Götzen–Dämmerung* staged an apocalyptic assault on the anti-
naturalism of Judeo-Christian thought, which could only stage the ritual of
salvation as a Golgotha. Against the idolatry of the cross he preferred the Dionysian revels, in which the god might be killed and his body scattered, so that
life might eternally recur. Indeed, for Nietzsche, the "intrinsic profound meaning of all antique piety" could be located in the sexual symbol.[11] As an insight
into imaginative activity rather than as an ideological exhortation, Nietzsche's
psychologizing has much to say about the general relation between sex and
creativity but little about the individual psychology of the sexual relation. In
Nietzsche's case, this seems a necessary consequence of his own enthrallment
to the Dionysian element of Hellenic culture. Woman is the idol of Nietzschean
theater—a mobile, unstable, procreant figure of Truth. Woman can never enact
the drama of love's wonted transcendence, never experience the sexual mysteries in the dimension of the personal. This I take to be the final import of
Nietzsche's claim to be the psychologist of the orgy.

At the close of *Twilight of the Idols* Nietzsche adverts to the importance of
this psychology in determining his first effort to transvalue values in *The Birth
of Tragedy*. In their "overflowing feeling of life and energy within which even
pain acts as a stimulus," the Dionysian orgiastic mysteries provided him with
the key to tragic feeling. To realize the eternal joy of becoming, Dionysian life
will sacrifice its highest type. The Apollonian temperament responds by representing the forsaken or sacrificed one in a clarified image. The Apollonian artist
would rescue, repair, and consecrate the sacrificed one in his discrete individuality. Nietzsche felt little sympathy with such Apollonian representations, which
idolized the individual and suspected the collective. The Apollonian cult of
individual suffering emerged, he argued, out of a devitalized instinct; it led to
pessimism, to the Aristotelian theory of tragedy as purgation, and the affective
drama of pity and terror. The sexual dithyramb affirms life and subdues pessi-

mism by resolutely embracing, indeed *postulating* pain and loss as part of the joy in creation. This Dionysian joy in the destruction necessary to all creation shadows Nietzsche's definition of Love as "the spiritualization of sensuality," which he hails as "a great triumph over Christianity." But he is the prophet who hails a further triumph, beyond the bounds of this study and one, I confess, that holds little appeal for me—the triumph he designates as "the spiritualization of *enmity.*" [12] The perspectivism of his gay science, which describes for us the ludic male in his most militant moods, bears little resemblance to the more subtle and concrete play of intersubjectivities which is the great theme and most civilizing activity of the novel.

In waging war against the "hollow" idols of modern thought, Nietzsche, I need hardly relate, provides no quarter for those ontological idols that First Love summons through the uncanny persistence of its feelings—those phantasms Nietzsche catalogs as "unity, identity, duration, substance, cause, materiality, being." [13] In demystifying and dispensing with these idolatries, Nietzsche can entertain us with "maxims and arrows," histories of errors and his own corrective propositions, but no narrative. Only the novelist can sound the idols of unity and identity, duration and cause, materiality and being, without smashing them. In the novelist's Apollonian representations we derive whatever understanding we can humanly possess of what is gained in creating and preserving the modern idols and what is lost in their destruction or—in what amounts to the same thing—their demystification. It is not enough to sound out idols unless one is willing to consider and, finally, judge, how hollow or resonant are the human vibrations they emit.

We are concerned, then, with the erotic and social idols that answer to the longings of the Apollonian temperament that would contain its rapture and projects its ideals within disciplined and individualized forms capable, as Stephen might say, of *arresting* the heart as well as transporting it. Bacon's nomenclature will help isolate the provenance of these idols, both in their general and in their particular, or local, representations: (1) The Idol of the Tribe: The Face; (2) The Idol of the Cave: Virginity; (3) The Idol of the Market Place: Comradeship; (4) The Idol of Theater: Beginning the World.

## THE FACE AS IDOL

The face is the first idol—of the child and of the tribe. In the ministering visage of the mother we receive our first intimations of our human nature; her face is the mirror in which the infant perceives the reflected image of its own integrity.

So begins what Juliet Mitchell speculates is the baby's "general fascination with human faces or human beings who are harmonious wholes at a time when the baby is unable to control its own movements." [14] The face is the first love of the human eye because it conjures up the being of both seer and seen, child and mother, in an ideal symbiosis. Moreover, as Mitchell reminds us, the loved face of the mother is, for the child, an initial attempt at self-portraiture. [15]

This general fascination with the face as an image of harmonious being persists in the adorations of later life. We seem to glimpse divinity in the answering gaze of the beloved or in those phantom faces of the portrait, the photograph, or the screen that enthrall us in a projected image of life. Through the face we come to know as well as to redream the world: For now we see as in a glass darkly, but then face to face. A complete narrative of human life would redeem this Pauline pledge of revelation in the fullness of time, but this narrative could be written only by a divine mind and interpreted only by a redeemed one. The impossibility of this textual apocalypse is a tragedy of comic proportions, as Beckett, inimitable in exposing the delusional structure of all human story, frequently reminds us. In *Molloy,* which can in fact be read as an exasperated satire on the Pauline conversion narrative, Moran, in the midst of his gradual metamorphosis into his "prey" Molloy, admits to a longing for a divine author. Moran, dutiful minister of powers he has never seen, confesses to his desire, long abandoned, to see Obidil, the idol (in both the administrative and metaphysical sense) of his existence. Obidil is the *almost* mirror image of that god of the Unconscious—Libido. Who else but Beckett would represent the mind's inner divinity in the ananym of a dyslexic!: "And with regard to Obidil, of whom I have refrained from speaking, until now, and whom I so longed to see face to face, all I can say with regard to him is this, that I never saw him, either face to face or darkly, perhaps there is no such person, that would not greatly surprise me." [16]

Whether god has disappeared, or died, or simply been denied existence by an unamazed skepticism ("perhaps there is no such person, that would not greatly surprise me") is a mystery that has lost its power, for Moran at least, to perplex. Rather it is man's capacity for perpetuating maleficent idols out of the bottomless "void" of his unconscious that convulses him with a strange laughter: "And at the thought of the punishments Youdi might inflict upon me I was seized by such a mighty fit of laughter that I shook, with mighty silent laughter and my features composed in their wonted sadness and calm" (162). Obidil, the primal "god," metamorphoses into Youdi, a figure of the Beckettian Super-Ego, who prohibits the ideal consummation of narrative desire: seeing face to face.

To see god is to die, a theological admonition that Beckett converts into an aggressive imperative—You die! Youdi, who will assume other names (for example, "Omniomni, the all-unfuckable," the sinister phallocentric idol of *Mercier and Camier*), provokes a strange laughter whose etiology, I will later attempt to show, is the aftershock of some earlier, traumatic seizure. As we shall see, the source of Beckett's traumatized narratives lies not in a transgression against the patriarchal gods of the symbolic order, but in the failure to comply with the self-silencing commands of the divinity who rules the Unconscious—the mother.[17]

For Thomas Hardy, fond of citing Novalis's epigram that Character is Fate, the human face, stressed or lined by experience, is the text which "fully confesses" the individual's truth: "In respect of character a face may make certain admissions by its outline; but it fully confesses only in its changes. So much is this the case that what is called the play of the features often helps more in understanding a man or woman than the earnest labours of all the other members together."[18] Hardy's moral dramaturgy consists almost exclusively in this play of features. Character and fate combine (literally) in the *complexion* of things. The complexion of events (a skein of intersecting causalities) permeates, then subdues, the natural radiance of the human countenance.

This complementarity between the complexion of events and their agents is what differentiates the human from what is mistakenly personified as such. In *The Return of the Native,* Hardy ascribes to Egdon Heath grandiloquent narrative powers: "The face of the heath," he relates, "by its mere complexion . . . could . . . retard the dawn, sadden noon, anticipate the frowning of storms scarcely generated, and intensify the opacity of a moonless midnight to a cause of shaking and dread." Egdon controls the dark times and determines the fearful moods of Hardy's tragic fable, yet remains itself "unmoved, during so many centuries, through the crises of so many things." It is the human frame that is unsettled or destroyed by the repeated shocks of that enduring crisis called modern life. Thus the complexion of the heath is described as one of "swarthy monotony," a mottled tone that distinguishes it from the vivid reds (of the blush and other marks of sexual chagrin) and pallid whites (of shock, horror, or sheer abnegation to the rule of overmastering events and luckless surprises) that define the range of hues in the human face.

Hardy's pictorial ambition to portray life in its telling but evanescent colorations is realized through portraits of astounding clarity. In these portraits we may glimpse the last vestiges of an idolatry of the *merely* human face of realistic narrative and the *first* glimpses of the eerie, mesmerizing portraiture of modern

physiognomy, of which, according to Pater, the Mona Lisa may serve as prototype and exemplar. This modern face is the face consumed by secret thoughts
or occult wisdom, a complexion either blanched by thought or suffused by the
blush of rapturous sensation.[19] The appeal, indeed *value* of the face as an existential portrait is established during the opening tableau of *The Return of the
Native*, which depicts the face of the sleeping Thomasin. Hardy describes her
face before it has composed itself into a waking pose: "The groundwork of the
face was hopefulness; but over it now lay like a foreign substance a film of
anxiety and grief" (41). Anxiety and grief, like the reddle that discolors Venn's
complexion, coat the hopeful countenance like a second, wizened skin. The
property of that foreign substance—care—to overcast the native hue of hopefulness with the "sickly cast of thought"[20] is demonstrated in Hardy's most
memorable facial icon for the plight of "modernity," the face as waste tablet. In
a rather quizzical description, the only passage Lawrence quotes at some length
in his study of Hardy, Clym Yeobright's face is compared to a waste tablet on
which are traced, in apparently indelible markings, the furrows of incisive—or
merely depressing?—thoughts:

> His countenance was overlaid with legible meanings. Without being
> thought-worn he yet had certain marks derived from a perception of his
> surroundings, such as are not unfrequently found on men at the end of
> the four or five years of endeavour which follow the close of placid pupi-
> lage. He already showed that thought is a disease of flesh, and indirectly
> bore evidence that ideal physical beauty is incompatible with emotional
> development and a full recognition of the coil of things. (162)

Lawrence complained that this symptomatic portrait depicts the relation between thought and the impressionable flesh as parasitic, while in fact, Lawrence
held, they were united in a true symbiosis: "One does not catch thought like a
fever: one produces it," Lawrence objected. "If it be in any way a disease of
flesh, it is rather the rash that indicates the disease than the disease itself."[21]
According to Lawrence, Hardy had misinterpreted the nature of the "affliction"
he saw as endemic to modern consciousness, mistaking its visible symptom—
the rash of irritable or distempered thought—with its origin in a deeper malaise, a "case of disease or unease of flesh."

What Lawrence disliked, even feared, in Hardy's portraiture was its modernity. The "disillusive nature" of the modern is represented by the lineaments
of Clym's face, lines etched not by vivid experience, but by corrosive realiza-
tions: "The view of life as a thing to be put up with, replacing that zest for

existence which was so intense in early civilizations, must ultimately enter so thoroughly into the constitution of the advanced races that its facial expression will become accepted as a new artistic departure" (147).

The face of the future, then, cannot picture life, but only, like Clym's face, decipher it. Such a face will fascinate not sculptors, but scribes:

> The lineaments which will get embodied in ideals based upon this new recognition will probably be akin to those of Yeobright. The observer's eye was arrested, not by his face as a picture, but by his face as a page; not by what it was, but by what it recorded. His features were attractive in the light of symbols, as sounds intrinsically common become attractive in language, and as shapes intrinsically simple become interesting in writing. (198)

Not the groundwork, but the finish of the face determines whether it is to be seen as a picture or read as a page. The page is the whitened field scored by the marks of incisive thought. The picture is a visual conjuration of being itself. It presents the illusion of an evokable presence and the special charms of portraiture: intrinsically simple and common features, the tinges of thought or mood that give the face its distinctive colorations. Clym's face has, apparently, no natural hue, only a pallor that resembles parchment. On this parchment the future inscribes hieroglyphs that make his face attractive (although only to a connoisseur of faces and not to those who, like Lawrence, prefer the living physiognomy to its symbolization in writing). Later Clym's mind will be described as "wrinkled," like a crumpled page from a waste tablet that time, like a dissatisfied novelist, makes ready to discard.

Clym's face, the palimpsest of his thoughts, is marked by the parchment pallor of death, or of, more accurately, those deadly recognitions that drain life of its blood, blanching it with the shock of unconscious thoughts become conscious and hidden fears confirmed. His face appeals to us as a text to be read, a legible rather than a lovable face. This differential play of features between Clym's devitalized "modern" countenance and Eustacia's self-delighting smile culminates in the complex interplay of looks in the novel's climactic recognition scene. Clym, newly apprised of Eustacia's role in the death of his mother, returns to Eustacia dressing before her glass, a picture of radiant life, "all carmine flush with which warmth and sleep had suffused her cheeks." Eustacia enjoys this moment of healthy if somewhat infantile narcissism, which has its predecessor and counterpart in the self-regarding smile with which Bathsheba greets her mirror image in the opening incident of *Far from the Madding Crowd*. The picture Bathsheba innocently reflects in her appreciative but private act of self-display is "a delicate one,"²² and Gabriel Oak, who witnesses it, and Hardy, who imagines it, would not think of interrupting this moment of self-delighting life. But the picture Eustacia both presents and observes dissolves in focus when "the death-like pallor in [Clym's] face flew across into hers" (386). Eustacia's face, no longer lovable nor loved, becomes a text in which Clym reads (wrongly) her exclusive culpability in his mother's death. When she questions the motive of his chilling intrusion, he responds: "You know what is the matter . . . I see it in your face." What Clym sees in Eustacia's face is the moral pallor of his own morbid consciousness communicated to her face and reflected there.

Eustacia's face is cruelly depicted here. Hers was not meant to serve as a waste tablet for thought nor to provide Clym with a convenient text of sexual treachery. Her face is a picture (as she herself knows!) to be adored; hers is the face-as-idol. Her impersonation of an infidel Turk in the mummery scene dramatizes her power to take on and cast off life, "her scope both in feeling and in making others feel" (167). The mummer's scene further complicates the representation of such female sublimity in showing us Eustacia not just with a costumed body, but with a masked face. Visored as the pagan Turk, she enacts and experiences a dark erotic destiny, the doom of Echo, "the power of her face all lost, the charm of her emotions all disguised, the fascination of her coquetry denied existence."

Hardy may be the last of our major novelists who could write about coquetry not as a subject for satire or censure, but as an object of fascination. Fascination is always the state of erotic transport eclipsed by an unwanted but inevitable shadow, the shadow of a future time when the beloved (man or woman) will no longer fascinate. The idol love creates is dependent on its maker to verify its power to inspire awe and delight. Eustacia understands this truth and remarks on its pathos when she complains to Clym, lost in the fascination of her face, that his passion is an affair of presence only: ". . . you occupy yourself, and so blind yourself to my absence" (231). Her rebuke foretells the troubles with sight literalized in the self-blinding labor of his reading. Clym is a forerunner to Jude, another Hardyesque idolater divided between the charms of the flesh and the disciplines of the book. But Clym, like Jude, is initially too dazzled by the world-transfiguring radiance of Eustacia's presence to heed any warnings about a future reckoning: "Let me look right into your moonlit face," he assures her, "and dwell on every line and curve in it! Only a few hair-breadths make the difference between this face and faces I have seen many times before I knew you; yet what a difference—the difference between everything and nothing at

all" (231–2). This difference between everything and nothing at all is the difference—"Half hidden from the eye"—that Wordsworth, the moonstruck lover
of the Lucy poems, made into a matter of egotistical sublimity: "Oh, / The
difference to me!" Yet the love which discovers this difference is fragile, as
Eustacia intuits, because the margin that defines a difference of such magnitude,
the difference between everything and nothing, is itself so slender, a matter of
a few hair breadths.

We should not, then, scan Eustacia's face for signs of legible meanings (we
are given Clym's face to satisfy that hermeneutic urge). Eustacia's face is a
theater that stages the supple play between existential and essential beauty that
Roland Barthes attributed to the captivating faces of the cinema "which
plunged audiences into the deepest ecstasy." For the idolatrous Barthes, "the
face of Garbo" was a sublime countenance that "offered to one's gaze a sort of
Platonic Idea of the human creature," one that pictured a transitional idol reconciling "two iconographic ages":

> A mask is but a sum of lines; a face, on the contrary, is above all their
> thematic harmony. Garbo's face represents this fragile moment when the
> cinema is about to draw an existential from an essential beauty, when the
> archetype leans toward the fascination of mortal faces, when the clarity of
> flesh as essence yields its place to a lyricism of Woman.[23]

Although we cannot see Eustacia's face, we are meant to believe in her archetypal essence as Queen of the Night. Through her self-exhibiting sex Hardy
presents to us that fragile moment in the history of narrative when the clarity
of female flesh as archetype (the post-Enlightenment obsession with the Eternal
Feminine) yields its place to a lyricism of Woman, which reaches its apotheosis
in the portrait of Tess, that pure and murderous woman. Tess's face is lovable as
a *lyric face* "that has nothing ethereal about it; all was real vitality, real warmth,
real incarnation":

> To a young man with the least fire in him that little upward lift in the
> middle of her upward top lip was distracting, infatuating, maddening. He
> [Angel Clare] had never before seen a woman's lips and teeth which
> forced upon his mind with such persistent iteration the old Elizabethan
> simile of roses filled with snow. Perfect, he, as a lover, might have called
> them off-hand. But no—they were not perfect. And it was the touch of
> the imperfect upon the would-be perfect that gave the sweetness, because
> it was that which gave the humanity.[24]

For the moderns who succeed Hardy, the face will never more inspire, through the delicate lyricism of its features, the fascination—and pathos—of mortal beauty. Only in the cinema, the art born out of a rapidly developing expertise in the arts of mechanical reproduction, will the face, magnified in close-up, exhibit anew its idolatrous powers. Indeed, for Ingmar Bergman, the close-up marks the "primary originality" of the cinematic vision. "Our work begins with the human face," he writes. "The possibility of drawing near to the human face is the primary originality and the distinctive quality of the cinema." [25] But the literary art, increasingly wary of such fascinations, will withdraw from descriptions of such tactile immediacy. It will give us "heads," not faces, blank and uninterpretable visages rather than blanched or tinted (hence morally expressive) countenances.

Orwell's *1984* may serve to illustrate the dehumanization that results from substituting inert picture for animate idol. The novel indeed reminds us how precious is the very ability to distinguish between a legible and a lovable face. In the world of Ingsoc, the face is neither readable nor lovable. It is the object of rote rather than readerly response; it does not fascinate, in the Hardyesque sense, but stimulates the reflexes of totalitarian identifications. The face of Big Brother, Winston Smith's mystical icon at the moment of his spiritual self-slaughter, and the face of Goldstein, which mobilizes anti-Semitic, zenophobic frenzy, are ideological pictures. They are not portraits infused, in the Wildean sense, with the character and spirit of their artist. These ideological icons are Pavlovian props whose sole function is to provoke an inflexible and absolutely conditioned response—enmity or love. In the totalitarian and non-narrative world of Ingsoc, the face is only representable in the rictus of conformist self-subjugation. Newspeak, we are informed, even has a word for "an improper facial expression" that brands as socially deviant any inflected—that is, idiosyncratic and individuating—counterresponse: *facecrime.*

In the cool fanaticism of O'Brien's description of the future that totalitarianism dreams for itself, Orwell depicts a world in which human affections are brutally defaced by a voracious, faceless power. O'Brien, whose own face had once suggested to Winston Smith a secret sympathy and kindred intelligence, envisions a time when human procreation, for Nietzsche the central affirmation of the Dionysian eternal recurrence, will be reduced to an "annual formality like the renewal of a rations card"; a world in which the orgasm will be abolished, while the imaginative pleasures of literature and the rational pleasures of science will be unknown. Yet even the analytical O'Brien must resort to vivid imagery to summarize the orgiastic rapture of the totalitarian fantasy-state:

"Always, at every moment, there will be the thrill of victory, the sensation of trampling on an enemy who is helpless. If you want a picture of the future, imagine a boot stamping on a human face—forever." [26]

Orwell's genius for exposing the affective manipulations of a political regime is nowhere more evident than in his depiction of the sadistic thrills craved by totalitarian man, whose lust for destruction is a constant somatic incitement. There is no conceivable way to discharge, in Freudian terms, such excitations in a single satisfaction. That is why Ingsoc must abolish the orgasm: people must not be permitted either the peace or the *tristesse* of the postcoital idyll. The body must be denied any evocative sensation that reminds it of its human nature, which for Orwell is its *first* nature. In the child's face, upturned in wonder or in love, we see the first steps toward claiming the birthright of an unmutilated humanity. Orwell as teller never reveals to us that face, the idol of a liberated humanity. But his tale suggests that a truly emancipated society will picture its rediscovered humanity as the child first glimpses its potential nature—in the face of the mother, she who wears no jackboots.

## THE IDOL OF THE CAVE: VIRGINITY

The face as idol testifies to the spiritual authority and emotional primacy of the mother. Orwell, a genuinely political man, is not too clever to dismiss the power of the maternal image to preserve the human affections from the hateful perversions of the will-to-power. First Love is at once the most primal and most subtle expression of this cult of womanhood and its affective symbolism, in which incestuous and religious longings fuse. In their fusion, the distinction between outside and inside is overborne, and a great harvest of emotional riches is gleaned.

Kierkegaard, in ascribing woman to the spiritual category "being for another," refines even as he suppresses this figuration of the mother as ideal or first nature. In "Diary of the Seducer" his Johannes is the aesthete who contends that Woman, as being-for-another, shares this category with Nature: "Nature as a whole exists only for another; not in the teleological sense, so that one part of Nature exists for another part, but so that the whole of Nature is for an Other—for the Spirit." [27] What holds true for the "whole" of women's existence also holds true for its particulars: "In the same way a mystery, a charade, a secret, a vowel, and so on, has being only for another." Woman, not only like but *as* Nature, remains an unintelligible category awaiting the impregnation of male Spirit, which alone endows matter with meaning, deciphers mysteries, solves charades, unriddles secrets, and articulates words out of vowels.

Feminist criticism has alerted us to the dangerous mystifications comprehended in this positing of Woman as being-for-another, who inspires speech but is herself silent, who suggests meaning but can never produce her own. What interests me here, however, is how this figure for Woman is materialized in the dialectician's dream-category—the pure being denoted by virginity:

> As being for another, woman is characterized by pure virginity. Virginity is, namely, a form of being, which, in so far as it is a being for itself, is really an abstraction, and only reveals itself to another. The same characterization also lies in the concept of female innocence. It is therefore possible to say that woman in this condition is invisible. As is well known, there existed no image of Vesta, the goddess who most nearly represented feminine virginity. This form of existence is, namely, jealous for itself aesthetically, just as Jehovah is ethically, and does not desire that there should be any image or even a notion of one. This is the contradiction, that the being which is for another *is* not, and only becomes visible, as it were, by the interposition of another.[28]

Virginity is the idol of the cave; it ministers to temperamental or subjective longings or dread. (Dread, which for Kierkegaard gives birth to the whole power of sensuousness, is the energy of Don Juan, the animating force of his "sensuous genius.")[29]

Kierkegaard's contention that virginity shuns representation, a self-withholding dictated by aesthetic rather than ethical considerations, is based on an insight shadowed by certain blindnesses. His insight is that the essence of virginity can be revealed only by the "interposition" of another. His blindness is in refusing to specify, or even to consider, the various forms this interposition might take, including, of course, the form of self-interposition. Novels, which shun solipsistic systems and embrace representations, refuse to regard individuals either as abstract categories or as pure essences (woman as Nature). The virgin as a novelistic being has a double nature: jealous guardian of her "invisibility," and "innocent" exhibitionist of her pristine body. In both capacities, she has been culturally instructed to preserve herself for "the firstcomer." And in the double, often comic role she must assume as both protector and displayer of her sexual wares, the virgin has a special place in the narratives of First Love.

We might understand the exhibitionism of Joyce's virgin, Gerty Mac-Dowell, as motivated by these contradictory impulses of spiritual pride and bodily display. In making painting the organizing art of her monologue, Joyce reminds us that virginity is a depicted state that poses for its possessor tragicomic problems in self-presentation. Gerty's self-display confirms rather than contradicts her virginal "being for another." Joyce depicts her exhibitionist game of hide-and-seek not as an indecorous performance, but as a psychological strategy to fulfill the female destiny culturally assigned to her. Gerty, in her mythological vestiture as Nausicaa, adorns herself to attract her "dreamhusband." We might say that it is Joyce's interposition as author that renders visible her virginity as the idol of Catholic Ireland: "Gerty MacDowell . . . lost in thought, gazing far away into the distance was, in very truth, as fair a specimen of winsome Irish girlhood as one could wish to see" (285–86). Joyce's clever use of "specimen" reminds us how natural types and cultural standards are often comically confused, but a more telling pun lurks in the sentimental adjective that specifies her maiden charm—winsome. For as Gerty's interior monologue all too plainly reveals, winsome is as winsome does: gazing into the distance, what she envisions is her eventual sexual triumph over her companion and sexual rival Edy Boardman (who squints and who prides herself in being petite though "she never had a foot like Gerty MacDowell, a five, and never would ash, oak or elm"!) (287). Assured by the superiority of her sexual charms and trusting to the superior quality of her feminine raiments, Gerty sets her sights on Bloom, confident that "he had eyes in his head to see the difference for himself." The poignant comedy of her performance is that she cannot project (as Molly can) an image which any newcomer might transfigure into idol. Rather she exhibits herself according to the outward conventions of feminine visibility and, consciously esteeming herself as a "votary of Dame Fashion," dutifully obeys the sartorial commands of her oracle, the *Lady's Pictorial.*

Gerty comically (and unknowingly) reveals to us the profound complicities between our most venerated cultural idols and the sentimental casuistries of a consumerism that literally advertises Woman as being-for-another. This complicity is formally reflected in Joyce's skillful interweaving of two ritual performances in the "Nausicaa" episode: Gerty's presentation of her body as a fashionably attired object to the fascinated Bloom (who as an adman appreciates her fastidious observance of the commercial pronouncements of Dame Fashion), and the rosary recited for the "men's temperance retreat by the missioner, the reverend John Hughes S.J." (290). The contrast between the ascetic purpose of the retreat and the intemperate glances that lead to the episode's masturbatory climax are obvious and pertinent. But equally if not more significant is Gerty's identification with the Virgin Mother, who theologically epitomizes the ideal of woman as being-for-another. In hearing "the old familiar words" of the litany of Our Lady of Loreto, "holy Mary virgin of virgins," Gerty finds her virginity transfigured and beatified. Mary, the virgin of virgins, both sublimates and reverses the Kierkegaardian notion of virginity as an invisibility awaiting interposition. Mary is the beatific being-for-another who actively interposes. She is the divine mediator, linked not to Nature but to Spirit in its feminized form. Intercession is the only power permitted to those resigned to their social and religious function as "being-for-another." It is as the devotee of the Virgin Mother that Gerty finds the image that defines her domestic role as a "second mother in the house, a ministering angel too with a little heart worth its weight in gold." Here we might detect the collusion of two apparently rival idolatries, one turned toward Dame Fashion, the other toward the Virgin Mother. Both conspire to subdue and domesticate Gerty's visible power to affect those who seek her emotional and sexual ministrations.

Her reward for saving herself and her womanly nature for her "dreamhusband" is that he would "love her, his ownest girlie, for herself alone." The awkward assonance in "ownest girlie" and "herself alone" is Joyce's way of rendering the "syntax" of a sentimental seaside girl who can arouse but never picture the passion of "real men." But Gertie is more than a simpering reciter of love's babble. Her foolish drivel comes from the very fiction that finds romance in the unsentimental economics of the patriarchal exchange. Two different pleasures in being first are endlessly retold and ideologically disseminated by such popular fictions: for the man, the pleasure of erotic primogeniture, the pleasure, that is, of being first in possession; for woman the pleasure of being loved alone, being loved, that is, not just for herself but against all others. Such are the rivalrous motives and struggles for sexual primacy dissimulated in the romantic cant of winsome Irish girlhood.

But to win some, Gerty must lose all. This is the irreversible law of sexual life, but it is precisely this law that the cult of virginity tries to dissimulate. Hence the social acumen and psychological prescience of Joyce's stylistic decision to depict virginity *sentimentally*. We might unleash our own dagger definition and propose that the virgin may be defined as she who would enjoy (sexual reality) without incurring the immense debtorship for the thing done. This definition is not proposed to disparage or mock Gerty's adolescent imagination. Rather it aims to suggest that the immaturity of the virginal mind consists in its inability to visualize, hence comprehend, the physical reality of sex as "a thing done." Whatever enjoyment Gerty derives from exhibiting herself, it is not, like Bloom's, an onanistic pleasure. Her pleasures belong to a less developed stage of autoerotism. She finds delight having her own body visually, never physically, embraced. Molly, in thinking about her daughter Milly's instinct for self-display ("I had to tell her not to cock her legs up like that on show on the windowsill before all the people passing they all look at her") invents her own inimitable epithet for the virgin-as-exhibitionist: the "great touchmenot" (631).

We might further understand Gerty's erotic status as a touchmenot by considering one of her forerunners in *Ulysses,* the nameless virgin at Hodges Figgis's window whom Stephen remembers earlier in the day. "She trusts me, her hand gentle, the longlashed eyes. Now where the blue hell am I bringing her beyond the veil? Into the ineluctable modality of the ineluctable visuality" (40). Despite the inward blast at his poetizing her gentle hands and longlashed eyes—now where the blue hell am I bringing her—Stephen's odd allusion to "beyond the veil" strikes one as a conscious naiveté. Defloration, if this is what Stephen has vaguely in mind, does not involve going beyond but through the hymenal veil. It is Stephen who reveals himself jealous, in the aesthetic sense, of exposing his own spiritual virginity, the foundation for the intellectual pride that is his most self-bruited attribute as artist. His rivalrous spirit makes him suspect this nameless virgin in her guise as a "lady of letters" seeking "the alphabet books you were going to write. Keen glance you gave her." Stephen's glance has the potential to bestow upon her the "ineluctable modality of the ineluctable visuality." Fearful still of entering into such exchanges, even visual ones, and so rending the veil by which woman preserves her disguise as being-for-another, Stephen quickly turns to unliterary women, those less likely to reveal their ineluctable modality as "real" characters or concrete objects of desire: "Talk that to someone else, Stevie: a pickmeup." Shunning the virgin, he once again forfeits the "occasion" of an artistically, if not emotionally, productive exchange. The alphabet books, like so many of his projected works, remain unwritten; the gentle hand ungrasped; these two events are not, as my argument should imply, unrelated.

Bloom, more eager for life as well as possessed of more pity, enjoys a different relation to Gerty MacDowell. Bloom's own temporarily forsaken idol, Molly, awaits him at home. We will meet up with her endearing form in a later chapter. This episode of voyeuristic dalliance, which culminates in a literal masturbatory climax, serves as a moral commentary on the onanism inherent in Johannes's dream-category of Woman as being-for-another. Woman reveals her being-for-another as pure spectacle, demonstrating that for women, *esse* is indeed *percipi:* "See her as she is spoil all. Must have the stage setting, the rouge, costume, position, music" (303). Woman must be theatricalized, securely framed within the setting of male desire, adorned and costumed, even positioned!—to elicit the full attraction of her "being-for-another."

Yet Bloom does have the imagination to "see her as she is" and, in fact, not spoil all. In his post-masturbatory *tristesse* (and discomfort), Bloom meditates on the "nature" of women in a more physical and social, less theatrical, sense: "Jilted beauty. A defect is ten times worse in a woman" (301). Here Bloom sympathizes with the sexual plight of virginal girlhood: engaged in rivalrous competitions, fearing the chagrin of being jilted, anxious lest she be fated to become a Nausicaa perpetually waiting on the shore. Bloom is not just voyeur, he is also witness, one whose polymorphous sexuality is more than matched by his novelistic empathy with natures different from his own. For him woman is being not for but as Another, her mysteries the mysteries of the world and its creative processes. For him woman as Nature is symbolized by the rich flow of her menstrual blood, linked to the cosmological tides that regulate the cycles of Creation: "How many women in Dublin have it today? Martha, she. Something in the air. That's the moon. But then why don't all women menstruate at the same time with the same moon, I mean? Depends on the time they were born I suppose" (301). Menstrual blood, as the one natural sign of womanliness, signifies woman's life-giving power and its profligate waste. It simultaneously signals a failure of conception and the proof that conception is still possible. Only the woman fated to perpetual virginity forfeits that power, and so the "natural" sense of her self as a life-generating being. Hence the complex pity and irony in Bloom's speculation, "Virgins go mad in the end I suppose" (301).

Let us leave aside the sexual politics of this supposition. What is novelistically pertinent here is that Bloom, following the most explicit exhibition of his voyeuristic and onanistic tendencies, still worries that virgins may be doomed to suffer a sexual fate general to *Ulysses* and, Joyce feared, to modernity as a whole: g.p.i., the general paralysis of the insane. Perpetual virginity, like the sexual promiscuity that can render one syphilitic, entails the risk of madness. The mad virgin has repressed the two desires that define woman's existence as being-for-another: the sexual impulse to serve Nature's procreative ends and the desire for self-representation. She is neither a Dionysian body nor an Apollonian being, a being who exists not for another, but, as Gerty says, for herself alone. This double repression produces, in the mixed world of modernity, that ambiguous double being, the *demi-vierge,* Lawrence's epithet for Lady Chatterley. Like Hardy's Sue Bridehead, Constance is neither maid nor wife, but some middling creature, born out of the self-negating, life-denying ethos of modernity.

It is only in one of his last imaginings, *The Virgin and the Gypsy,* which he dedicated to Frieda, that Lawrence attempts to recuperate the virgin as a narrative as well as ontological idol. Lawrence's novel describes the dissipation of postwar English life, in which physical and emotional energy is expended to maintain a "complete stability where one could perish safely." [30] The visionary symmetry of this work is existential and onomastic. The virgin's own identity is conditioned by two personages—the mother who deserted her, and who is referred to only as She-who-was-Cynthia; and the nameless gypsy who, in the climactic episode, rescues her from a flood, whose prototype is the flood that concludes *The Mill on the Floss*. Lawrence is both attracted and repelled by such watery death-rituals (one remembers the marsh flood that takes Tom Brangwen's life in *The Rainbow* and the drownings in the early episodes of *Women in Love*). He is, however, staunch in keeping faith with George Eliot's symbolic reading of disaster, interpreting such catastrophes as figures of a spiritual destiny accomplishing itself in the naturalized medium of history.

Thus the virgin's physical rescue portends her spiritual awakening, a rebirth signaled by her relearning the significance of proper names. The novel's last sentence, which concludes her convalescence and the narrative, links the virgin's recuperation with an almost shamanistic appreciation of the power of the name: "And only then did she realize that he had a name." The fable that begins by trying to efface the memory of She-who-was-Cynthia, literally a woman who disappears from public sight, concludes with the effort to restore public (and readerly) awareness of He-who-is-Joe-Boswell, the last Laurentian avatar of inviolate humanity:

> His race was very old, in its peculiar battle with established society, and had no conception of winning. Only now and then it could score.
>
> But since the war, even the old sporting chance of scoring now and then, was petty well quenched. There was no question of yielding. The gypsy's eyes still had their bold look: but it was hardened and directed far away, the touch of insolent intimacy was gone. He had been through the war. (110–11)

The gypsy's "curious indignation against life" can be assuaged, as in mythological lore, only by the virgin's touch of insolent intimacy. Lawrence, atavistic as well as cosmological in his response to modern problems, recalls to us the original force of his oppositional words. Hence the fine precision of his phrase—insolent intimacy—the intimacy that goes against and reaches across the customs of "established society" (*insolent,* from the Latin *insolens,* denoting whatever is *not* according to established customs). He would transgress the taboo on the virgin as "a great touchmenot."

## THE IDOL OF THE MARKET PLACE: COMRADESHIP

The divorce of touch from the intimacy of contact was for Lawrence the final, subtle degradation of sacred Eros in "white sex," the "cold nervous 'poetic' personal sex, which is practically all the sex the moderns know." Lawrence, like Joyce, links "white sex" to sentimentality, i.e., "something to be flowery and false about, but nothing to be hopeful about." [31] Feminist assaults on Lawrence's sexual mythologizing tend to deprecate his insights into this dialectical "conspiracy" between the sentimental cult of womanhood and the nervous "ecstasies" of white sex that leave bodies "utterly out of touch." I want merely to recover their critical (and indeed puritanical) force and redirect attention to Lawrence's still cogent sense of the loss of real intimacy in modern life.

The intimacy that is most out of touch is subsumed under the name of comradeship. Comradeship is an idol of the market place, a phantasm that gives an irregular definition to the sex relation and the decorums that regulate human contact. It is a word that enjoys remarkable favor in the works of early modernist rethinking of the sex-relation. In *Jude the Obscure*, comradeship represents the dream of a passionate love without physical passion: "I did want and long to ennoble some man to high aims," Sue confesses to Jude; "and when I saw you, and knew you wanted to be my comrade, I—shall I confess it?—thought that man might be you." [32] Sue's recurrent usage of *comrade* to evoke her instinctive relation to men and her "noble" longings for them is not casual. As a term of relationship, *comrade* originates in a consciousness of physical place and placement. It originates in the Spanish *camarada*, "chamber-mate," and especially designated the comraderies of bivouacking soldiers. *Comrade* incorporates some of the military (or militant) progressivism of this pale bachelor girl who, as Hardy in his droll postscript reminds us, takes no sexual pride or comfort in being "licensed to be loved on the premises." Yet it also uncomfortably reminds us of Sue's experiment in chaste cohabitation with an undergraduate who later dies, it is implied, a victim of baffled desires. Arabella shares nothing in common with her mates *but* locality. Sue, however, wastes the proximity of bodies that allows Nature to accomplish her work and sends an undergraduate to his death because of her indifference to the "natural" ends of cohabitation.

The enthralled Jude feels enjoined to a similar heroic, if difficult, ascesis: "If he could only get over the sense of her sex, as she seemed able to do so easily of his, what a comrade she would make" (173). Sue's individual sexual practices and proclivities are registered in her surname. *Bridehead* denotes a woman who can neither remain a maid nor become a wife. But her desire to transcend "the sense of sex" can become the basis of a social idealization, where it assumes the common name of comradeship.

Pater, in his translation of the early French tale *Li Amitiez de Ami et Amile,* employs *comrade* to convey what he sees as "the entire personal resemblance between the two heroes." He ascribes to the story of Amis and Amile "that curious interest of the *Doppelgänger,* which begins among the stars with the Dioscuri, being entwined in and out through all the incidents of the story, like an outward token of the inward similitude of their souls." [33] The masculine force of comradeship as an outward token of inward similitude seems psychologically pertinent to Sue's boyish androgyny, and anticipates the egalitarian passions and revolutionary practices of a coming era and its different sexual and social ideals. Yet Sue's personal sense of comradery, like Pater's, is essentially nostalgic, even atavistic. In Gertrude Stein's *Q.E.D.,* we encounter a more modern exploration of comradeship as a rational form of sexual and social contacts. Adele, who initially fancies herself an "apostle" for the middle-class ideal, propounds the "ideal of affectionate family life, of honorable business methods." When her future "teacher," Helen, objects that such views mean "cutting passion quite out of your scheme of things!" Adele responds that passion

> has no reality for me except as two varieties, affectionate comradeship on the one hand and physical passion in greater or less complexity on the other and against the cultivation of that latter I have an almost puritanic horror and that includes an objection to the cultivation of it in any of its many disguised forms. I have a sort of notion that to be capable of anything more worth while one must have the power of idealising another and I don't seem to have any of that. (59)

Adele, a sure-footed thinker but a stumbler in feeling, divides and diverts desire into two idolatrous byways: affectionate comradeship and physical passion. She attributes her preference for comradeship to her lacking the power of idealizing another, her horror of passion to the "Calvinist influence that dominates American training." In the course of the novella, the rapture of her first passionate embrace will annihilate the artificial division she has proposed, and with it, her moral and time sense: ". . . for the first time in Adele's experience something happened in which she had no definite consciousness of beginnings. She found herself at the end of a passionate embrace" (78). Intimacy of contact initiates the transvaluation of her own American values. She soon comes to accept the mystifications of passion and to acknowledge, not without self-irony, that her attitude toward passionate feeling "was degrading and material, instead of moral and spiritual." *Q.E.D.* concludes on the note of impasse or, in Stein's word, deadlock. Adele, champion of affectionate companionship, wrestling out with her conscience her pain and desire for Helen, laments, in her final letter to her, the loss of her "power of coming near you" (133). This, as we shall see, is a resolution-in-impasse not unique to Stein's lesbian love story. It is a formal inevitability in First Love narratives that make comradeship their erotic and social ideal.

E. M. Forster's *Howards End,* the novel Lionel Trilling took to be about England's fate, illustrates the allure as well as the limits of comradery. For Forster, comradeship is not, as for Stein, strictly a matter of personal preference. It represents the genius of English moral and sentimental life. In *Howards End* we may test the durability of comradeship as an idol of the market place. The wych elm of Howards End symbolizes the unifying powers of comradeship as a social and political as well as personal ideal. The wych elm evokes a communitarian traditionalism that contrasts sharply with the class vicissitudes and fashions of modern life, a life riven by differences: a proletarian Bast, a bohemian Schlegel, and an enterpreneurial Wilcox. Its function, an important one in the novel devoted to the proposition that the inner and outer life might be redeemed if they would "only connect," is to herald the future of England in the Zeitgeist of Comradery. It is Margaret Schlegel, the one destined to inherit Howards End, who assigns to the wych elm the rôle of comrade:

> No report had prepared her for its peculiar glory. It was neither warrior, nor lover, nor god; in none of these rôles do the English excel. It was a comrade, bending over the house, strength and adventure in its roots, but in its utmost fingers tenderness, and the girth, that a dozen men could not have spanned, became in the end evanescent, till pale bud clusters seemed to float in the air. It was a comrade. House and tree transcended any similies [sic] of sex. Margaret thought of them now, and was to think of them through many a windy night and London day, but to compare either to man, to woman, always dwarfed the vision. Yet they kept within limits of the human. Their message was not of eternity, but of hope on this side of the grave. As she stood in the one, gazing at the other, truer relationship had gleamed.[34]

Sue Bridehead's call for comradeship is socialized here, although comradeship is still esteemed a power transcending, without eliminating, the stridencies as well as the similes of sex. For Forster, comradeship is a kind of rhetorical hoping (or willing) that body and spirit might commingle, not in eternal but in mortal embrace. Forster endows this vision of comradeship with a breadth—or girth—that replaces the appeal to sublimity in his fiction. This replacement is motivated both by Forster's personal desire to see power evanesce into tenderness—as it does in the organic contours of the wych-elm—and by his political conviction that the Sublime, a revolutionary and leveling emotion, however appealing imaginatively, is finally unacceptable for a novelist who speaks for a democratic humanism. Forster reserves his esteem for "the comradeship, not passionate, that is our highest gift as a nation" (268).

Yet the politics of comradeship involve Forster in a quite different set of cultural questions, upon which Margaret Schlegel muses as she strolls the grounds of Howards End:

> Why has not England a great mythology? Our folklore has never advanced beyond daintiness, and the greater melodies about our country-side have all issued through the pipes of Greece. Deep and true as the native imagination can be, is seems to have failed here. It has stopped with the witches and the fairies. It cannot vivify one fraction of a summer field, or give names to half a dozen stars. (267)

Comradeship is a politic virtue that flourishes in an antimythological culture. It rarefies rather than vivifies the native imagination. Comradeship is capable of faery imaginings, but it can produce no inspiriting mythology that makes palpable to us the great energies and superlative beauties of the cosmos. Comradeship contributes to communal virtue, but cannot participate in the procreative powers infusing the natural world.[35]

Sexually, affairs are scarcely more vivid. *Howards End* dramatizes two ways of falling in love—Helen's way, which is to love a cause or a place rather than a man, and Margaret's way, which is to love what she can discern in the inner life of a man. But it is Helen's way that provokes Forster to state his ideal of sexual nobility: "Helen forgot people. They were husks that had enclosed her emotion. She could pity, or sacrifice herself, or have instincts, but had she ever loved in the noblest way, where man and woman, having lost themselves in sex, desire to lose sex itself in comradeship?" (311). Forster's ideal of comradeship explains why in *Howards End* sexual irregularity does not end in Hardyesque disaster. Ultimately, Forster's vision is different in kind from Hardy's brooding, passionate evocations. We might isolate their differing sexual politics by remarking that Sue Bridehead's ideal comradeship is too potent or virile a product of her inner yearnings, too potent, that is, for Forster. Forster's imagination, normally so resourceful in converting the inner life into social currency, cannot see how *so much* inner life can possibly, as he puts it, "pay," possibly because, unlike Hardy, he can't quite imaginatively pay the tragic price.

The price, of course, can be simple and awesome—the cost is Death. Forster wants to discount the cost by substituting the idea of death for the natural debt Eros exacts for its excesses. He has Helen Wilcox articulate how this mortal accounting might be rendered, without exceeding human means. Helen speaks to her future lover, Leonard Bast, of the difference, the infinite difference according to her, between death and the idea of death:

> "Death destroys a man: the idea of Death saves him." Behind the coffins and the skeletons that stay the vulgar mind lies something so immense that all that is great in us responds to it. Men of the world may recoil from the charnel-house that they will one day enter, but Love knows better. Death is his foe, but his peer, and in their age-long struggle the thews of Love have been strengthened, and his vision cleared, until there is no one who can stand against him. (239)

The tones of the chapel reverberate in this paean to Death's disciplinary powers over the passionate Spirit. In *Jude the Obscure* Hardy transforms this paean into a bitter narrative catastrophe—a double infanticide and suicide. In positing the comradeship of Death and Love, Forster has fashioned a humanist folktale, but he has missed the resounding note of true myth. Indeed Forster capitulates to the spiritual provincialism endemic to a folklorist culture at the conclusion of *Howards End.* He ultimately refuses to heed the voices of those goblins of malignity Helen had earlier heard in the sublime stirrings of Beethoven's Fifth Symphony. We will see in *The Rainbow* how D. H. Lawrence, a bold cosmological thinker, incorporates those goblins who undermine human belief into the representational design of his Cathedral. Their mocking countenances represent a counterresponse to the passionate human demand for Unity, for assumption into the Whole, which the Cathedral symbolizes.

Forster could never undertake that dialogue of spiritual expostulation and reply because his speech deserted him just on that linguistic verge where the novel disappears into myth, and world-description expands into cosmology. Forster may be the deeper pessimist because he cannot affirm a point just beyond the ken of human sight, shimmering on the human horizon of what we know and see and feel, where Love and Truth might be symbolized as one radiant arc. Lawrence saw the consonance of Love and Truth figured in the natural and sacred sign of the Rainbow. Forster, in merely thinking about their confluence, cannot envision a rainbow, the sacramental or outward sign of the inward grace of Eternity. For him, rather, the visible world is the theater in which Love and Truth combat each other: "Love and Truth—their warfare seems eternal. Perhaps the whole visible world rests on it, and if they were one, life itself, like the spirits when Prospero was reconciled to his brother, might vanish into air, into thin air" (230). The cosmic reconciliation of Love and Truth is figured as fraternal or comradely. Forster forswears the high Romantic vision of an apocalyptic mating that would consume the ramparts of the world in glorious and passionate flame. To evanesce, not to be consumed—this is the projected end of Forster's comradeship. *Maurice,* directly inspired by Edward Carpenter's Whitmanesque belief in the Love of Comrades, concludes with the disappearance of its hero and his working-class lover, a disappearance which leaves no trace "except a little pile of the petals of the evening primrose, which mourned from the ground like an expiring fire." [36] Perhaps, then, it was not just the failure to enact the recommendations of the Wolfenden Report that led Forster to suppress *Maurice,* written immediately after *Howards End,* for fifty-odd years. Though Forster tells us that "happiness was its keynote," he can only imagine such happiness in "the last moment of the greenwood," where "it was still possible to get lost" (254). Forster's tales, like Helen's loves, are husks that enclose his emotion, but cannot liberate it. To that *A Passage to India* eloquently if sadly attests, in portraying a hero, Fielding, who convicts himself of traveling light, and of a heroine, Mrs. Moore, who perishes before she can communicate the burden of the echoes that haunt her.

I began my discussion of comradeship with Hardy's *Jude the Obscure* and I end it with Forster's *Passage to India* to emphasize how comradeship, taken as either a sexual or a social ideal, concludes in narrative impasse. Both works represent that puzzling phenomenon of a last novel written long before death claims the author. Though differing in temperament, and fashioning different fictions of the world, both Hardy and Forster conclude their novelistic careers in the same desperate impasse. Each failed to reimagine the terms of a rebeginning, without which any relation, comradely or otherwise, remains *without a story to tell.* We can look to Joyce for a way out of this impasse created by end-of-the-world feelings. The last story of *Dubliners,* "The Dead," evokes these end-of-the-world feelings, although it is not Joyce, only his false messenger-angel, Gabriel, who succumbs to a vision of the final end. Joyce was ingenious in finding beginnings in his endings, as *A Portrait of the Artist as a Young Man* confirms. This Joycean bildungsroman opens with a child's disconnected bab-blings and inchoate impressions: a moo cow advancing down the road to encounter Baby Tuckoo. The material of maternal fantasy blends with the race wisdom of nursery rhymes to form the first, stammering words of Joyce's cosmic fairy tale. Joyce's gift for comedy makes light of beginning his novel of human emergence at the point where it is hardest to do so—at the *very* beginning.

## THE IDOL OF THE THEATER: BEGINNING THE WORLD

Joyce inaugurates his "portrait" of the artist by recalling those tales of self-emergence and world-venturing known as fairy tales, tales in which the child begins to realize the potential heroism—and hence narrative interest—of his own life. In such self-mastery the novel of bourgeois individualism had found its ideal. The Victorian fathers, Thackeray and Dickens, satirized but never discredited the promise of self- and world-mastery when they spoke of their heroes and heroines "beginning the world." Thackeray, with characteristic duplicity, equivocates at the opening of *Vanity Fair* about "the real truth of the matter" when he remarks that for Becky Sharp the "newness of the world" may be a convenient—and exploitable—fiction: "At all events, if Rebecca was not beginning the world, she was beginning it over again." The "real truth" surfaces only at the conclusion of the novel, when Thackeray, prompted by the futility of human desires and the puppetry of human agency, returns his marionettes to the imagination's playhouse.

Beginning the world is given more sentimental treatment in Dickens's *Bleak House,* where in the chapter of that name, Richard Carstone, in his death delirium, still dreams: "I will begin the world." "Not in this world, O not in this," laments the Dickensian narrator, the cankerous other who rails against England's infectious social evils. It remained to the matriarch of the realist tradition, George Eliot, to suggest how "beginning the world" is the constant labor of history. In the prelude to *Middlemarch* she invokes the child-pilgrimage of St. Theresa as "a fit beginning" for those whose "passionate, ideal nature demanded an epic life." St. Theresa, we are informed, found her epos in a religious order, but Eliot's narrative is dedicated to the memory of all those creative spirits who have found their ardor dissipated and dispersed by the moral meanness and social hindrances of the actual world, who have sunk into oblivion and who find their patron saint in a "Saint Theresa, foundress of nothing." Eliot found a beginning in the acceptance of a diminished end, affirming, as is well known, the unhistoric acts that contribute to the growing good of the world.

The ideal of self-mastery comprehended in "beginning the world" is the one idol of the realist tradition that the moderns could not dispense with and still remain within the "system" of novelistic representation. Instead, they transfigured it. Hardy, whom I, like W. H. Auden, have taken to be the indispensable guide in chronicling the transition between the Victorian and the modern world, eventually abandons all hope in ever beginning the world. He depicts a different dispensation, that of the Immanent Will with its cruel and inevitable ironies. And yet Hardy's pessimism in no way dampens the narrative excitement and interest of his tales. The interest of Hardy's novels emanates almost exclusively from his tragic characters, those grand "native beings," as Lawrence recognized them, who still possess the vitality to imagine and pursue new beginnings when all the world, like a Greek chorus, admonishes them against doing so. Hardy's tragic characters are ruled by the emotional logic, as I will call it, of first initiatives. Having failed to begin the world, his noble beings, most impressively Tess and Jude, are determined to begin again. They interpret their early failures, as Eliot interprets St. Theresa's child-pilgrimage, as a fit beginning that tempers their idealism with practical experience of the world, not a monitory sign of the oblivion that awaits them.

For the moderns who follow him, Hardy's irony may be the vehicle, but never the inspiriting tenor, of their quest for beginnings. Lawrence, as we shall see, criticized Hardy for having mistaken his quarrel with society for his quarrel with God. Lawrence, as *The Rainbow* attests, held fast to his faith in the perpetual newness of the world and to his conviction that creative individuals can still be said to begin the world, both for themselves and, in their prophetic capacity, for others. Joyce, too, entertains prophetic longings that defy all attempts to parody or mock them into submission. The compass of Joycean irony is far-reaching, extending even to the heavens where Leopold Bloom and Stephen, on a fateful June night, see their destinies inscribed in the stars. But for the logic of his tale he must rely on the circular reasonings of Molly Bloom, who neither seeks nor needs further proof of God (Augustine's proof) than the sun's rising every morning. Molly reminds us that the world is created anew each day. Beginning the world is a diurnal myth, not a piece of dainty Victorian folklore.

Only Beckett, of the authors I consider, may be rightly regarded as our poet of impending ends. It is the "epos" of nothing that he sings. As a subject of contemplation, the world reveals only one meaning, a meaning comprehended by the word *defunctus,* the last word of his monograph, *Proust.* Beckett's unblinking view is announced in the inaugural sentence of his first novel, *Murphy:* "The sun shone on the nothing new, having no alternative." One does not begin the world, but circulates through it, a figure of contumely, ridicule, and abuse. The Victorian hero or heroine may attain the status of social or moral cynosure. Beckett's characters attract our attention as public eyesore. The mere sight of Murphy, "that long hank of Apollonian aesthenia," inspires the local denizens of the Brompton Road to transports of hilarity—"Thou surd!" (77). Beckettian man is an irrational integer who can never indulge the rational fantasy of Joycean man that the world might reveal the compass of the soul or imaginatively blossom into the Utopia that echoes Bloom's name as it reflects his measure: Flowerville.

I do not know whether it is accident or necessity that determined that when the young lovers of modernity began their world, God was dead or in hiding or yet to be created anew in their image. I associate—in Beckett's phrase, rightly or wrongly—the death of the gods with the birth of First Love. The idols of First Love awaken, as the pagan idols were wont to do, consciousness of a truth and a power. The conquests of First Love are equal in kind (certainly not in degree) to the Olympian conquest Gilbert Murray describes in his rich evocation of Hellenic culture, *Five Stages of Greek Religion*.

> Its gods could awaken man's worship and strengthen his higher aspirations; but at heart they knew them to be only metaphors. As the most beautiful image carved by man was not the god, but only a symbol, to help towards conceiving the god; so the god himself, when conceived, was not the reality but only a symbol to help towards conceiving the reality. That was the work set before them. Meanwhile they issued no creeds that contradicted knowledge, no commands that made man sin against his own inner light.[37]

First Love is the invention of modern narrative, designed to fill the emptiness left by the death or the desertion of the gods. As a symbolic and idolatrous state it discloses to us the possibility of a time-disregarding love. But with this difference, perhaps: First Love often does issue creeds that contradict the accepted knowledge of the world, give commands that make man sin against his own inner light.

To tell the tale of that difference separating the Olympian conquest from the modern debacle requires a storyteller well-versed in the drama of Unfulfilled Intentions. It requires Thomas Hardy, the novelist who shows us the harsh conditions under which First Love manifests itself to the modern understanding. *Tess of the D'Urbervilles* will serve as our exemplary instance of the troubled questions that surround a "first" love, dramatized in this novel in the brutal form of a seduction-rape:

Why it was that upon this beautiful feminine tissue, sensitive as gossamer, and practically blank as snow as yet, there should have been traced such a coarse pattern as it was doomed to receive; why so often the coarse appropriates the finer thus, the wrong man the woman, the wrong woman the man, many thousand years of analytical philosophy have failed to explain to our sense of order. (62–63)

In "First Love" we have the myth that gives us the explanation, in both Hardy's and Gertrude Stein's sense of the word, for an otherwise senseless appropriation of the finer by the coarse, the right by the wrong, the inner by the outer forces. Yet its explanations still manage to keep faith with the finer inner determinations of the Spirit and abjure the coarser rationalizations of the self-seeking Letter. First Love is one of the narratives that rescue the modern imagination from the servilities and desecrations of modern history.

In designating Tess as a "Pure Woman," Hardy affirms his belief in such spiritual recuperations: "Was once lost always lost really true of chastity? she would ask herself. She might prove it false if she could veil bygones. The recuperative power which pervaded organic nature was surely not denied to maidenhood alone" (84). As a moral question, the recovery of chastity may be a subject fit only for casuists to settle. Hardy's apposite use of *veil* as a predicate and not a nominative word suggests that the truth of chastity has little to do with the presence or absence of the hymen. What interests Hardy as a chronicler of human life is the *particular* form that nature's recuperative power takes in human life: the power to imagine and fashion new beginnings. This is the power of "unexpended youth, surging up anew after its temporary checks, and bringing with it hope, and the invincible instinct towards self-delight." It is this profound "appetite for joy" that First Love, in its myriad idolatries, affirms.

# THREE

# *THE RETURN OF THE NATIVE*: FIRST LOVE, GUILT, AND REPARATION

# WRITING'S PRIMAL SCENE

T HE TITLE OF Hardy's first major tragic novel, *The Return of the Native*, comprehends a profound crisis in the nature of modern feelings about the physical and social world. Raymond Williams, in his magisterial work, *The Country and the City*, has defined this crisis "as something that is still very close to us wherever we may be living: something that can be put, in abstraction, as the problem of the relation between customary and educated life: between customary and educated feeling and thought." Williams elaborates on "what is meant, in idea and in feeling, by the return of the native":

> This has a special importance to a particular generation, who have gone to the university from ordinary families and have to discover, through a life, what that experience means. But it has also a much more general importance; for in Britain generally this is what has been happening: a moving out from old ways and places and ideas and feelings; a discovery in the new of certain unlooked-for problems, unexpected and very sharp crises, conflicts of desire and possibility.[1]

It is this felt contrast between a world that appears as both "rooted and mobile, familiar yet newly conscious and self-conscious" that gives Hardy's work its characteristic and historically significant "structure of feeling."

It is, foremost, an idolatrous structure of feeling. For the return of the native depicts not just the sharp crises that unsettle the relations between educated and customary life, old and new modes of feeling and thinking about the world. It also describes the revisitings of animistic conceptions long thought outgrown in the evolution of human development. The return of the native encapsulates those "primary processes" of the unconscious that resist the incursions of historical change or social pressure, that revolt against the "recently learnt emotions" of educated attitudes and sophisticated views. The return of these primal feelings is recorded in the pandemic idolatries and fetishistic observances that survive in Hardy's world, nowhere with such fidelity as in his chronicles of First Love. First Love brings the conflict between desire and possibility to its crisis; its idolatries dramatize the painful and divided loyalties of the native torn between his "deep," primal feelings and his newly acquired learning. The body and the book—these two idolatrous figures compete for the love and fealty of Hardy's passionate men and women—Clym Yeobright, Angel and Tess, Jude and Sue.

This competition is invariably staged against the august background of myth. Wessex is the regional name for Hardy's country, but his landscapes finally suggest to us a panorama inhabited by titanic and preternatural powers. Indeed, of all our major English novelists, Thomas Hardy most understood— and suffered—the human habit of populating the world with phantom divinities. In the contagious anthropomorphism that afflicts Hardy's vision, but also empowers it, the Immanent but faceless Will that rules the world is embodied in the tragic face of things. The face of things, as we shall see, is no conventional figure in Hardy's mythic imaginings. The face, the idol of the tribe, is the primary image that unites Hardy's mimetic and idolizing instincts. *The Return of the Native* opens on such a "natural" landscape of personification: the wild face of the heath on which Time, according to the initial chapter title, makes little impression.

Of that little, much is made. For Hardy, the gaunt sublimities of the Heath, "emphatic in its admonitions, grand in its simplicity," appeal "to a subtler and scarcer instinct, to a more recently learnt emotion, than that which responds to the sort of beauty called charming and fair." I want to excavate this narrative site to uncover the subtle, repressed instincts that compose, like so many geological formations, the granite face of Hardy's pessimism. For it is these instincts that discover, in the course of their vicissitudes, the inevitably tragic nature of First Love.

D. H. Lawrence, Hardy's most creative interpreter, regarded Hardy's fiction as the last efflorescence of genuine tragic feeling, the feeling of being, in Lawrence's words, "close to the body of things," where there can be heard "the stir that makes or destroys us" (*P.,* 415). Nature was the Great Mother, "the unfathomable womb" whose improvident cycles of generation disregard as they offend the human "conceit of self-preservation and of race-preservation" (*P.,* 400). Lawrence could only see in the heath a "primal impulsive body" of titanic energies and inexhaustible instinct, a body *without* distinguishing features and certainly without the individualizing, heart-entrancing features of a *face.* For Lawrence, the delights of excess are not idols or texts, but the flowers or "Bloom's End" of the bud of being. Hardy's Nature, Lawrence avers, is too prodigal to be implicated in that conceit of self- and race-preservation that we call writing.

But it is precisely this "conceit" of writing that unites place and person in the originative figure of Hardy's fiction: the tragic face of things. When we first glimpse the face of the heath, which Hardy dreams is the home of "that traditionary King of Wessex, Lear," it *is already* contorted into "a lonely face, suggesting tragical possibilities." The heath never relaxes its features, and so never yields to that lyrical portraiture of place we identify with pastoralism. Its mask-like face is coated by a kind of historical skin, scarred by those Celtic tribes and dyed barbarians who "left their marks here, as writers on paper beside writers on parchment" (456). The heath, according to Hardy's somewhat labored archaeological conceit, is a primal scene of writing. It partakes of the paradoxical destiny of the textual, its markings, like all human objects of cultivation, being subject to "unforeseen factors [that] operate in the evolution of immortality."

The heath is, however, a text whose ancient markings can only be deciphered in that Lear-like moment when the heath is roused to reciprocity, reflecting in its savage face the wild passions buried in the heart of the human. Only then does it reveal its face "to be the hitherto unrecognized original of those wild regions of obscurity which are vaguely felt to be compassing us about in midnight dreams of flight and disaster, and are never thought of after the dream till revived by scenes like this." As the "hitherto unrecognized original" of these dreams of flight and disaster, the heath assumes the aspect of the Uncanny or Unheimlich, the un-homelike, non-native. Freud defined the Uncanny as "something which is secretly familiar [heimlich-heimisch], which has undergone repression and then returned from it."[2] The uncanny apparition that dominates Egdon appears, at first glance, to be "a sort of last man . . . musing for a moment before dropping into eternal night with the rest of his race." But this exposed and illuminated figure, defiant and Promethean, is female. Through this logic of reversal and substitution, the last man—the ghost of some ancestral Celt who will outlast, it seems, time itself—is revealed to be the primal woman—the Queen of the Night, regent of the dark womb of time. This uncovering of the original and familiar (female) in the belated and apparently alien (male) links the riddle of destiny to a sexual knowledge long forgotten or denied (and thus classically "uncanny").

The Uncanny is oddly personified in another female figure, (or, more precisely, figurehead) in the novel, the Quiet Woman, whose emblem provides the legend for a communal gathering place. The quiet woman is represented as a beheaded woman (thus deprived of face and mind) who carries her severed head under her arms, whether as a reproach or as an admonition, the novelist does not specify. But it is this gruesome figure which accumulates all those anxieties—castration, death, self-silencing, and the power of injurious thoughts—which are activated, according to Freud, by our encounter with uncanny sights or occurrences. This silent woman cannot speak for herself,[3] but as a monitory figure she visually asserts the presence of dumb fate, whose workings inspire that dread that emotionally is the basis of the tragic conception of life.

## THREE WOMEN: NARRATIVE NUMBERS

*The Return of the Native* stages this anxiety dream-play as a five-act tragedy, whose opening movement is denominated by the part-title "Three Women." This narrative numbering is not fortuitous, but predictive and symptomatic. "Three Women" establishes the dominant pattern of the tragedy as a series of repetitive, compulsive behaviors that take the form of an irresolute or unhappy return: the return of Thomasin after her elopement with Wildeve; the return of Diggory Venn to the home of the love who rejected him; the revival of Wildeve's passion for Eustacia. That these events transpire under the reign of "Three Women" indicates that these natives return not only to a place once forsaken, but to a presiding power, in some cases a power they themselves partially constitute—the hegemony of three women whose own uneasy relations are further destabilized by the advent of Clym.

Freud, whose attention was arrested by such recurrent and apparently indicative numbering, remarked the uncanny regularity in which the number three appears in fables involving acts of ostensibly free choice—the choice of the three caskets in *The Merchant of Venice,* Lear's tripartite division of his kingdom and his preference for the third and silent daughter. He was startled by an "astounding contradiction whenever our theme occurs": "The choice between the women is free, and yet it falls on death," observes Freud. "For after all, no one chooses death, and it is only by a fatality that one falls a victim to it." [4] By way of this contradiction, Freud arrives at the emotional bedrock of such wishful reversals: "Choice stands in the place of necessity, of destiny. In this way man overcomes death, which he has recognized intellectually. No greater triumph of wish-fulfillment is conceivable. A choice is made where in reality there is obedience to a compulsion; and what is chosen is not a figure of terror, but the fairest and most desirable of women." [5] The *appearance* of a meaningful and free choice overlays, but cannot contravene, the dictates of Necessity. This astounding contradiction leads Freud to speculate: "We might argue that what is represented here are the three inevitable relations that a man has with a woman—the woman who bears him, the woman who is his mate and the woman who destroys him; or that they are the three forms taken by the figure of the mother in the course of a man's life—the mother herself, the beloved one who is chosen after her pattern, and lastly the Mother Earth who receives him once more."[6] The maternal archetype that justifies the traditional analogy between terrestrial and human body projects the fateful nature of First Love as Mother Love. Those who fail to appreciate the significance of *amor matris,* objective and subjective genitive, as the First Love after which all subsequent loves take their image, fail to appreciate not only the significance of birth, but the meaning of death.

If, then, the heath embodies the fateful agency of the Great Mother, "Three Women" designates her form as a composite trinity: the Morae or Fates who rule human destiny. The character of this female trinity is the mythological subject of Hardy's extravagant prose rhapsody to the Queen of the Night, triform goddess of the moon. Robert Graves emphasizes the genealogy that connects the Three Fates with the triform goddess, and further specifies her manifestations as Nymph, Maiden, and Crone,[9] female characters distributed and sublimated but never effaced in the novel's "realistic" presentation of Eustacia, Thomasin, and Mrs. Yeobright. The power of three women may be denied, dissimulated, or unspoken, but is yet everywhere latent, waiting to be roused to reciprocity. Dumb fate even has a local habitation and a name in the Quiet Woman Inn, site of the novel's multiple catastrophes: here Thomasin returns, shame-ridden after the canceled marriage; here Christian ill-advisedly plays and wins a lottery, an episode in which luck soon converts to lucklessness; here the drowned bodies of Eustacia, Wildeve, and Clym are laid out; here Clym is restored to life, after having been given up for dead.

*The Return of the Native* respects and narratively executes the will of three women as the hidden force behind these tragic entanglements and catastrophes. Damon Wildeve is the first object of female machinations in Hardy's sardonic drama of sexual selection. His remarkable name suggests as much, being an odd amalgam of untamable nature and the first female. He is a type for the feminized male, that is, either a narcissistic double of the female (implied in Hardy's observation that women instinctively respond to Wildeve while men find no reason to admire him) or an embodiment of the manhood women dream for themselves. Lawrence, so alert to any hint of diverted or inverted sexuality, intuited though never explicitly averred this when he called Wildeve "the eternal assumption" (*P.,* 402). This odd description locates the hidden impulses of Wildeve's romantic character in a long-sought, though perpetually deferred manhood.

The confused, almost delirious sexual fable subsumed under Wildeve's name refers to a principle that Hardy does not, as narrator, directly admit to or comment upon: that manhood is a state conferred by female desire. With a presumption usually reserved for divinities, Eustacia regards Wildeve as "some wondrous thing she had created out of chaos" (84). So, too, in the novel's folkloric subplot, where mythical relationships are played out in the counterpoint of comic pastoral, Christian anxiously confesses that "'Tis said I be only the rames of a man, and no good for my race at all" (28). Christian's misfortune? To have been born on a moonless night. Nativity is fate, and it is cast by the moon. Christian offers a "shattered recitative" of a man unmanned by the unpropitious conditions prevailing at his own nativity, a misfortune related and understood by the succinct folk formula—"No moon, no man." The moon, Queen of the Night, confers masculinity. Thus her absence or displeasure (no moon) foretells castration (no man). The feminization of Christian is further symbolized, rather openly (as is Hardy's way), by his winning of the lottery prize, the gown piece intended for the bride's trousseau, which he is encouraged to keep for luck.

Only one man successfully circumvents or balks the will of three women, and he is Diggory Venn. Thomasin rejects him as a lover, Mrs. Yeobright objects to his class status, Eustacia regards him as a strange ally, then adversary, to her own romantic designs; yet he outloves, outlives, and outwits them all. Venn's exemption from the rule of female numbers is symbolized by his lurid coloration, which incarnates his "weird" nature. *Weird* is, of course, a fateful term, linking Venn's eerie sheen to the etymological origin of *weird* in *wyrd*—the Anglo-Saxon word for "destiny" whose base sense derives from *weorthan,* "what is to come." Dice are Venn's accessories, emblems of what is assigned by lot or fantasy. The play of the dice defines a realm which is neither fateful—the domain of moral law—nor deliberately inconsequent—the field of play or of the dance, the realm of (temporary) self-forgetting and self-rejoicing. Gaming is distinct from human art or industry[8] in that it engages human fancy, but cannot be disciplined by its power. For William Dare, the villain-gamester of *A Laodicean,* the irresistible attraction in gaming is, as his name clearly announces, in the "spectacular piquancy" of defying the odds. Later in the novel, the hero George Somerset will be drawn to the roulette tables, which he regards as a visual representation of "a network of hopes."[9] He can find no excitement in what appears to the "eye of perfect reason" as "a somewhat monotonous thing—the property of numbers to recur at certain longer or shorter intervals in a machine containing them—in other words, the blind groping after fractions of a result the whole of which was well known" (298). The complex syntax of this thought simply reveals that Somerset is no gambler. The genuine gamester is blind to these demonstrations of pure, if convoluted, reason; he provides, as Hardy sardonically observes, "one testimony among many of the powerless-ness of logic when confronted with imagination" (298). As a potential figure for the demonic artist, the gambler forswears whatever is monotonously predict-able because this totality is everywhere self-consistent and therefore unevent-ful, unnarratable. Numbers are fateful only when placed in certain charged combinations or distributed at certain critical or irregular intervals. It is the *fraction* of any instant, it is the event singled out of the whole that incites the gambler's desire to risk his individual portion even though defeat (succumbing to the odds, the law of averages) is already foreknown.

Such daring in the face of the foregone conclusion offers us a parable of the fond foolishness of the novelistic imagination. In *The Return of the Native* this struggle of the singular against the hegemony of the whole is played out in the phantasmagoric night scene wherein Damon Wildeve outplays Christian and strips him of his winnings, only to be bested by a greater daimon, Venn, who seems to have total mastery over the dice, "magical machines" (265), those engines of the uncanny. Wildeve lures Christian into gambling with three tales about men "born to luck," an irony entirely lost on the ingenuous Christian, who earlier had lamented his luckless nativity. Yet Wildeve is both seducer and seduced in this venture, and he is seduced by his own mystifications—that is, by the allure of his own stories about streaks of luck. When Venn appears on the scene and dares Wildeve to continue gambling after Christian departs, Wildeve is ready to risk all. A game results which is a study in contrasts, set in a night of preternatural contrasts: the unearthly light given off by the natural illumination of glowworms, the nervous and excitable Damon mastered by the "daimon" Venn, twice described as machinelike in the deliberateness of his motions, an emotional daimon versus the daimonic automaton. Venn punc-tuates his winnings by reciting back to Wildeve the ironic conclusions of his own tales of luck, thereby appropriating not only Wildeve's ill-gotten winnings, but his ill-conceived narratives: "Won back his watch, won back his money, and went out of the door a rich man," Venn taunts Wildeve "as stake after stake passed over to him" (273). Venn wins steadily, but Wildeve, enmeshed in the network of (futile) hopes, casts one last die. He rolls an ace; Venn matches him. Wildeve rerolls, again an ace; Venn casts the die, it splits. The unitary, numinous One is shattered before the uncanny counterimage of the split die. Luck can achieve no finer narrative climax: the cast of the die, proverbial for the irrever-sible venture, despoils and splits the image of its own integrity. And as luck runs out, so does the narrative hope for a timely deliverance, whose most obvious gambit in the Victorian novel is the unexpected inheritance. In such a material reprieve relief is sought from the sordid conditions that are the breeding ground of Bovaryism. Wildeve's inheritance, coming at such an "opportune time," actually precipitates, rather than postpones, the tragedy.

Narratives of luck are always compromised by the moral disquiet that attends the novelist's decision to ignore or challenge the austere code that governs the classical novel, a code more incumbent upon the novelist as a seeker of truth than the fantasy, no matter how morally inspired, of a distributive justice. No novelist makes the stakes so high and the risks so obvious as Hardy, who perpetually reminds us that tragic narrative is always luckless. Hardy's ingenuity as a storyteller depends on his native understanding of those implacable laws of necessity that cannot be apprehended through the rational, demystifying representations of realism tracing the minute links between demonstrable causes and their certain effects. Hardy's narratives belong to another order of organization and insight, whose analogue, I have claimed, is the bad dream or the uncanny occurrence. With these occurrences, luck has nothing to do. Luck depends on the slippage of fractions within the whole, but in Hardy's dark fables of life, the tragic monotony of the whole always reasserts its controlling, if hidden, presence. That monotony can, however, take on deceiving forms—the uncanny appearances we call, often dismiss or despise as, coincidences, but which for Hardy constitute the inner form and severe truth of luckless narrative. Venn is only a moral accessory who ministers to this inner truth. It is the reckless Eustacia, venturing and desiring all, who precipitates the crisis that discloses the inner mythos of the novel, in all its depth and devastation.

## THE DISINVITED

Eustacia Vye—her surname, which links her to the hazards of competition, reverberates with the mythic power of a primal word. It assigns her the lot of the embattled. Her antagonist appears to be less a person than a sexual condition: "God! If I were a man in such a position I would curse rather than sing" (302). Such is Eustacia's reproach to Clym when, "set upon by adversities," he sings a song, thus cheerfully—to her maddeningly—accepting his blind and reduced state. Her Promethean refusal to abide this insult to her *nature* resembles in the form as well as the content of its expression what Karen Horney termed "the masculinity fiction,"[10] a female protest against masochism, passivity, the "truth" of castration (as both physical loss and social privation). For Eustacia, who has lived her life as a series of militant impersonations—an infidel Turk, a "witch," and a social outlaw—Clym's resignation represents an insupportable attitude, unworthy of her name. Hers is a name inherited, importantly, from the matrilineal line, further evidence that power in this novel is transmitted, mediated, and wielded primarily through female agency. Eustacia's father, who assumes his wife's name to hide his earlier vocation as bandmaster, is the source of that class chagrin that spawns Bovaryism and all its grand illusions: Eustacia's imperious conviction that she *deserves* a greater man than Wildeve and has been fashioned to command a larger stage than the heath and, knowing very little of the world, can only call this dream of life—Paris.[11]

*Vye,* as a variant spelling of *vie,* provides yet another antithetical meaning to her "native" character. *Vie* derives from the French *envier,* "to invite," a word which, through aphaeresis, became associated with gambling and now retains its present sense of the competitive and contentious. This verbal origin subliminally survives in the narrative, shadowing the novel's most "avertable" incident and its tragic *perepetia*—"The Closed Door," structurally the fourth and fatal act of the tragedy. Mrs. Yeobright intends to effect a reconciliation with her son, but is "inadvertently" refused or denied entry into his house. Eustacia's failure to admit her mother-in-law while Clym lies sleeping, murmuring, "Mother, Mother," is the beginning of a series of misunderstandings leading to Mrs. Yeobright's death, Clym and Eustacia's estrangement, and the final catastrophe. Each link in this chain of events is forged to mimic the appearance of inadvertency: Eustacia, caught in a compromising "conjuncture" (as the chapter title rather officiously regards it) as she converses with Wildeve, delays in opening the door for Mrs. Yeobright, thinking Clym will answer her knockings, while he in turn remains asleep, "unconscious" of his mother's presence. The mother, too, seems victim to heedless but fatal responses, mistaking the furze hooks outside the cottage door for a sign of Clym's *conscious* presence within and interpreting "the sight of a face at the window" as a sign of heartless rejection. This critical moment of failed encounter is staged as a series of natural but wrong conjectures that leaves each character feeling aggrieved by a manifest wrong. This manifest wrong, however, is but the displacement of a hidden, latent guilt.

For the "innocent" semblance of the sleeping son conceals a troubled unconscious intention: to ignore or banish, just on the threshold of entry, the uninvited guest who, *not* accidentally, is the mother. The closed door, an ever-present stage prop in Hardy's tragedies, is linked to a symbolism of obstruction and impassability that, as Dorothy Van Ghent was the first to recognize, signifies the presence of a forbidden crossing, a dangerous threshold, or a sexual, economic, and class barrier.[12] *The Return of the Native* identifies this consciousness of limit and represents it as engaged in a drama of repression, what I call the drama of the disinvited. Freud describes the "general vicissitude" suffered by an instinct as it tries to gain access to consciousness precisely in such unhospitable metaphors:

> The general vicissitude which overtakes the *idea* that represents the instinct can hardly be anything else than that it should vanish from the conscious if it was previously conscious, or that it should be held back from consciousness if it was about to become conscious. The difference is not important; it amounts to much the same thing as the difference between my ordering an undesirable guest out of my drawing-room (or out of my front hall), and my refusing, after recognizing him, to let him cross my threshold at all.[13]

In Hardy's drama, the vigilant are never successful in banishing the unwanted visitor. The undesirable guest will appear, just as Eustacia, the outcast, makes her way into the Christmas gathering; she, however, is only the *uninvited*. The uncanny guest whose presence is more dreaded than desired is familiar to us in the person of the mother and her unmanning love. Mrs. Yeobright is the dream-figure the sleeping son calls out for, but cannot wake to acknowledge. Clym's earlier admission that he could never recollect a clear dream of Eustacia assumes in this episode the suspicious form of a telling symptom. As a lawful object of his passion, Eustacia need not be banished from the threshold of consciousness. The door to conscious avowal is closed only to the mother, and closed, moreover, at Alderworth, another name riddled with portentous meanings: the place, as the archaic prefix *alder* ("of all") suggests,[14] of supreme or all-worthiness, the patriarchal site in which Clym could establish his own home and recapture his masculine identifications after his "effeminate" career in Paris, where he trafficked in vanities. At Alderworth Eustacia may reap the manhood the mother sows, but only as a rival, not as a natural successor or approved double for the mother.

   This rivalry between mother and wife often appears to originate "outside" male consciousness, that is, in the sexual competition of women vying for the love of a "worthy" man. But *The Return of the Native* ascribes this conventional romance plot to the mythic oppositions within Clym's own (representative) mind. How Hardy himself conceived of these antagonisms has been a source of some contention and confusion. In a letter to his illustrator Hardy ascribed a hierarchy of significance to the novel's "Three Women": "The order of importance of the characters is as follows—1 Clym Yeobright 2 Eustacia 3 Thomasin and the reddleman 4 Wildeve 5 Mrs. Yeobright."[15] Michael Millgate, one of Hardy's most astute interpreters, is baffled by this Lear-like ordering of characters, particularly since Mrs. Yeobright is "a strong character, strongly presented."[16] I would suggest that it is the mother's emotional primacy that necessitates this repressive order—and ruse—in which the first is presented last. Clym's filial devotion, which is primary and mythic, is the real passion in this oedipal tragedy, and not his love for Eustacia, which is secondary and "novelistic," a matter of personal "fascination."

Within the novel, Hardy disguises the nature of this mythic attachment by ascribing the superior, speechless rapport subsisting between mother and son to a "magnetic"—that is, an invisible but iron—attraction: "Indeed, how could it be otherwise," the narrator comments disingenuously of Clym's filial devotion to his mother, "when he was a part of her—when their discourses were as if carried on between the right and the left hands of the same body?" (223). This unitary body is undemonstrative about its own self-love. In one of his most puzzling authorial commentaries Hardy asserts: "Of love it may be said, the less earthly the less demonstrative. In its absolutely indestructible form it reaches a profundity in which all exhibition of itself is painful. It was so with these" (222). "Of love it may be said"—Hardy's attempt at an amatory maxim offers us a seductive but resistible sentiment. Profundity and indestructibility—these are attributes of Eros, which is deep and eternal, and they are "etherealized," according to Hardy, in mother-son love. But why should love recoil from exhibiting itself—and recoil with pain—*unless* it is the love that bespeaks the incomplete separation of the son from the maternal body, the love that constrains the son to converse—silently, magnetically—with and against the mother's discourse of chastisement and rebuke?

## THE MOUTH OF OEDIPUS

In this unspoken and unspeakable discourse between mother and son, the "quiet woman" ceases to be a figure for place or person and becomes instead the generative figure for the novel's erotic rhetoric. The silent communications between mother and son do not comprise, as Hardy claims, the sign of their unrepresentable, because ethereal and profound, love; they designate the existence of a mythic unity that is interrupted and finally ruptured when Clym begins to gravitate into the novelistic field, where he can love Eustacia. "A slight touch in the shaping of Clym's destiny" illustrates this growing rift. Clym retrieves an urn excavated from a heathen barrow to please his mother's antiquarian tastes, but "on second thought" gives it to Eustacia, who has "a cannibal taste for such churchyard furniture" (224). Mrs. Yeobright is no allegorist, but she can detect, as anyone could, the symbolic transference from old (first!) love to new in Clym's turning a funereal receptacle into an amatory token. This transfer of affection from mother to mistress is a "natural" sequence interrupted or obstructed by the disapproving and prohibitory silence of the mother. When Clym returns home from an assignation with Eustacia, he feels a guilt so pronounced that he *imagines,* never actually hears, his mother's sexual accusation: "What red spot is that glowing upon your mouth so vividly?" (225). When his mother actually objects to his impending marriage and new plans for life, Clym tries to appease her by rededicating his mouth to a "higher vocation": "I no longer adhere to my intention of giving *with my own mouth* rudimentary education to the lowest class. I can do better" (227, emphasis added). But later a red spot marks the site of the adder bite that kills Mrs. Yeobright, already spiritually wounded by Clym's defection to Eustacia. Lips stained with pleasure, a foot swollen with poison—an aggressive orality links the son's amatory adventure with the mother's spiritual and bodily afflictions. The mouth in Hardy can impress a mark (the "stain" of sexual contact and possession), communicate an intention or bestow a gift (speak and instruct), or inflict a wound (lacerate and destroy). Hardy's importunate orality expresses itself through this multiple sexual iconography: the kiss of rapture, the bite of death.[17] Only Tess's "pouted-up deep red mouth" is more passionate and more fatal.

Clym's investigation into his mother's death concludes in a startling physiognomic detail which confirms this destructive orality. On the afternoon that Clym learns *from a child* the answer to the riddle of death that has tormented him, he disavows Johnny Nunsuch's literal report of his mother's dying accusation: " 'Cast off by my son!' No, by my best life, dear mother, it is not so! But by your son's, your son's—May all murderesses get the torment they deserve!" (384). Clym cannot supply the proper name of the guilty one, nor her relation to himself. Instead he invokes the accusatory noun of the morality play—*murderess.* But his inward apostrophe, "dear mother," which is placed almost in apposition to "my best life," implicates him in a story of fatal attachment, a story told not on the written page but in the telling configuration of the lines on his face: "The pupils of his eyes, fixed steadfastly on blankness, were vaguely lit with an icy shine; his mouth had passed into the phase more or less imaginatively rendered in studies of Oedipus."[18]

Clym's legible face now discloses the hidden text of his desire, a text made familiar to us by an uncanny depiction of Oedipus, the sexual researcher whose inquisitiveness concludes in self-confirming guilt. Damning testimony is delivered by the mouth that loves and destroys, kisses and wounds. Clym's is the mouth of Oedipus that has passed into the phase more or less imaginatively rendered, not by Freud, but by Melanie Klein in her studies of the child's emotional life. Klein, who in a sense wrote the prehistory for Freud's history of oedipal development, finds in the infant's oral sensations the prototypes of adult feelings of frustration as well as gratification. Her account of pre-oedipal life posits, rather notoriously, the nursing infant's elementary but formative reactions to the"good" and "bad" breast, reactions that eventually determine and explain his future relations to objects and persons: "The need to cope with frustration and with the ensuing aggression is one of the factors which lead to idealizing the good breast and good mother, and correspondingly to intensifying the hatred and fears of the bad breast and bad mother, which becomes the prototype of all persecuting and frightening objects."[19]

The baby's ambivalent feelings of love and hate culminate, during the first year of life, in what Klein characterizes "the femininity phase." During this phase infantile aggression against the bad object (to be destroyed, torn apart, mutilated, or at any rate *expelled* from the angry and frightened unconscious) threatens as it overshadows the loving relation to the "good object" that nurtures and satisfies: "For at this stage of his development loving an object and devouring it are very closely connected. A little child which believes, when its mother disappears, that it has eaten her up and destroyed her (whether from motives of love or of hate) is tormented by anxiety both for her and for the good mother which it has absorbed into itself."[20] Clym's discovery of the true circumstances surrounding his mother's death can be seen as reactivating the ambivalences of that "certain phase of development" (the phrase, be it noted, is Hardy's) in which the aggressive urge to harm the bad mother (who fails to satisfy) converts to anxiety about the fate of the good mother whom the subject has internalized as a good, even revered, object. John Paterson's study of the manuscript revisions would suggest that this is the dynamic that Hardy, belatedly but firmly, intended when he altered the circumstances surrounding the mother's death, circumstances that would confirm Clym in his self-recriminations.[21]

Klein thought that such early but complex fantasies later developed into the more elaborate constructs we familiarly identify as the work of imagination.[22] Her analysis of the correlation between anxiety and guilt helps us account for the "magical thinking" (Freud's "omnipotence of thoughts") that is a distinctive feature of Hardy's fiction-making and his own self-understanding.

An early memory recounted in Hardy's self-authored "biography" suggests precisely this anxious fascination with the power of his own thoughts, of *thinking* itself, to do damage to himself and to others. Hardy recalls the "one event" of his early life that "stood out . . . more distinctly than any": "He was lying on his back in the sun thinking how useless he was and covered his face with his straw hat. The sun's rays streamed through the interstices of the straw, the lining having disappeared. Reflecting on his experiences of the world so far as he had got he came to the conclusion that he did not wish to grow up."[23] Young Thomas Hardy "innocently" confided to his mother his conclusions on the uselessness of his, of all, existence, and "to his great surprise she was very much hurt, which was natural enough considering she had been near death's door in bringing him forth. And she never forgot what he had said, a source of much regret to him in after years."

Hardy never seems to doubt the truth of his pessimistic feelings, only the wisdom of communicating them to his mother. That negative feelings, once represented to others, can work harm is a disturbing thought to a novelist of tragic existence. Yet the curious episode also casts a revealing light on the close but anxious relation of mother and son. According to Robert Gittings, Jemima Hardy was the formative and strongest presence in Hardy's life. Gittings tells how she created and commanded the center of a "firelit evening kingdom" in which children's rhymes and country verses, family histories, rural tales and native lore were recounted, stories that were later to appear, transformed, but with their essential lineaments still recognizable, in even the most bizarre of Hardy's tales of Wessex life.[24]

The numerous witches who populate his narratives accumulate around them Hardy's ambivalent feelings toward the mother's moral and magical virtues. Fairy tales, of course, recognize this connection between powerful mothers and fearful witches as a matter of common—narrative—sense. The witch figures prominently as a *complicator* of plots in Hardy's fiction, but always as an embodiment of that double figure—the good/bad mother who both protects and destroys. We encounter a figure of the good witch in Hardy's relatively innocent early pastoral, *Under the Greenwood Tree*. The witch Endorfield appears there as an ambiguous figure whose "repute" falls somewhere between "distinction and notoriety."[25] Endorfield is a "Deep Body" practiced in amatory charms, but she proves to be a practitioner of benevolent witchcraft. Her sorcery is worked through common sense and is identified with cunning of a superior but hardly supernatural sort. She counsels Fancy Day to feign an illness brought on by frustrated love, but this amatory ruse is regarded as the white magic of women's lore. Endorfield is admired for those "old dexterities of witchery" that facilitate matters of the heart and fancy (the traditional "field" of the novelist).

In *The Return of the Native* acts of imitative magic—the fashioning of images, the devising of plots—are associated with more unhallowed arts. The diabolic spells and incantations of the mother-witch, Susan Nunsuch, replicates the mother-child dyad that is the original object of the novel's imitative magic. Nunsuch is a double of Mrs. Yeobright, the "good" mother who mistrusts Eustacia as a rival for her son's affection. In her protective but malignant fervor, Nunsuch becomes a figure of fearful powers who busies herself with "a ghastly invention of superstition, calculated to bring powerlessness, atrophy, and annihilation on any human being against whom it was directed" (423). The novelist's plastic art in embodying character finds a dread counterpart in Nunsuch's creation of a wax model, a fetish doll fashioned "by warming and kneading, cutting and twisting, dismembering and re-joining the incipient image" until it resembles Eustacia. The mother devises destruction in the manner attributed to the Three Fates, cutting the thread of human life. Her violation of the Eustacia doll she has fashioned recalls the savagery of Dionysian dismemberings of the victimized body. In Nunsuch, Hardy openly recognizes one cause of the novel's tragic happenings in the maternal will-to-destruction *and it is this maternal will that the novel executes.* It is as the mother's rival that Eustacia's imaged form is impaled,[26] burned, and effaced in one of the more sadistic scenes in the history of the "classical" novel. The aggressive orality that is responsible for generating such fantasies asserts its presence in the black-magical assault on the integrity of the human image: Eustacia's doll-form, already mutilated by the voodoo like ceremony of pin-sticking, is then subjected to a trial by fire in which a long flame "arose from the spot, and curling its tongue round the figure eat [sic] still further into its substance" (359). The uncanny dream-premonition of flight and disaster foretold at the novel's beginning finds grisly confirmation in Nunsuch's unhallowed *fantasy* of mutilation.

In the emotional dialectic proposed by Melanie Klein, the damage done in fantasy is the first step in imaginative thinking, but it is by no means the last. We should be relieved to learn that in Klein's dark account of our struggle for emotional connection, guilt and anxiety announce the presence of love. They are the harbingers, the first definitive signs of a sympathetic *human* nature:

> Side by side with the destructive impulses in the unconscious mind both
> of the child and of the adult, there exists a profound urge to make sacri-

fices, in order to help and to put right loved people who in phantasy have been harmed or destroyed. In the depths of the mind, the urge to make people happy is linked up with a strong feeling of responsibility and concern for them, which manifests itself in genuine sympathy with other people and in the ability to understand them, as they are and as they feel.[27]

This strikes me as an admirable description of what pertains to the distinctly *novelistic* imagination: a sympathetic understanding of other people as they are and as they feel. But to accept this version is also to accept Klein's account of the origin of this (novelistic) capacity for sympathetic identification. In her later researches into the psychology of expiation, Klein linked love, guilt, and reparation to the same developmental stage. The impulse to make reparation (the origin, arguably, of conscience and of human law) itself originates in the desire to restore the damaged integrity of the good mother whose body (particularly her procreative organs) the child has damaged in fantasy: "In our unconscious phantasy we make good the injuries which we did in phantasy, and for which we still unconsciously feel very guilty. This *making reparation* is, in my view, a fundamental element in love and in all human relationships."[28]

The motive in such acts of reparation is always, in Klein's resonant phrase, "the motive of *restoring* damaged comeliness"[29] to the well-beloved if ill-fated objects of our love. We can see how this motive inspires Clym's acts of atonement. Hearing of Eustacia's death, Clym feels that he is guilty of a double murder: "She is the second woman I have killed this year. I was a great cause of my mother's death," admits Clym, "and I am the chief cause of hers." *But in his mind the death of his mother and the death of Eustacia represent the same offense, played out in identical form—the drama of the Disinvited:* "I spoke cruel words to her, and she left my house. I did not invite her back till it was too late" (449). Here Clym blames himself for Eustacia's death, accepting the guilt he had earlier disavowed when he denied that he had turned his mother away. "My great regret," says the guilty son and husband as he passes into his oedipal phase of moral enlightenment, "is that for what I have done no man or law can punish me!"

As an allegory of the "crime" of repression, this drama of the Disinvited conforms to the canons of *psychological,* not legal, justice: aggression against the disinvited mother (murdered in fantasy) is atoned for by the reparative urge of the contrite son, whose first penitential act is to restore the face of the mother to its original status as beloved idol. When Clym confronts Eustacia with evidence of the insult against his mother, he demands that she recall her obliterated image: "Call her to mind—think of her—what goodness there was in her: it showed in every line of her face!" (390).

A more poignant instance of Hardy's reparative imagination is his description of the drowned Eustacia, one meant to recall, then oppose, and finally supersede, the daimonic image-making of the "bad" mother, Nunsuch. Nunsuch conceived of Eustacia's body as a ravaged doll, but Hardy's last glimpse of her reinstates the mythic character of her rebellious womanhood. This is Hardy's final amending look at Eustacia, who, "as she lay there still in death, eclipsed all her living phases":

> Pallor did not include all the quality of her complexion, which seemed more than whiteness; it was almost light. The expression of her finely carved mouth was pleasant, as if a sense of dignity had just compelled her to leave off speaking. Eternal rigidity had seized upon it in a momentary transition between fervour and resignation. . . . The stateliness of look which had been almost too marked for a dweller in a country domicile had at last found an artistically happy background. (448)

In attributing a translucent whiteness to Eustacia's deathly pallor and in lingering, as if in homage, over the sculpted mouth, Hardy attempts to accord her lifeless yet still eloquent body the stateliness of human statuary, which Ruskin held was the most noble of human representations.

Wildeve, Lawrence's type for the male's eternal assumption, undergoes a similar symbolic restoration. His corpse, like Eustacia's, is said to be overcast by a "luminous youthfulness," as if the sculptor Death replaced what life took away—the radiance of a hopeful countenance. Only Wildeve's scarified hands are evidence of a death-struggle. Death was a labor for the indolent Wildeve, whose Wildeve's Patch was notoriously left uncultivated. Now the legend of violent, tragic death is incised on his "finger-tips, which were worn and scarified in his dying endeavors" (449). That legend itself is both reparative and clement. Even the narrator is touched by the pathos of this corpse still bearing the marks of its death-torment. Taking the position of even the "least sympathetic observer," he pronounces that Wildeve, whom no woman could dislike and no man truly honor, "was born for a higher destiny than this." Early death is justified as an imaginative mercy. Misfortune, philosophizes the narrator, had struck Eustacia and Wildeve gracefully by "cutting off their erratic histories with a catastrophic dash, instead of, as with many, attenuating each life to an uninteresting meagreness, through long years of wrinkles, neglect, and decay" (453).

Hardy actually provides an orthodox psychoanalytic explanation for the symbolic reparation performed by an aggressive and guilty imagination: "It is an unfortunate fact than any particular whim of parents, which might have been dispersed by half an hour's conversation during their lives, becomes sublimated by their deaths into a fiat the most absolute, with such results to conscientious children as those parents, had they lived, would have been the first to decry" (468–69). This is a shrewd "classical" analysis of an "unfortunate fact": death converts parental whim into irrevocable fiat in the minds of conscientious— and morally imaginative—children. However, the rational knowledge that parents would have decried this law enacted in their name is imaginatively useless. The inability of rational deliberation to banish irrational guilt is one of life's "little ironies," one Hardy explored in "For Conscience's Sake," which begins: "Whether the utilitarian or the intuitive theory of the moral sense be upheld it is beyond question that there are a few subtle-souled persons with whom the absolute gratuitousness of an act of reparation is an inducement to perform it; while exhortation as to its necessity would breed excuses for leaving it undone."[30] A casuistical subtlety shadows Hardy's Pauline insistence that reparation, like charity, seeketh not its own. The claims of Necessity delay and deaden the impulses of the moral sense to repair past wrongs. The subtle-souled child-man, like Thomas Hardy, can be induced to imagine, can be induced to *value,* only moral acts of absolute gratuitousness. Anything less is work undertaken for the world's rather than for conscience's sake. The iron creed of evangelical Christianity shadows Hardy's pictures of struggling life and his moral ambivalence in painting them.

We should remember this when we try to make sense of Hardy's way of giving a guilty complexion to the face of things, even to those acts of most innocent appearance. Dramatic evidence of this imaginative necessity is given in the novel's final reparative act, which signals and confirms Clym's deep identification with his "best life"—Mrs. Yeobright.[31] Clym makes his final amends to the last—and first—of the novel's three women by taking on the role and powers of the first of women: the mother. He appropriates the mother's role in order to circumvent the maternal will of the "bad" or frustrating mother, consenting to what Mrs. Yeobright opposed—Thomasin's marriage to Venn. This ending, which in his footnote Hardy the "realist" repudiated as lacking the austerity of tragic form, possesses, for Hardy the moral fantasist, the beauty, the sound economy, of a gratuity: "My sex owes you every amends for the treatment you received in days gone by." Thomasin may well be startled by Clym's admission and his peculiar locution—"my sex"—which makes gender the culprit! Of course his blessing, like his confession of "general" masculine wrongdoing, is gratuitous, for Thomasin will marry Venn no matter what Clym says or feels about it. Indeed, Clym's self-explanation will appear sententious unless understood as imaginative reparation for the fantasized past. For Hardy is the novelist who dramatizes the effects wrought in the human world by injurious *thoughts* as well as injurious acts; emotionally he conforms to the pattern of that boy moving in the feminized phase more or less rendered in studies of Oedipus by Freud, Klein, or other portraitists of our early but lasting, our first and guilty love. This love is the prototype of all those disasters of the mind's own creation; it is the initial object of that imaginative thinking we call tragedy.

FOUR

# EROTOLEPTIC NARRATIVE: HARDY'S *JUDE THE OBSCURE*

THE LETTER KILLETH, the chilling epigraph to *Jude the Obscure,* is no idle admonition. The murderous force of the literal everywhere prevails in this novel intellectually fascinated and morally bound by the laws governing the origin, development, and obsolescence of letters. Think what a different life Jude might have led if he had only heard of Grimm's law! Indeed Hardy seems to take a grim satisfaction in dramatizing how men and letters share a similar destiny: inevitable corruption of innocent originals. Life in Wessex may take the form of a Greek tragedy, but it is haunted, if not inspired, by a Pauline terror of the letter.

Perhaps nowhere is the word more dramatically fateful than in the neologism—*erotolepsy*—that Hardy adopts to describe the somatic and spiritual disturbances that afflict and finally overmaster Jude's virile idealism. As the combining form *-lepsy* specifies, erotolepsy is a more violent and imperious manifestation of Eros than the indolent or melancholy show of madness classically recognized as erotomania. Erotolepsy designates a species of that bodily transport so important to Pater's *Greek Studies* and Nietzsche's recovery of the Dionysian origins of tragic experience. As tragic man, Jude is subject to *seizures* by the divine Eros, a diagnosis confirmed by Hardy's pun on the folly, at once genealogical (the Fawley name) and characterological, that rules his dark, non-Apollonian destiny. Erotolepsy compels the self-tutored Jude "as a violent schoolmaster a schoolboy he has seized by the collar, in a direction which tended towards the embrace of a woman for whom he had no respect, and whose life had nothing in common with his own except locality" (64). Eros seizes upon Jude as a recalcitrant but apt pupil in the *ars amores.* The war between flesh and spirit, the central agon of all Hardy's work, is waged under the generic banner of eroteleptic romance. Jude's passions are divided between a love of letters, which "killeth," and his love of women, who give, but also take away, life. In Hardy, who has a decided taste for compounded ironies, such overdeterminations are to be expected, but in *Jude the Obscure* they prove fatal and portend the death of novel-writing itself.

That death culminated a series of traumatic "mutilations" chronicled in Hardy's self-authored *Life and Work of Thomas Hardy.* Hardy's account of these last years, " 'Tess,' 'Jude,' and the End of Prose," dwells on the disabling effect of Grundyism on fiction-writing; he refers repeatedly to novels "finished, mutilated, and restored." However, as perhaps befits a modern thinker, Hardy recounts a dismemberment or *sparagmos* that has become strictly textual. Hardy's feelings, which motivate the end of novel-writing, are complicitous with the shattering insights of the novels themselves into the disastrous nature of our human, especially our first, loves. I will be expatiating on this complicity in the pages that follow. I want only to remark here the striking coincidence that finds Hardy observing the death of his belief in a heroic culture of letters while paying ironic tribute to the power of woman as deviser of human destiny, this time not through the elaborate displacements of *The Return of the Native,* where fate is personated in the classical figure of three women (the Morae), but through the direct replacement of the divine (paternal) dispensation with a feminine one. Hardy's heretical substitution is sardonically summarized, if not legitimated, by the narrator's laconic observation that "if God disposed not, woman did" (228).[1] In this transposition we can detect, among other things, how Hardy's satire on the Christian dispensation is accompanied by a pagan, reprobate awe of the female mysteries.

This awe of woman's primary governance over human life gives the novel its aura of precocious feminism, which Hardy funnily alludes to in his postscript of 1912. There Hardy relates how Sue, "the slight, pale 'bachelor' girl," was hailed by a critic as "the first delineation in fiction of the woman who was coming into notice in her thousands every year—the woman of the feminist movement" (26). Hardy is too accomplished a novelist to ignore the emergence of a new social type—"the intellectualized, emancipated bundle of nerves that modern conditions were producing, mainly in cities." Yet Hardy also admitted to Sir Edmund Gosse that Sue was "a type which has always had an attraction for me."[2] Like Jane Austen, solicitous in defending her Emma, whom she fears no one will much like but herself, Hardy seems to defend Sue in a way he never felt necessary for his Tess (who, at any rate, is conspicuously lovable).

Yet both women are implicated in the same erotoleptic agency that translates the occasions of first love into the plot of disaster. This plot, in which Love is inexorably betrayed by the idols of its own creation, remains a remarkably stable object of imitation throughout Hardy's career. First love initially appears in Hardy under the aspect of "Fascination." Fascination, which serves Hardy as the part-title for his first major tragedy, *The Return of the Native,* recounts an enthrallment (as revealed by its Latin origin *fascinatus,* 'bewitchment'). Fascination originates in the magical attraction of opposites and concludes in that chagrin of spirit which Hardy allegorizes in *Tess of the D'Urbervilles* as the birth of Sorrow, the Undesired. Sorrow, as either a narrative or an allegorical figure, can claim no mythic lineage, but is proverbial. Fascination is Hardy's theme as a *rural* novelist whose fiction represents the ethos of a folk culture experienced in the ways of instinct-propitiation.

But Fascination is a tale often told in conjunction or in competition with a love story which evokes the presiding spirits of a literary rather than a folk culture. Hardy identifies this love in *Jude the Obscure* as Shelleyan, which he carefully distinguishes from Platonic love. It is the love of Laon and Cythna, Paul and Virginie, a love that does not divert or sedate the erotoleptic, but gives it spiritual form. Shelleyan love does not originate in the magnetic attraction of opposites, but is born of the Spirit of "Sympathy" or "Similitude of feeling." Fascination comprehends the love story of Bathsheba and Sergeant Troy, Eustacia and Clym, Tess and Alex, Grace and Fitzpiers, Jude and Arabella. Shelleyan love projects its essential longing in the incestuous imagery of affinity and twinship: Clym and his mother, Tess and Angel, Jude and Sue are coupled as a primary and indivisible unity, conjoined by the sympathy of like for like. Fascination is but an episode whose firstborn is Sorrow; Shelleyan love endures as spirits endure, "folded within their own eternity." Fascination is carnal and finds its purpose incarnate in the child, figure for love's self-perpetuating joy—or unexpected sorrow. Shelleyan love originates in an insubstantial vision and seeks thereafter to unite with "the shadow of that idol of my thought" that Shelley calls "epipsychidion": "this soul out of my soul," at once "sister, spouse, angel, and Pilot of Fate." Shelleyan love dreams of a visionary assumption into a state of transcendent unity:

> One hope within two wills, one will beneath
> Two overshadowing minds, one life, one death,
> One Heaven, one Hell, one immortality,
> And one annihilation.
>
> ("Epipsychidion," lines 584–87)

And Shelleyan love perishes as myths perish, by the leaden and fatal literalism of irony:

> The winged words on which my soul would pierce
> Into the height of Love's rare Universe,
> Are chains of lead around its flight of fire—
> I pant, I sink, I tremble, I expire!
>
> (lines 588–92)

Hardy, self-proclaimed "chronicler of moods and deeds" (308), records this trembling expiration of Shelleyan love. Indeed he is unsurpassed as a novelist of such romantic debacles. Yet Hardy the realist knows that the novel can never, as novel, follow the Shelleyan quester darkly, fearfully afar into the realm where "high hearts are wrecked." The novel must traffic with the viscous materials of life; its commerce is with the here and now, not the transcendent elsewhere. The ideal is not an agency, as in Shelley, of the spirit's self-slaughter. It is the concrete reality of life which defeats desire in Hardy's dark allegories of love.[3]

These allegories involve his idealists and lovers in the language and contradictions of an Omnipresent Irony. Hardy speaks bitterly in *The Woodlanders* of the "Unfulfilled Intention, which makes life what it is," thus installing irony as the First Cause and Final Effect of his narrative world. Hardy is a storyteller given to recounting tales of impotent loves and failed ambitions, which accounts for the sexual as well as metaphysical despondency that characterizes their mood. To dramatize this contrast between Ideal Intention and actual existence was, as Hardy wrote to Sir Edmund Gosse, his narrative object in *Jude the Obscure,* one that justified the scandalous and droll account of Jude's first encounter with Arabella. "The 'grimy' features of the story," wrote Hardy, "go to show the contrast between the ideal life a man wished to lead, and the squalid real life he was fated to lead. The throwing of the pizzle, at the supreme moment of his young dream, is to sharply initiate this contrast."[4] The pizzle, as phallic projectile, describes, in its flight, the distance that separates what is wished from what is fated. It is a distance between two different orders of conception, one "symbolic" and ethereal, the other literal and corporeal. The sexual sense of conception is what marks this initiating contrast as a supreme, but also comic, moment of vocational crisis: Jude, convinced of his spiritual calling, responding helplessly to Arabella's erotic summons. Contributing to the droll piquancy of this contrast is Hardy's theological "wit" in showing how Jude's rapt contemplation of Christminster as an Alma Mater, a divine mother, is diverted toward Arabella, who is about her "father's business." The implicit Christological pun elaborates the contrast between a ministry of spirit whose product is the book, and a life spent in physical labor (beginning with childbearing and including pig-jobbing).

But it is only the end of Jude and Arabella's "love story" which marks this opposition between mental and bodily labors as tragic; its beginning is at worst grimy and squalid, at best, the stuff of old comedy. Jude, immersed in the ideal world of letters, imagines himself in the society of his revered teachers.[5] He rehearses the curriculum of his planned study and, thrilling to a majestic litany of names, strolls in anticipation of the mental company of "Livy, Tacitus, Herodotus, Aeschylus, Sophocles, Aristophanes—" (57). It is, of course, at this particular juncture that Arabella's pert "Ha, ha, ha! Hoity-toity!" is first heard, signaling the possibility of an altogether different kind of company. She recalls him from his cloud-cuckoo-land; and indeed their encounter is—as Hardy's dash cunningly designates—more Aristophanic than Sophoclean, which would be fitting for a scene devoted to the spectacle of phallic display.

However, in interpreting this scene, it would be well to remember Lawrence's defense of Arabella, which exonerates her of *sheer* vulgarity. For Lawrence, Arabella is not only Jude's first love, but also his true mate (but then Lawrence religiously allows that the phallus is the real engendering power in Nature and is suspicious of any work of the spirit antagonistic to that life-producing power). Their courtship begins when Jude abandons his reading to follow the old idols of the flesh. Their marriage ends on a scene of their "last difference," a final quarrel which recapitulates their radical dissimilarity: Arabella, with grease-laden hands, tosses Jude's "dear ancient classics" on the floor, declaring, in the spirit of outraged Nature, "I won't have them books here in the way" (89). The battle of the books concludes with Jude extracting a promise from Arabella to leave the books alone. Her assent, a reluctant "I do," is a grim reenactment of the marriage vows and intensifies the opposition between Arabella's grease and Jude's identification with sacerdotal grace. This old pun on *grease/grace,* common to the Elizabethans, verbally materializes the "shop-soiled condition of the marriage theme," for which Hardy ironically accepts responsibility in his postscript of 1912.

Hardy's grim pun on the sanctity or sordidness of the marriage service presents the battle between flesh and spirit as a verbal combat. Arabella's greasy smudges are traces of the latent materiality of spiritual figures. She hurls the characteristic part of the pig at the male dreamer, just as she later effects her seduction by teasing him with her adept manipulation of an egg, which she causes to appear and disappear in obedience to a biological rhythm as yet completely mysterious to Jude: "Now mind you don't come near me. I don't want to get it broke, and have to begin another" (75). Arabella rescues these literal images of sexual parts from the "folly" of synecdoche; she does not mistake the part for the whole, and so rescues Jude from the onanism potential to his idealism.

Arabella's name provides another confirming instance that the linguistic is character is fate. *Arabella Donn* is one of Hardy's antithetical names; it reveals the hidden unity between Nature and Art, at least in the realm of female comeliness. Arabella's attractiveness as a "substantial female animal" is the product of adornment (false hair) and artifice (producing dimples on demand). Arabella or "Bella" is arable, a cultivated beauty. Her last name is a less conventional but more adroit indicator of what Hardy terms her "instinct towards artificiality"

(79). Don[n], which claims verbal ancestry in *dominus,* "master," is a concealed but proleptic jibe at Jude's scholarly ambitions, echoing, as it does, the honorific for the fellows of Christminster (Oxford). But *Donn* works more directly as a pun on the bodily adornments Arabella dons to lure the aspiring don into more carnal pursuits. In this she differs spectacularly from Sue, who in a crucial moment dons Jude's own clothes and so assumes in his eyes the raiment of divinity. Sue is the idolized other-as-double who represents the promise of a self-unity enjoyed, presumably, only by the gods.

Thus Jude's religious passion, which initially obstructs his erotolepsy, ultimately transfigures it. This reversal is pedantically (that is, appropriately!) dramatized in the way Arabella encourages a nonreading, Sue a rereading, of the New Testament. Jude, the "incipient scholar," would "begin at the beginning" of the Greek Gospels, but he never proceeds beyond the opening words after he meets Arabella. A rhetoric of beginnings is insistently and ironically deployed in describing Jude's first love, anticipating the thematic contours of Jude's career as a series of failed or balked initiatives. Jude's initial act of scholarly dereliction leads Hardy to brand him, as he rises from his desk, with the tragic epithet, "the predestinate Jude." Hardy's preterition here is eroteleptic, not theological. It is always a woman, as Jude soon realizes, who checks his aspirations by seizing his sexual attention: "Strange that his first aspiration—towards academical proficiency—had been checked by a woman, and that his second aspiration—towards apostleship—had also been checked by a woman" (238). Women are not disposed to champion male aspirations presumably because they prefer to initiate their *own* beginnings.

For Arabella, the beginning is biologically conceived (a pregnancy); for Sue it is textually instituted. Sue recounts to Jude how she once had devised a "*new* New Testament" (emphasis mine), rearranged in "chronological order as written, beginning the book with Thessalonians, following on with the Epistles, and putting the Gospels much further on" (172). The effect of this recomposition, Sue claims, was to make the book "twice as interesting," presumably because textual, not narrative, order is what interests her. Sue's enthusiasms are quite scribal, which Hardy emphasizes by initially presenting her to Jude's (and our) eyes at work lettering religious manuscripts in a "seed-bed of idolatry," a workshop run, tellingly, by women. Sue is a fashioner of idolatrous images and religious bric-a-brac, monkish if not quite papist in her "business." Of course, her religious temper, more accurately reflected in the plaster images of Venus and Apollo she smuggles into her rooms, is Hellenic rather than Hebraic. Gibbon, "the sly author of the immortal chapter on Christianity," not Pusey the Tractarian, is her authority on Judeo-Christian culture.

Sue's experiment in textual criticism extends to the Old Testament, where it is more conventionally applied to the Song of Songs. Sue, an advanced thinker, instructs Jude in the new biblical hermeneutics that de-allegorize and naturalize the Song so as to recover its initial, *literal* emphasis on ecstatic sexual love. Yet in recovering the carnal sense of Solomon's Song from patristic commentary and protesting against the allegorical reading of the Bride as the "Church profess[ing] her faith," Sue so personalizes the text that it seems to refer to her own name, Bridehead. In this name is comprehended the ambiguity of her own sexuality. Her personal construction reminds us that she is the "Bride" who does not represent but replaces the Church in Jude's complicated ecclesiastical romance. In a dizzying series of transferences, Jude's desire "precipitates" itself in Sue's "half-visionary form" (109), a description I think we can take to mean that Sue is Jude's Shelleyan self-specter. (When Jude burns his own photograph, Sue's immediately replaces it as a kind of soul-fetish.)

But Jude's love for his "Bride" obviously involves a more carnal sense of devotion to this epicene shadow of the idol of his thought. Jude's idolatry ministers to the dominant fantasy of the novel: that heredity and social law can be circumvented or erotoleptic fate averted simply by beginning life anew. Again and yet again, Jude rededicates himself to a love or to a vocation, *as if for the first time.* He acts in defiance or in ignorance of the claims of an accomplished and all-determining past. There is no last or final term to Jude's emotional logic; there is only the rapture of the first time recaptured, not in memory, but in present or narrative time. In *Jude the Obscure* this logic—let us call it the erotoleptic logic of first initiatives—determines that Jude's new love for Sue metaleptically assumes the form of an idyll, which locates love beyond the realm of physical or historical forces, arenas of sexual selection, competition and contention. *Jude the Obscure* has such an idyll, in Jude and Sue's day trip to Wardour Castle: "There duly came the charm of calling at the College door for her; her emergence in a nunlike simplicity of costume that was rather enforced than desired; the traipsing along to the station, the porter's 'B'your leave!' the screaming of the trains—everything formed the basis of a beautiful crystallization" (156). *Crystallization* is not an innocent term here—it is the neologism Stendhal proposes to describe "the impulse of folly that makes us see all beauties and perfections in the woman we are beginning to love, but also many bolder ellipses."[6] Crystallization is the distillate of fascination's expert alchemy: "The crystallization about your mistress, that is to say her *beauty,* is nothing but the sum of the fulfillment of all the desires you have been able to formulate about her." Like all alchemical solutions, crystallization is a philosopher's folly, as Hardy's portrait of an erotoleptic scholar sadly illustrates. Hardy finely details the elements that contribute to this crystallization—Sue issuing from the very portals of the "College" already identified as a "paradise of the learned"; the porter's greeting that gives these self-conscious lovers a sense of their own unremarkableness, raising their hope that they might love as other unremarkable people love—without dire consequences. Sue romanticizes their outing as a journey outside "every law except gravitation and germination." This seems her only real concession to the laws that govern corporeal bodies in the natural order of time.

What Hardy emphasizes in this crystallization is the restless Shelleyanism it condenses and fulfills. Jude is drawn to Sue as like is to like; the law of kinship, subject to class ironies in *Tess,* in this novel assumes a transcendental aspect. When their idyllic trip ends with Sue's being barred from her lodgings, she insists on identifying herself as an outcast Ishmaelite. Jude offers her the shelter of his room, drapes her in his own garments, and then worships the idol he has materialized as an apparition of Ganymede. Sue's self-characterization as Ishmaelite is sensitive to the social implications of their love. Jude's comparison introduces the note of reversion Stendhal detects in all crystallization: as Ganymede, Sue embodies a fantastical, cherished boyhood beloved by the father of gods. In fact, she confesses to Jude on this expedition that she "crave[s] to get back to the life of [her] infancy and its freedom" (158). Sue's sexual particularities, which Edmund Gosse remarked would "fill the specimen tables of a German specialist," are discomfiting not only on their own terms, but for what they elicit, in fantasy, from Jude himself, who in this as in other instances seems to be Hardy's most unblinking self-portrait. Hardy himself maintained that a "clue to much of his character and action throughout his life is afforded by his lateness of development in virility, while mentally precocious."[7] Jude's manhood is as much reflected as it is refracted in Sue's womanhood.

Sue's peculiar sexual character found an unexpected defender in Lawrence. He regarded society's failure to accommodate her extraordinary nature as a sign of modernity:

> Why must it be assumed that Sue is an "ordinary" woman—as if such a thing existed? Why must she feel ashamed if she is specialized? . . .
>
> She was not a woman. She was Sue Bridehead, something very particular. Why was there no place for her? Cassandra had the Temple of Apollo. Why are we so foul that we have no reverence for that which we are and for that which is amongst us? . . .
>
> If we had reverence for what we are, our life would take real form,

and Sue would have a place, as Cassandra had a place; she would have a
place which does not yet exist, because we are all so vulgar, we have nothing. (*P.*, 510)

What Lawrence stresses is the need to establish a new place, as yet unimagined,
for such "particular" individuals. But Lawrence suggests the kind of place it
must be, a place to be linked, like Cassandra's, to the sacred precincts of prophecy, of Apollonian enlightenment and ritual abstinence. Lawrence's metaphor
of place does not refer to Sue's own figure for her desire, but is nevertheless
coextensive with it. Sue's progressive if perilous experiments in cohabitation
are explicitly linked with the self-testing practice "deliberately sought by the
priests and virgins of the early Church, who, disdaining an ignominious flight
from temptation, became even chamber-partners with impunity" (213). Neither Sue nor Jude pause to consider Gibbon's warning that "insulted Nature
sometimes vindicated her rights."

## THE TABOO OF VIRGINITY

In support of Gibbon's authority, Hardy offers at once a less politic and more
cynical observation: "Love lives on propinquity but dies of contact." Gibbon's
remark strikes us as worldly; Hardy's, disillusioned. It is the remark of a man
who apparently prefers the beloved in his vicinity, but not within his domain.
Moments of crisis in Hardy's fiction generally transpire before closed doors (*The
Return of the Native, The Woodlanders*), blocked entrances (Tess trapped in the
tomb), or unscalable walls. These architectural and amatory figures of blockage,
frustration, or indecision suggest that Hardy conceived of the benefits as well
as the hazards of propinquity in structural and strategic terms. The part-title
"At Christminster" takes as one of its epigraphs Ovid's rendering of the beginning stages of the love between Pyramus and Thisbe, a myth that complements
the Hardyesque vision of amorous destiny as one ruled by the figure of the wall:
"Notitiam primosque gradus vicinia fecit; / Tempore crevit amor" ("Contiguity
caused their first acquaintance; / love grew with time"; *Metamorphosis,* book 4,
lines 59–60). Initially that wall whose very existence denotes vicinity is the wall
of Christminster itself, which encloses the promised land from which Jude is
excluded: "Only a wall divided him from those happy young contemporaries of
his with whom he shared a common mental life . . . Only a wall—but what a
wall!" (105). Through those condensations that permit Hardy to translate literal
constructions into figures for the Spirit, the wall that impedes Jude's Christ-

minster "sentiment" is replaced, through an ingenious but inescapable series of metonymic associations, by the proper name that predicates Sue's sexual existence as a hymenal creature. Hardy, always a bold fabulator of names, denotes Sue as a "bridehead," recalling Hymen's double existence as perforative wall and presiding spirit of marriage. Jude's erotolepsy and Sue's sexual inaccessibility are thus twin or mirror images of each other (as the language and acts of their exchanges intimate), and together reflect what we might call the ontology of virginity that in no way assumes an innate nor even a characteristic sexual innocence. Tess is a pure woman; Sue is a woman more variously compounded.

The ambiguous relationship that obtains between virginity and First Love can be more easily examined in a tale Hardy wrote in collaboration with Florence Henniker.[8] The story is titled "The Spectre of the Real." This title, I think, cryptically alludes to that presence that can never be pictured, that invisible but perforative wall, the hymen. The tale begins as a story of youthful sexual misadventure (the most common and unremarkable type of "first love"), which both parties agree to have been pure folly. Years later the heroine, Rosalys, is about to marry a Lord Parkhurst, who has no knowledge or even suspicion of her earlier elopement. Hardy often satirizes the romance of elopement, but in this story what is emphasized is the seemingly providential series of events which brings the heroine's former lover, presumed dead, home again. Although Rosalys is legally entitled to "presume" her husband's death after seven years without word of him, she is less sure of her moral ground in proceeding with the nuptials. On the eve of her wedding, however, her former lover promises never to return or to contest his legal status as defunct. He drowns immediately after leaving Rosalys with these assurances, thus morally as well as legally absolving her of fraud or possible bigamy.

Hardy, as any of his narratives will testify, is unreasonably fond of such casuistical subtleties and often lets them dictate the finer moralities of his ironic tales. The "rescued" heroine is, then, according to formula, safely married, and departs on her wedding-tour. On the brink of this channel (and narrative) crossing, the story takes an uncanny turn. The narrative shifts, almost brutally, to a newspaper report of Lord Parkhurst's suicide:

> We regret to announce that this distinguished nobleman and heroic naval officer, who arrived with Lady Parkhurst last evening at the Lord Chamberlain Hotel in this town, preparatory to their starting on their wedding-tour, entered his dressing-room very early this morning, and shot himself through the head with a revolver. The report was heard shortly after

dawn, none of the inmates of the hotel being astir at the time. No reason can be assigned for the rash act.[9]

In the interval between evening arrival and morning departure, the aristocratic groom apparently encountered the specter of the real. What other motive could be assigned for his suicidal act? What else could transform the bridal bed into a deathbed but firsthand proof of what Joyce sardonically termed the preordained frangibility of the hymen? In a letter to Henniker, Hardy insisted that "the ending, good or bad, has the merit of being in exact keeping with Lord P. 's character."[10] This is an odd remark, particularly since Lord P. has no character, only a title and its legacy of representative attitudes. A different merit attaches to this ending, which hints at, but never avers, the invisible but essential presence of the hymen in the sexual and social transaction known as marriage. Virginity is a specter of the real; it can exist either with or without the physical evidence of its existence. Lord P. killed himself because he was a literalist, and wanted in body what his bride in fact offered him in spirit—the fruits of her first love.

Sue Bridehead's proper name, which defines her with an inspired if characteristically overdetermined linguistic precision, suggests that she is such an enigmatic figure precisely because she would both conceal and expose this partiality for maidenheads. Her name defines the logically untenable wish to be neither wife nor maiden, but to define a place or status between these two states. Sue cannot disclose this hidden desire, only point to it, as she does when, quoting Browning, she urges Jude to "twitch the robe / From that blank layfigure your fancy draped." What Sue wants Jude to see is her own blankness as a lay figure who may consent to cross-dressing but not to sexual redressing. She chooses this moment to reveal that she consented to live with a man "by letter," unconscious of his strict construction of terms: "But when I joined him in London I found he meant a different thing from what I meant." Sue's sense of contract, in which the spirit, not the letter, of cohabitation is fulfilled, proves victorious, yet even she confesses that a better woman would not have remained as she began.

Sue's actions are motivated by an antiliteralist logic which is, Hardy says, "extraordinarily compounded, and seemed to maintain that before a thing was done it might be right to do, but that being done it became wrong" (239). Her emotional logic, which directly contrasts with Jude's "logic of first initiatives," is a hymenal logic of a necessarily perverse and, I believe, modern kind that dreads the consummation of the first principles it predicates. For Sue to act on her feelings is equivalent to canceling or destroying them, a contradiction that Derrida explores in his double session on Mallarmé's *Mimique,* in which this hymenal logic is analyzed as an obsession with fictionality. What seems pertinent to our understanding of Sue's nominal identity as "bridehead" is Derrida's emphasis on the generative ambiguity of the hymen that "sows confusion *between* opposites *and* stands *between* the opposites at once. What counts here is the *between,* the in-between-ness of the hymen." [11] By virtue of its strategic placement, neither fully inside nor outside the female body, the hymen designates all the decided ambiguities of *entre*—in-between-ness, and its homonym in French, *antre*—cave, natural grotto, or deep dark cavern. (Is this condensation what Hardy instinctively grasped in naming the mistress of the house where Sue lives with other maidens "Miss Fontover"?) In Derrida's polymorphous play on *entre/antre,* which is more extensive than I have indicated here, [12] the hymen is prestigiously placed within the heart of the imaginary itself: as an impermeable but perforative membrane, the hymen is the oracular site ready to receive or disseminate the phallocentric Logos, desirous of cavities and caves.

Such a Derridean excursus, however, would eventually account for Sue's vacillations by positing the essential fictionality of the self. There is some truth, but not enough, in this understanding of her "character." Hardy himself diagnoses her neurosis as a historically conditioned and symptomatic "abnormalism," a cautionary instance of "modern nerves wed to primitive feelings fated to disaster." Yet is not Hardy's psychologizing marked by one of the four errors Nietzsche identified in his *Twilight of the Idols*—the error of mistaking the effect for the cause? For it is not the modern nerves of the pale bachelor girl that unsex her, but Sue's primitive feelings that unnerve her. Michael Millgate, who endorses as he explicates Hardy's reading of Sue's nervous sexuality, suggests that Sue's name roots her in anthropological ground. Bridehead, Millgate notes, is "a Dorset place-name (for the source of the River Bride, near Little Bredy)." Millgate then ventures that, as Hardy had been reading *The Golden Bough,* "it is perhaps worth noting that Frazer's discussion of the corn-spirit mentions that in parts of Scotland the last handful of standing corn at harvest-time was called 'The maidenhead or the Head.'" [13] Whether it originates as a place-name or as a harvest name, *bride-* or *maidenhead* expresses the heathen concern with those forces or states that promote—or hinder and obstruct—fertility. Millgate's speculation thus complicates and deepens his more conventional interpretation of Sue as a woman "fatally inhibited by the 'head,' by intellectuality and a revulsion from the physical." [14] I will only propose, on the basis of Millgate's own source work, that Sue's compound name refers to a *specific* personal revulsion that is subject to communal taboo, the taboo, as Freud identifies it, of virginity.

Freud, still unrivaled in explaining the persistence of the archaic in the symptoms and symbols of modern thought, believed the taboo of virginity was originally linked to a complementary taboo against menstrual blood. These taboos in turn formed part of general prohibitions against murder and blood-lust that regulated primitive society. But he further recites an explanation I find useful in understanding Sue's final reversion to archaic thought. Freud associates the taboo of virginity with a "perpetual lurking apprehensiveness" that appears most strongly "on all occasions which differ in any way from the usual, which involve something new or unexpected, something not understood or uncanny." Freud, in his canny way, locates the source of this apprehensiveness in the "fear of first occurrences." [15]

This fear of first occurrences governs the love story of *Jude the Obscure* and gives Hardy's familial and folk plot a startling anthropological clarity. Every "new beginning" or "turning point" that Jude undertakes in emotional obeisance to his logic of first initiatives occurs on the site of landmarks in danger of being obliterated, Hardy complains, by modern (and perishable) designs "unfamiliar to English eyes." In this novel, so concerned with acts of architectural restoration, Hardy's reparative imagination works to re-inspirit these sites by recalling to us those unquiet, indwelling spirits who once were controlled or appeased by honoring taboo. Violation of taboo leads to a curse transmitted across generations: in unconscious but prescient recognition of this fact, Jude and Sue first meet at the Spot of the Martyrdoms.

The Spot of the Martyrdoms seems to commemorate the two fears commingled in the taboo of virginity: the fear of first occurrences, itself an adumbration of the fear of blood. The narrative distribution of amorous episodes confirms this essential structure of sacrifice, which the novel's Christological imagery does more to obscure than to reinforce. The perforation of the hymen is traditionally the bloody act that signals the spiritual as well as literal (or legal) fulfillment of the marriage contract. Yet in her first marriage Sue clearly remains a "Bride," as she confesses to Jude, and it is this abbreviation that is one of his pet or love names for her. The truncation already signals that impending catastrophe of defloration she dreads.

To whom or to what then can Sue, guardian of her own virginity, entrust the task of defloration, the first occurrence that will alter her nature—and confute her name—and make her at once a better and a diminished woman? This question is not rhetorical, but pointed, for Sue's conformation to the customs (if not delights) of the marital bed is the ethical dilemma confronting her. Her solution to this dilemma demonstrates her genius for adapting ancient practices to modern instances. Again, Freud will provide the relevant cases for us:

> The customs of primitive peoples seem to take account of this *motif* of the early sexual wish by handing over the task of defloration to an elder, priest or holy man, that is, to a substitute for the father. There seems to me to be a direct path leading from this custom to the highly vexed question of the *jus primae noctis* of the mediaeval lord of the manor. A. J. Storfer (1911) has put forward the same view and has in addition, as Jung (1909) had already done before him, interpreted the widespread tradition of the Tobias nights (the custom of continence during the first three nights of marriage) as an acknowledgment of the privilege of the patriarch. It agrees with our expectations, therefore, when we find the images of god included among the father-surrogates with defloration.[16]

This tradition of ceremonial defloration is revived in Sue's perverse request that Jude "give her away" to Phillotson. "You are 'father,' you know. That's what they call the man who gives you away" (191). Sue is being conventionally minded in assigning Jude, the groom's former pupil, the paternal role of married relation. The reversal, read in Freudian terms, could suggest her wish that Jude be the one to deflower her, but Jude, so cruelly tormented by this novel revival of ancient custom, can only see that Phillotson's age gives him the literal qualifications for the role of "father of the bride": "Phillotson's age entitles him to be called that." Two literal constructions compete with each other, and Sue, victimized by her own undecidable logic of virginity, seems doomed to remain perpetually confused on the question of who is her real husband and to whom—as Bride—she must surrender her virginity. She remains in a kind of ritual bondage to her "fear of first occurrences," perhaps because she exists beyond the reach of a language or a logic—of an erotoleptic force—that would seize or transport her out of her in-between-ness and deliver her into a sexually and civically authorized place.

Freud suggests that the resistances accommodated by these taboos are of a psychological rather than sociological importance; they express the anger and resentment of the maiden whose "frigidity" is symptomatic of her "masculine protest" against castration. The pig's "pizzle" is the manifest presence of this latent castration anxiety, but as a totemic object, it is associated, in broad folk humor, with an amorously determined Arabella. A more modern form of this protest, Freud rashly speculated, was "clearly indicated in the strivings and in the literary productions of 'emancipated' women." [17] What interests me here is not the clinical truth but the psychological value of Freud's explanation in uncovering the archaism lurking in Hardy's portrait of Sue as the pale bachelor girl, already identifiable as a distinct modern type destined to revert to a "fanatic prostitution" (380). This projected catastrophe is as serious, if not as spectacular, as Jude's histrionic death on Remembrance Day. Sue's gradual involvement with Jude is marked by images or incidents of animal cruelty that dramatize mutilation anxieties. The lacerated leg of the rabbit caught in a gin is a literal instance of mutilation that is figuratively elaborated and incorporated in Jude's criticism of the "artificial system of things": "Is it that the women are to blame; or is it the artificial system of things, under which the normal sex-impulses are turned into devilish domestic gins and springes to noose and hold back those who want to progress?" (238). All of Lawrence could be read as an extended answer to the unsettlements of this question. Hardy, I would venture, lets the question defeat him. He cannot bring himself to blame women, nor to exonerate them for the cruel fate of male erotolepsy. Hardy can dream of a future in which normal sex-impulses will abet rather than hinder "those who want to progress," but he cannot envision a future that is anything but a reversion to the archaic forms and dead letters of the past. Like Sue's Voltairean redactions of the New Testament, Hardy's erotoleptic narratives, however progressive in spirit, are sex-tragedies transfixed by the spectacle of "the dead limbs of gibbeted gods."

Only once in the novel does the spirit reciprocate the letter in full and reconciling affection. The fateful exchange occurs as a drama of a kiss given in pledge of physical as well as spiritual surrender:

> They had stood parting in the silent highway, and their tense and passionate moods had led to bewildered inquiries of each other on how far their intimacy ought to go; till they had almost quarreled, and she had said tearfully that it was hardly proper of him as a parson in embryo to think of such a thing as kissing her even in farewell, as he now wished to do. Then she had conceded that the fact of the kiss would be nothing: all would depend upon the spirit of it. If given in the spirit of a cousin and a friend she saw no objection; if in the spirit of a lover she could not permit it. "Will you swear that it will not be in that spirit."
>     No: he would not. (237)

Jude's refusal to submit to Sue's casuistical divorce of the spirit from the letter of the kiss leads to a look, simultaneously exchanged, that issues in a long and unpremeditated embrace in which these lovers "kissed close and long." The kiss, the narrator claims, "was a turning-point in Jude's career." It is hard to mobilize our suspicions against this erotic peripety which concludes with a unique Hardyesque auto-da-fé: Jude Fawley returning home to burn his books, the "leaves, covers, and binding of Jeremy Taylor, Butler, Doddrige, Paley, Pusey, Newman and the rest . . ." Again a woman conquers the Church fathers; once more Jude's erotolepsy triumphs over his love of divine letters. Yet this time Jude is liberated rather than trapped. His renunciation of the book frees him from a hated religious imposture: "In his passion for Sue he could now stand as an ordinary sinner, and not as a whited sepulchre." The replacement of Love for the Law ushers in a period of happiness, which has no history (the domain of scribes) and so goes unrecorded in the novel. We know of its existence only because it produces not books, but children, living proof of Sue's camaraderie.

What finally countermands and divides this Shelleyan union is what we could call the novel's rhetorical genetics. Darwinian logic might predict that the offspring of the substantial Arabella and the virile Jude would produce the child fittest to survive, but Hardy's cross-matchings are more sensitive to elective than to biological affinities. Sue and Jude's offspring are spiritually "healthy"; that is, no pathological morbidity afflicts them. They appear to be the well-adjusted offspring of a spiritually compatible, if sexually tense, coupling. Oddly, it is the union of the idealistic dreamer and the substantial female animal that produces a figure of depressed consciousness—Little Father Time. Little Jude, both as diminished replica of his father and as harbinger of the coming universal wish not to live, is the necessary end term that gives decided, if morbid, direction to Hardy's sexual allegory of Unfulfilled Intention. The child, once a rival of the book, becomes a bookish figure for the letter: that is, little Jude becomes Little Father Time, signaling his transformation from a biological or narrative figure (the child of human parents) into a rhetorical one.

This triumph of the letter over the spirit takes a specific literary form in Hardy's conscious parody of Wordsworthian childhood. Through a sardonic interpolation of the Intimations Ode, Hardy demonstrates how "the inception of some glorious idea" gives rise in the transparent and susceptible natures of the young "to the flattering fancy that heaven lies about them then" (48). Wordsworth's intimation of a recuperable prophetic power is dismissed as the illusion of a "milk-fed infancy." But Hardy pays a price for these demystifications. He forgoes, in his repudiation of Wordsworthian childhood, the logic of Wordsworthian consolation. Wordsworth could acknowledge that "nothing can bring back the hour" of childhood joy and yet still find "Strength in what remains behind; / In the primal sympathy / Which having been must ever be"

("Ode: Intimations of Immortality," lines 180–83). Hardy is not only grieved at what has been, but also dreads what is to come. His dark reasoning inverts Wordsworth's consoling proposition that the child is father to the man. The desponding "Little Father Time" would not father a man, but would die a child. He is no child of joy, but a figure of age masquerading as juvenility.

The murder-suicide that represents Hardy's cathartic disavowal of Wordsworthian childhood represents the grisly cost of little Jude's hapless masquerade, and exposes it as an error of the literalist imagination. "Done because we are too menny"—the testament of Father Time's motives—reflects the confusion of all allegorical figures in the presence of abundant but unaccommodated life, the life, that is, with which the novel, as secular narrative, is concerned. Father Time lacks the wisdom that not only gives life, but can interpret it charitably, that is, novelistically. His error, as any church doctor—good Lord, even his own father!—might have taught him, is to confuse the spiritual with the literal sense. He dies a victim of Sue's feminine instruction, mystified by the words of a woman who can neither fully explain nor fully conceal the material troubles that beset all living creatures. Perhaps he takes her words as a kind of indictment against his own existence as an allegorical figure whose meaning is fixed and delimited. His rejection of multiplied meanings and propagating life is not so much childish as precocious. His suicide is taken as the harbinger of a *universal* wish not to live, rather than a localized pathologic reaction to life. As a despondent figure and a beleaguered interpreter of modern conditions, Little Father Time presages the modernist crisis of representation, in which the will not to live takes the form of the refusal to narrate.

The coming of the universal wish not to narrate is the baleful dysangelism of this novel, which seems to welcome its own extinction once it discovers the flight of spirit from its verbal precincts. Hardy's narrative is structured in a way that suggests the crumbling of those metaphoric tenements that housed the Penates of the novel, its tutelary divinities and sanctities. The transformation of Christminster, the first object and site of Jude's desire, is the most spectacular instance of the frangibility of the walls that enclose us as well as separate us from the ideal life. Christminster, as many critics have noted, is first glimpsed as mirage, and yet as a place its existence is enduring. What is precarious is Jude's imaginative relation to the initial image of his First Love. Christminster undergoes a series of metaphoric substitutions that replicate but can never recapture the majesty of Jude's original eidolon. The mirage of Christminster is replaced by the actual institution; it is then reproduced in the miniature model Jude and Sue display in the itinerant exhibition were Jude and Arabella re-meet, thus building up the structure of reoccurrence so demoralizing to a narrative so in love with first things and so fearful of repeated things. Finally Jude's "Heavenly Jerusalem" is reincarnated as a perishable good, the Christminster cakes which Jude and Sue sell. This last metaphoric declension, in which a spiritual image is replaced by a material commodity, bitterly reflects the wisdom that man does not live by bread alone. The Rhadamanthine strictness of this degenerative process accounts for the remarkable folktale that seems to pertain to Jude and Sue's unauthorized love. On entering a church, they overhear a story about a satanic experiment in church "restoration"; in the relettering of the Ten Commandments, all the *not*s were expunged. The Blakean inversion appears to counsel obedience to Instinct's imperatives—the body's *thou shalt*s. But Hardy, like Phillotson, is a feeler rather than a reasoner about such revolutionary prescriptions. His belief in the possible realization of desire in a Blakean utopia of the redeemed body is compounded in equal parts of sympathy and suspicion.

Eventually suspicion conquers sympathy and Hardy can only satirize, albeit regretfully, Jude's empowering belief in original acts. The novel that begins with a supreme contrast between a pig's pizzle and a young man's dreams concludes with a most bitter contrast between the hurrahs of strong-lunged young men and the whispers of the tubercular Jude, citing Job's lamentation: "Let the day perish wherein I was born and the day it was said there was a manchild conceived." To cite this text is to invoke authority for self-extinction. The coming universal wish not to live finds its most terrible expression in this wish to reach into the womb and annihilate life at its inception. It will find its most comic expression in Beckett's Neary, who curses the day he was born and then, in a bold flashback, the night he was conceived. Both curses are the inspirations of erotoleptics whose sexual transports find their natural end in a fatal dream of checked conception.

Nietzsche, in one of his skirmishes as a self-proclaimed untimely man, observed that "in England one must rehabilitate oneself after every little emancipation from theology by showing in a veritably awe-inspiring manner what a moral fanatic one is. That is the penance one pays there."[18] Nietzsche was speaking of George Eliot and her strict adherence to Christian morality after she had dispensed with the Christian God. But it is Hardy's *Jude the Obscure* which provides a grim exemplification of the moral exactions that give to English fiction its "consistency." Hardy's last novel dramatizes the recidivism of "English" morality in the pitiable spectacle of a child's murder-suicide and a wife's fanatic prostitution. Yet it is not Sue, sacrificing herself to fulfill the letter of the marriage bed, but Jude, crying out against the fruit of the conjugal bed, whose moral fanaticism, like Job's, is identical to despair. Perhaps Hardy did not abandon narrative letters simply because of the public outcry against the antimarriage sentiments of his novel—he and others have survived obloquy of that sort—nor even because the spirit of the pale Galilean did in fact conquer his robust passion for his pagan idols—Venus and Apollo. For the worst may not be that the letter killeth. That epigram encapsulates the cathartic agency, not the tragic wisdom, of Hardy's fable. The worst may be that the letter cannot give life. A novelist cannot remain a novelist if he succumbs to the moral fanaticism of that creed. Was it the sterility rather than the murderousness of the letter that led an emancipated but desponding Hardy to compose out of the mythic materials of First Love his final drama of oblivion?

# ANGELIC LAWRENCE:
## *THE RAINBOW*

NGELIC LAWRENCE MUST seem a deliberate provocation to those who see in the Laurentian messenger the Satan or Adversary of all the progressive "isms" of modern times: liberalism, socialism, nationalism, feminism, indeed humanism in its comprehensive, modern sense. But I see no way around this provocation, if I am to pursue my interest in the modern imaginations and renunciations of the myth of First Love. The gospel Lawrence preaches is that Love must be dissociated from the dream of personal precedence. We cannot be the first one, not because we have not come first, but because, in the sad pun that rules Lawrence's life, we are not yet one. Love must separate itself, Lawrence proclaims, not only from the idea but from the grammar of first persons.

W. H. Auden suggested that such teachings have been discredited because Lawrence's *kerygma* no longer seems good news. Auden's witty pun captures current feelings about Lawrence as a prophet whose proclamations sound like ineffectual—because inopportune—jeremiads, the misogynist ravings so fiercely denounced in Kate Millett's *Sexual Politics*. Repudiation, however, was a reaction that Lawrence anticipated and internalized as part of his fictional dialectic. As a novelist, he is most compelling in describing the self-limiting and reactive emotions, particularly in their virulent forms: the jeer of derision and the blast of self-mistrust. For Ursula Brangwen, the heroine of *The Rainbow*, the instinct for repudiation is the individual's primary defense against modern life. She complains of "spitting out of her mouth the ash and grit of disillusion, of falsity. She could only stiffen in rejection, in rejection."[1] The body stiffening in rejection is the characteristic posture of the modern, its standard attitude of revolt: Mrs. Dalloway stiffening at the top of the stairs; Stephen Dedalus's spiritual contractions in revulsion against Dear, Dirty Dublin; the crampings that afflict the Beckettian body. But Lawrence also recounted how this atavistic gesture, like the infant's moro reflex, could indicate the last insistent twitchings of life-in-embryo resisting the soul's couvade.

For Lawrence is self-evidently the novelist whose subject is the modern "life of the nerves." The phrase appears in Lawrence's brilliant novella, *St. Mawr*, whose canny opening line, "Lou Witt had had her own way so long that by the age of twenty-five she didn't know where she was,"[2] encapsulates, with the gnomic efficiency of parable, the willfulness that explains why the modern is also a lost generation. The surname Witt is a further satiric refinement on the mental acuity that does not compensate for, but aggravates, that vitiation of instinct which is such a pronounced feature of modern life. Lawrence shared

Nietzsche's deep aversion to the modern fetish for "rationality at any cost, life bright, cold, circumspect, conscious, without instinct," believing, like Nietzsche, that "as long as life is *ascending,* happiness and instinct are one." [3] For him, as for Nietzsche, the modern repudiation of the instinctual body was a sign of decadence, of descending (or in Lawrence's term, "disintegrating") rather than ascending life. The conscious wit of modern culture did not spiritualize or redeem, but devitalized an already decadent civilization even further. Yet Lawrence's prescription against this devitalization, unlike Nietzsche's, is to *relax* the will. Stylistically, this prescription is carried out in Lawrence's effort to break up and break through the sediments that congeal on the surface of everyday or novelistic language. Lawrence's incantatory style, sibylline and jaunty by turns, aims at dispelling concentrations of linguistic energy that are in danger of solidifying into inert rant (Lawrence is a dynamic ranter) or petrified narrative formula. Even the most formidable defender of Laurentian prophecy, F. R. Leavis, admits that such prophetic ventures can degenerate into exasperated tirades, but such lapses, I would contend, merely demonstrate that Lawrence is a novelist who is too wise to forgo playing, on occasion, the fool. Whatever his personal or narrative distresses, he will not cling to his wit if it means losing his way.

Yet Lawrence never, for all his meanderings, severs his connection with the Creative Sources—both literary and organic—from which the "life" of the novel derives. This connection is triumphantly affirmed, then severely tested, in Lawrence's beleaguered epics of modern life, *The Rainbow* and *Women in Love.* They were originally conceived as composing a double novel, but then were divided into separate testaments, the former serving as verbal witness to the advances, the latter to the apocalyptic depredations, of the Creative Tradition. Lawrence's Odyssean narrative, *The Rainbow,* predates his strife epic, *Women in Love.* This reversal is dictated by the Great War and Lawrence's gradual loss of faith in his visionary epos. We can determine what Lawrence's genius was capable of imagining when it was unencumbered by dejection in *The Rainbow.* This novel attempts an epic recounting of human life in its historical evolution and cosmic significance. Its sheer ambition links Lawrence to the grandiose tradition of nineteenth-century realism that culminated in the magisterial panoramas and psychological precisions of the Tolstoyan novel. But *The Rainbow* is also remarkable for the pressing topicality of its theme, through which Lawrence articulates his hope for the coming age: "woman becoming individual, self-responsible, taking her own initiative." [4]

The attempt to write a novelized epic of becoming does involve Lawrence in certain generic contradictions, however. As Lukács and Bakhtin have long recognized, the epic and the novel are to be distinguished primarily in their attitudes toward time and history. The epic represents the past in the enclosed form of an accomplished or a canonized history. The novel, on the other hand, represents the indeterminacies of the living present. The epic memorializes, the novel records. Lawrence attempted to resolve this contradiction by fashioning his "epic of the human soul" according to the model of Genesis. Genesis recounts the absolute beginning of the world in divine fiat, whereas the classical epic, on less assured ground with its gods, begins in medias res. Lawrence resolved the contradiction between the epic and novelistic treatments of time by reinstituting at novel's end the covenant which promises both a renewal and a fulfillment of human history. *The Rainbow* finds its spiritual resolve and narrative resolution in a vision of human destiny which proclaims fulfillment in the prospect of a new beginning.

Lawrence accomplishes this reversal by revaluating the devaluations of *Jude the Obscure,* the novel that seems to have haunted him most in his *Study of Thomas Hardy.* Hardy's dysangelism (to borrow, as I have earlier, Nietzsche's term) is reflected in the metaphoric degeneration of Christminster as a figure for the spirit's desire. Christminster is first beheld as a mirage in which the visible world is subsumed into a visionary projection of the Heavenly Jerusalem. But this visionary architecture is reduced and literally miniaturized in the itinerant model Jude fashions. Finally the only surviving trace of Jude's dream of a celestial city is the perishable bread of Christminster cakes. Lawrence's angelism reverses the degenerative course charted by Hardy's pessimism. In *The Rainbow* the figures for inchoate human desire acquire substance and clarity over time, until they cohere in the enduring form of a divine architecture—the rainbow arch that connects heaven and earth, the divine and human world. The rainbow arch that symbolizes this eternal connection is first glimpsed as a human creation—in the marriage of Lydia and Tom Brangwen, which forms an arch "to span the heavens." This figure of fleshly union is then projected outward until it reaches the realm of God, where it is beheld by the redeemed Ursula as a sign of the earth's new architecture set against the overarching heavens. The novel concludes by looking forward to its own human beginning, an Einsteinian ellipse more promising and complicated, in its typological transpositions, than Joyce's *Ulysses,* which is, at any rate, a more resolutely Aristotelian narrative.

The "unbegotten hero" of this epic of becoming is the angel who will be born at the end of mankind's pilgrimage through the universe of material forms. This angelic being is foretold in Lawrence's *Study of Thomas Hardy,* the work which, as H. M. Daleski and Mark Kinkead-Weekes have shown, imaginatively conditioned Lawrence's double novel.[5] Lawrence speculates there, less apropos of Hardy's than of his own fiction, about the evolutionary development of humankind. In his own version of the origin of the species, human life arose out of an organic reaction against "homogeneous inertia":

> So on and on till we get to naked jelly, from the naked jelly to enclosed and separated jelly, from homogeneous tissue to organic tissue, on and on, from invertebrates to mammals, from mammals to man, from man to tribesman, from tribesman to me: and on and on, till, in the future, wonderful distinct individuals, like angels, move about, each one being himself, perfect as a complete melody or a pure colour. (*P.,* 432)

To be noted in this evolutionary progression from naked jelly to the perfected form of the angels: occupying the privileged vantage point of epic, in medias res, is the Laurentian "me." This "me" is Janus-faced. It grammatically designates Lawrence the visionary, he who discerns the "naked being" stripped of its accidental, *personal* qualities and who foretells the coming of wonderful distinct individuals who exist as angels exist—as a perfect essence, like the complete melody or the pure color. This "me' also refers, more impersonally, to the impoverishments of the individual in modern culture and modern parlance. Lawrence's liberties with the grammar of the first person singular reflect his impatience to move beyond the evolutionary state designated and maintained by the very language of persons.

In his essay "Democracy," Lawrence notes that "a *person* is given in the dictionary as an *individual human being,*" but then proceeds to argue, appealing to etymological testimony, a fundamental distinction between the words *person* and *individual:*

> The derivation this time helps. *Persona,* in Latin, is a player's mask, or a character in a play: and perhaps the word is cognate with *sonare,* to sound. An *individual* is that which is not divided or not dividable. A *being* we shall not attempt to define, because it is indefinable.
>
> So now, there must be a radical difference between something which was originally a player's mask, or transmitted sound, and something which means "the undivided." The old meaning lingers in *person,* and is almost obvious in *personality.* A person is a human being *as he appears to others;* and personality is that which is transmitted from the person to his audience; the transmissible effect of a man. (*P.,* 710)

Lawrence's objection to the novel of bourgeois realism, with its conscientious documentation of social effects, is that it resonates or vibrates too deeply to the sounds made and transmitted by persons. He will later satirize the modern personality in his portrayal of Lord Chatterley, the author whose books, "entirely personal," are popular because they are "curiously true to modern life, to the modern psychology, that is."[6] The "modern" psychology is a psychology of persons. Its practitioners rely on the insinuating intimacies of talk, the personal talk with which Lord Chatterley both seduces and defrauds his wife into modern marriage. Chatterley, the word-purveyor, is depicted as the Satan in his own Eden, tempting Connie Chatterley with "the paradisal promise: Thou shalt have men to talk to!" (4). As a popular novelist, Chatterley captivates his audience as he had captured his wife—through his genius for transmissible or *verbal* effects. His idolatry of persons appears related to his status as a childless aristocrat, anxious to bequeath his *personal* effects to a future that he cannot otherwise father.

Yet Lawrence recoils from, even as he recognizes, the pathos of dead and dying things (like persons and personalities). For him the homeopathic talking cures of modern psychology agitate rather than soothe the neurasthenic ego. He repudiates the chatty personalism of such ego-psychologies, just as he seems determined to overrule Freud's contention that the hero of the novel is his majesty, the Ego, a fantastical projection of the writer's "I" or "me." The novelistic person, counters Lawrence, is either an anachronism or a shrewd pretender who ought to give way to a figure Lawrence calls the "unbegotten hero." The Unbegotten hero—or heroine—is the individual whose being cannot be divided and disseminated. This figure is indivisible and cannot be dispersed into the various personae of its social roles; he or she comes into being only in that rapture of self-consummation known to the angels.

Lawrence's angelic figure for the interrelatedness of sexuality, consciousness, and life is not subservient to any doctrine—or grammar—of personal limits. Lawrence's career as a psychological novelist can be seen, in fact should be seen, as an attempt to overstep the limits separating genuine impulse from the secondary propagations of the consciousness. His tumescent prose expends itself in transgressing those designated limits, showing them to be mental and diaphanous limits only. Prophetic language is the force that can bridge, with luck abrogate, the "fissure" of sexuality.[7] In the ascendant and exploratory phase of Lawrence's visionary utterances, instinct and consciousness are always beheld as one.

The chapter title, "Widening Circle,"[8] reiterated throughout the novel to

mark critical moments of human growth and advancement, indicates this symbolism of expanding and ascending life. Lawrence often refers to this ascension
as a spiritual trespass, thus exposing a common religious fallacy, based on fear
and self-mistrust, that confuses sin with any act of self-overcoming. He would
not have us be forgiven our trespasses, but encouraged in them. The jocularity
of this proposition is as important as its unconventionality. The young Lawrence, who entertained a Wagnerian personification of himself as Sigmund in
his second novel, *The Trespasser,* speculated in a letter to Blanche Jennings
about the history of trespassing: "It was a word invented in Hell—or before
socialism, eh?"⁹ Some of this idiosyncratic mixture of the colloquial and the
portentous infuses his account of the love scene that brings Tom and Lydia
together: "And the dawn blazed in them, their new life came to pass, it was
beyond all conceiving good, it was so good, that it was almost like a passing—
away, a trespass" (81). The biblical idiom for decreed eventualities—"and it
came to pass"—is gently converted into the vernacular "passing away," where
it designates a positive spiritual trespass: the death of the old life and the assumption of the new. The stripping of *trespass* from its accretions of sin, accomplished by Lawrence's canny transliterations, indicates the difference between
the fervid moralist's understanding of human action and the novelist's chronicling of human ways. Lawrence the novelist is a chronic trespasser of forms. He
continually oversteps the theoretical limits imposed by an unimaginative realism
or a servile naturalism, limits that would confine the novel to a strict imitation
of a world *already known* if yet imperfectly understood. Through such trespasses, he recaptures the spirit, if not the precise letter, of Odyssean epic,
whose hero is always committing such infractions.¹⁰ The Laurentian spirit is
eager to venture out into the unknown, where it can meet its Fate.

    To describe this spiritual transit, *The Rainbow,* unlike *Sons and Lovers* and
*Women in Love,* which both begin in social time, opens on the landscape of
prehistory, where only place (the Marsh farm, defined by the coursings of the
Erewash), but not time (relayed through the indefinite formula "for generations"), can be specified. The Marsh Farm is inhabited by a generic clan (the
Brangwens) of primordial men and women who establish, in their elementari-
ness, the fateful structure of human relationships as Lawrence beheld it. They
"lived full and surcharged, their sense full fed" by the teeming fertility of the
Marsh. Within this natural economy, no personage—that is, no *named* self who
takes part in the social and civic order of life—exists. The work ordained for
consciousness in demarcating the "me" from the "not-me," the central preoccupation of Laurentian psychology, is yet to be performed. The first stammering
attempts to distinguish the inside from the outside are represented as a function

of the sexual division of labor. Only after this primary differentiation is made can the boundary between self and other be drawn.

And here Lawrence introduces a startling reversal that upsets all the draconian precepts of nineteenth-century mythographers like Bachofen, who interpreted the dethronement of Mother Right as the liberation of the luminous Male Spirit. He alleges that it was primordial man who acted as custodian of the body's inwardness: ". . . the limbs and the body of the men were impregnated with the day, cattle and earth and vegetation and the sky, the men sat by the fire and their brains were inert, as their blood flowed heavy with the accumulation from the living day" (42). Men occupy the place or *topos* of fecund Nature. The male body, impregnated by the germinating seeds of the living day, is burdened by the weight of its own fertility: its limbs are sluggish, its mind inert at the close of the day, the time of dream or reverie. Women, though they experience the "drowse of blood-intimacy," are more wakeful, attending to intimations of the beyond. They occupy the place or *topos* of culture; the fruit they bear is knowledge, the harvest of the mind: "But the women looked out from the heated blind intercourse of farm-life, to the spoken world beyond. They were aware of the lips and the mind of the world speaking and giving utterance, they heard the sound in the distance and strained to listen."

Lawrence has a predilection for the word *utterance* to describe the lambency of prophetic speech. He is sensitive to the necessary *outwardness* of utterance and seems concerned to avoid the implication, even through casual synonym, of the sealed inwardness of prophetic inspiration. Utterance reaches out; words are to be propagated and disseminated, not in the Derridean but in the apostolic sense. And it is women who are the conveyers of this good news because they are the first to desire "an intimacy that was not a blood-intimacy." To this end they set their sights on "the far-off world of cities and governments and the active scope of man, the magic land . . . where secrets were made known and desires fulfilled." Lawrence's use of *man* in this sentence is, I believe, generic, although later he will identify (in order to denounce) the far-off world of cities and governments as a man's world. But in his initial mythic placements, the Brangwen men "faced inwards to the teeming life of creation, which poured unresolved into their veins," while the Brangwen women stationed themselves on the threshold of outgoingness. Woman, before she is *personated*, stands for education, that leading outward which alone permits self-development. The enticements of knowledge, not the blind lurchings of intuition, urge woman on to speculative trespass. It is through knowledge, as the vicar instructs the Brangwen women, that we "learn entry into the finer, more vivid circle of life."

Lawrence at once acknowledges a literary debt and seems to insinuate a natural sequence of genres when the outgoing Brangwen women first fix their imaginations on the romance figure of Mrs. Hardy, the squire's wife. In the village gossip "they had their own Odyssey enacting itself, Penelope and Ulysses before them, and Circe and the swine and the endless web." Is Lawrence being bemused, condescending, ironic when he concludes, in remarkably chaste summation, "So the women of the village were fortunate. So long as the wonder of the beyond was before them, they could get along, whatever their lot" (45)? Perhaps. But Lawrence's more generous point appears to be that the women have access to the beyond; that they speak its wondrous language of self-initiative.

This language of self-initiative, of consciousness extending and ascending into the beyond, is articulated in three successive ages of verbal trespass. I am not generally partial to schematism in interpreting so resolutely antischematic a form as the novel, whose essential material is the fluidity and indetermination of life. And Lawrence is himself a great satirist of the pretenses that give systematic thought their dazzle (when Lawrence is being systematic he is careful to present his thoughts as deliberately fanciful and unaccountable). Yet Lawrence also appreciates numerological virtuosities, and in *The Rainbow* the symbolism of three exerts a kind of spell over his narrative presentations. First there is the three-generational structure of the novel, which, as Kinkead-Weekes has argued,[11] seems to have been conceived in some measure to conform to his description of prophetic speech in *Study of Thomas Hardy:* "Always the threefold utterance: the declaring of the God seen approaching, the rapture of contact, the anguished joy of remembrance, when the meeting has passed into separation. Such is religion, religious art, and tragic art" (*P.,* 450). This triadic sequence of utterances is not superimposed on the novel, however. Rather it is a structure that seems to emanate from the novel's benign apocalypticism, which seeks to reverse as well as redeem the established cycles of recorded history. *The Rainbow,* the finest example of Lawrence's religious artistry, moves, typologically, in a counterdirection to canonical history. It begins with scenes of Annunciation and concludes with the first apparition—the rainbow—by which God signaled his intention to keep faith with the Flesh.

Northrop Frye, the most generative of typological critics, can help us discern the forms and the motives of Lawrence's linguistic trespasses and typological reversals. In his study of the Bible's "Great Code," Frye translates Vico's historical schema into more specifically literary language, a translation that I find useful in considering Lawrence's prophetic utterances:

According to Vico, there are three ages in a cycle of history: a mythical age, or age of gods; a heroic age, or age of an aristocracy; and an age of the people; after which there comes a *ricorso* or return that starts the whole process over again. Each age produces its own kind of *langage,* gives us three types of verbal expression that Vico calls, respectively, the poetic, the heroic or noble, and the vulgar, and which I shall call the hieroglyphic, the hieratic, and the demotic. These terms refer primarily to three modes of writing, because Vico believed that men communicated by signs before they could talk. The hieroglyphic phase, for Vico, is a "poetic" use of language; the hieratic phase is mainly allegorical; and the demotic phase is descriptive.[12]

Read as a revelatory epic, *The Rainbow* depicts the *verbal* longings that prompt us to venture into the unknown. These longings are first expressed in the demotic or vernacular language of common desires, are refined and extended in hieratic speech and gesture, but are satisfied, literally, only by the novel's last words—the numinous hieroglyph of the divine Logos "built up in a living fabric of Truth."

Because Lawrence's model for the creative mutations wrought by the Creative Logos is Genesis, *The Rainbow* presents this visionary accession as the book of generations. His family chronicle is composed, according to biblical conception, of three testamentary periods, connected to each other not only sequentially but in their formal integrity as love stories. Only the last tale of the modern age, Ursula's initiation into the "man's world" through her love for Skrebensky, is a tale told self-consciously as a story of "First Love." The novel's generational structure thus confirms the primary assertion of this study—that First Love is a modern invention. So let us provisionally designate these tales of generation by the utterances peculiar to them. And, in keeping with Lawrence's own *kerygma,* which insinuates the primacy of woman's rule over the lips and minds of the world, let us further designate these ages by their regnant female figures:

> Lydia, or the Triumph of the Demotic;
> Anna Victrix, or the Rout of the Hieratic; and
> Ursula, or the Restoration of the Hieroglyph.

## LYDIA, OR THE TRIUMPH OF THE DEMOTIC

My account begins where Tom Brangwen, the first Brangwen who finds life's meaning in a love story, begins—suspicious of life's commonplaces. Tom's lack of creative initiative can be traced to self-mistrust: "For him there was nothing palpable, nothing known in himself, that he could apply to learning. He did not know how to begin." Tom does not know how to begin because he has no idea where the boundary separating inward (realm of inchoate desire) and outward (domain of definite life-forms) is drawn. His first impressive encounter with the outside world, an introduction to "a small withered foreigner of ancient breeding," alerts him to the human potential for spiritual trespass: "There was a life so different from what he knew it. What was outside his knowledge, how much? What was this he had touched? What was he in this new influence? What did everything mean? Where was life, in that which he knew or all outside him?" (60). In the light of this newly acquired vision of the outside world, the "homestead of his nature" dwindles into "the mean enclosure of reality," which he stubbornly refuses to reenter. In a "fever of restless anger," he dreams of foreign parts, "stubbornly resistant to the action of the commonplace unreality which wanted to absorb him" (61).

Lydia Lensky emerges from this dream of foreign worlds and shows him that the outside is nothing stranger than—nothing is as strange as!—the world of historical acts. Lydia is the character who transforms the legendary account of the Brangwen works and days into a real history. She brings into the novel an experience of concrete kind—the actual struggles of the Polish Rebellion of 1863. It is her experience that makes traditional chronicle possible—indeed necessary, if her past is to be adequately told. In recounting her personal history, the novel assumes the familiar and unalarmed cadences of direct narration: "She was the daughter of a Polish landowner, who, deeply in debt to the Jews, had married a German wife with money, and who had died just before the rebellion" (86). No Brangwen is defined in these specifics of class, nationality, and historical period. Human history is given concrete expression in the events of her life: her marriage to an intellectual and political agitator, the death of her two young children, the years of exile and bleak widowhood. Her story represents Lawrence's homage to nineteenth-century realist fiction, which insisted on figuring its characters against the complex ground of social and historical reality.

Tom feels excluded from the realm of historical events by the symbolic obstruction of Lydia's wedding ring, which "stood for the life in which he could have no part." But he oversteps the circle of her concluded life, overborne by the "logic of the soul" that ignores the facts and materials of history as "only words." Tom and Lydia thus meet and in a sense remain foreigners to each other as "personalities" with definite histories, attachments, relations, obligations.

Herein lies the singular importance of the novel's initial trespass: "How Tom Brangwen married a Polish lady."[13] Lawrence's exogamous bow to the world honors a primary cultural interdiction: the rule of intermarriage and the enforcement of the incest taboo. Anthropologically, the reluctance to countenance the foreign or unknown is reflected in the incestuous longings to mate with one's own kind, to wed the represented known, rather than the unincorporated unknown. Anna's marriage to her cousin Will, the intertestamentary love story of the novel, delineates a threshold where the "clan" distinction between inside and outside becomes problematical. Lawrence makes this threshold a point of dramatic and perceptual trespass: their counsinship and eventual marriage mark the horizon that verges on but does not encompass the "greater ordering of the stars in the dark heaven travelling, the whole host passing by on some eternal voyage."

This heavenly host is the angelic destination of the human soul. Less obvious, but perhaps more important, this vision of a greater ordering of stars establishes the ironic limits as well as the mystical reaches of Lawrence's formal venture into family chronicle, the most bourgeois and earthbound of narrative forms, concerned as it is with property and other inheritable effects, like the Buddenbrooks' bad teeth or the Brangwens' impatient temper. The Brangwens seem less awed than the narrator by the distant and impersonal prospect of eternal pilgrimage; their ingenuity is expended in personal reckonings with what I have called "narrative numbers." They seem, that is, less immediately preoccupied with what comes next than with who shall go or be placed first. Ursula addresses this issue with a directness Hardy's idealists never managed when she asks her grandmother: "Did you like my grandfather best?" Ursula poses the riddle of the past as the riddle of precedence: does time or the heart determine who comes first in one's life? Lydia's answer, which unfolds in pages of remembrance, becomes an extended commentary on the parable "In my father's house there are many mansions": "She loved both her husbands. To one she had been a naked little girl-bride, running to serve him. The other she loved out of fulfilment, because he was good and had given her being, because he had served her honourably, and become her man, one with her" (302). For Lydia, this parable may not solve the mystery of future space (where the soul is destined to abide), but it does settle the question of future time (what the soul is destined to become). Heaven, she determines, is all-accommodating, a determination which carries with it a practical corollary: no one, therefore, need "take all upon himself." Lydia sensibly reproves her first husband's distinctly male presumption (in which he exhausts his will and finally his life). It is the presumption to be first in all things: sexually as the initiator-god to the girl-bride eager to serve him, publicly as the political eminence who can change history itself. Lydia is the first to utter *The Rainbow*'s gospel of history: "You are not the beginning and the end." Lawrence intends us to find both consolation and resolve in the thought that Life entails a vast and infinite promise that cannot be symbolized or exhausted by any one person. The human significance of Lydia's history is thus revealed only at the moment when its individual—that is, its novelistic—value can be dissolved and absorbed into a past "so big, that all it contained seemed tiny; loves and births and deaths, tiny units and features within a vast horizon" (304).

The narrative equivalent to this cosmic reabsorption is the flood that sweeps across the Marsh. A larger reality inundates commonplace existence, submerging the "tiny" individual in its vastness. Yet Lawrence's religious art does not advocate the worship of the blind force of the Creative Mysteries. He reserves the deepest feelings of his devotional imagination for the eidolic body of the beloved dead, those who have been claimed by the Flood of Reality or absorbed into the cosmic vast. The drowned body of Tom Brangwen is the novel's first sacred eidolon. Tom's body, "laid in line, inviolable, unapproachable," makes visible "the stripped moment of transit from life to death" (294). Description, which Frye deems the expressive mode of the demotic, is put to sacred use in this passage, which recalls the reverential depictions of the dead in *The Return of the Native*. What is described here is not a contingent or impermanent reality, the beloved body before it deteriorates or disappears. Human transit is for a brief instant arrested, as if change itself had momentarily, but impressively, revealed itself to be not a process, but a state interposed between life and death, partaking neither of the fluidity of the one nor of the irrevocability of the other. Tom Brangwen achieves in death a sculptural perfection: "He was a majestic Abstraction made visible now for a moment, inviolate, absolute." This majesty, in a solemn if familiar paean to phallic mysticism, betokens the sublimity of the inaccessible male, whom Lydia salutes: " 'I shared my life with you, I belong in my own way to eternity,' said Lydia Brangwen, her heart cold, knowing her own singleness." Absent from this funereal scene is the *intimate* note; no personal feelings intervene to disturb the cold integrity of the male body perfected "beyond change or knowledge, absolute, laid in line with the infinite." Lydia has survived the flood of the demotic and rescued from this historical catastrophe the finely articulated *point* of human life: we are *single,* but we are not the sole beginning nor the final end. Ursula, fearful of her own destiny, clings to her grandmother, her gateway to the great space of the past, in which her individuality is not obliterated, but rightly placed within an all-accommodating tradition. History is the common name for this tradition and it is a matter of female transmission and inheritance.

Men seem to enter this tradition only as baffled visionaries or stumbling interpreters. Tom Brangwen shares his wife's transfiguring love, but unlike her he cannot compose a complete sentence, much less a complete narrative, to communicate the truth of his life. He can only propose an ahistorical figure for a human destiny not yet realized: angelism. On the wedding day of his step-daughter, Anna, he proclaims that the true mating of the male and female in marriage creates an Angel: "If we've got to be Angels," he proposes as a kind of wedding toast, "and if there is no such thing as a man nor a woman amongst them, then it seems to me as a married couple makes one Angel": "For . . . an Angel can't be *less* than a human being. And if it is only the soul of a man *minus* the man, then it would be less than a human being" (177). His ravings are passed off as the product of too much brandy, but the narrative insists that "Tom Brangwen was inspired":

> "An Angel's got to be more than a human being," he continued. "So I say, an Angel is the soul of man and woman in one: they rise united at the Judgment Day, as one Angel——"
> "Praising the Lord," said Frank.
> "Praising the Lord," repeated Tom.
> "And what about the women left over?" asked Alfred, jeering.
> The company was getting uneasy. (178)

It is hard to determine whether Alfred's jeering reflects or provokes the general—and modern—uneasiness with such prophetic inspirations. Even Tom, the seer, is unsettled by the prospect of the female souls who on the last day will be left over in a sorry, unbalanced accounting. The human arithmetic of Tom's angelic forecasts, unlike Lawrence's own narrative numbers, does not add up, even should we trust to God's fairer apportionments on Judgment Day. Ursula's question about two husbands had recognized that life unfolds in specific and irreversible times, but Tom's vision of angelic couplings and transfigurations disregards such "novelistic" considerations of our life in time. He remains essentially the Tom of the novel's beginning, resenting the claims of "the customary life" and overwhelmed by the "facts of daily life [which] encompassed everything, being legion." The voice of the everyday life is the voice of Legion, whose speech is inflected by psychological nuance, social prejudice, political faction, and religious passions; the speech, that is, not of angels, but of demons. This demon voices the pathos of the world desecrated by history. All that is inalienably and fiercely romantic in Lawrence commends to him the demon whose name is Legion.[14] But he would command that demon to get behind him, not stray beyond him. Lydia heeds that voice; Ursula must learn to resist it. But it is Anna who would triumph over it.

## ANNA VICTRIX, OR THE ROUT OF THE HIERATIC

The love story of Anna and Will is further evidence that the Brangwen chronicle is devolving toward a female command—or myth—of human destiny. During their marriage, the Brangwens' verbal patrimony is dissipated in the squabbles of sexual factionalism. If my account seems to conflate domestic with divine politics, it may be because Anna and Will seem to monopolize as they incarnate the language depicting the cycle of Christian Redemption, from the Annunciation and Gethsemane to the Resurrection and entry into Paradise. Their love story is also told among repeated references to the great paintings of the tradition that exemplify the marvels of the iconographic imagination: Fra Angelico's *Entry of the Blessed into Paradise* (whose "real, real, angelic melody" makes Anna weep with happiness) or Rubens's *Fecundity*. These works of art seem to be invoked primarily for their pictorial suggestion of the typological pressures on Will and Anna to give definitive form to their marriage. The language of types and antitypes becomes the verbal ground—often battleground—of their courtship and marriage.

The urge to transform life into allegory is partially attributed to Anna's discomfort with the demotic mode of ordinary life. She is described as a changeling, who does not feel at home in the commonplace. The only recorded triumph over the girl who will eventually be given the august epithet *Victrix* is when a neighboring gentleman-farmer teases her until she speaks dialect (126). Otherwise she "glanced with strange, mystic superstitions that never found expression in the English language, never mounted to thought in English" (141). Despite the potency of her mysticism, Anna is suspicious of hierophantic symbols. She is the first character in the novel to pose the riddle of existence as primarily an *exegetical* dilemma. Her hermeneutic confusions provoke existential distress; hearing "things expressed, put into words," makes her spirit recoil, "her mind [reverting] often to the torture cell of a certain Bishop of France, in which the victim could neither stand nor lie stretched out, never" (143). The prison-house of language, confining verbal orthodoxies to cramped and close quarters, repels her; she clings to a godhead apprehended as "the Great Mystery, immediate beyond all telling" (141).

Then Anna meets Will Brangwen, who insists on the "telling" of the Great Mystery through the canonical language of established Christianity. For him this language is not a prison-house, but a cathedral. Though Anna comes to love him, she can never love his version of the Creative Mystery. She relentlessly challenges Will's faith in Christian lore, ridiculing "the ecstasy into which he could throw himself with these symbols." She is Victrix because she makes him, finally, ashamed of his ecstasy in mystical figurations like the Lamb, "the symbol of Christ and His innocence and sacrifice": "Whatever it means, it's a lamb! And I like lambs too much to treat them as if they had to mean something" (202). Her jeers hound him until he takes cover under the mantle of shame, cloaking his veneration of symbols that he can no longer defend or profess.

Anna's most vigilant mistrust is reserved for the Cathedral and the theological symbolism it incarnates, a mistrust that is the subject of an entire chapter in her life and in this novel. The symbolic import of Anna and Will's visit to Lincoln Cathedral has been intelligently analyzed by many critics. What I want to emphasize is not what the Cathedral "stands for"—womb envy, orgasmic mysticism, the allegorical tradition[15]—but its importance as a verbal tenement for human vision. In other words, I am interested not so much in what a cathedral means, but in what it means to be inside—or outside—one. To be inside is to be "seized" by the power of "Absolute Beauty," which is the power, Lawrence suggests, of all representations that figure "the Great Conclusion of the Whole." To be outside is to observe gargoyles mocking the grand conclusions of Absolute Beauty with those deformations specific to imperfect, disillusioned, or skeptical life. The gargoyles speak the language of Legion: "they jeered their mockery of the Absolute, and declared for multiplicity, polygeny [sic]." In refusing to affirm the Great Conclusion of the Whole in which Beauty and Truth are figured as one, in declaring, that is, for indeterminacy and multiplicity, Lawrence seems to be reconsidering, if not criticizing, the architectural metaphors that stabilized the agitations of *Sons and Lovers* and *Study of Thomas Hardy*. Paul Morel, for example, relates to Miriam how destiny presents itself to him in the language of spatial configurations. He confesses that he is transported, or inspired, by his "love of horizontals":

> . . . the great levels of sky and land in Lincolnshire, meant to him the
> eternality of the will, just as the bowed Norman arches of the church,
> repeating themselves, meant the dogged leaping forward of the persistent
> human soul, on and on, nobody knows where; in contradiction to the
> perpendicular lines and to the Gothic arch, which, he said, leapt up at
> heaven and touched the ecstasy and lost itself in the divine.[16]

Paul illustrates here a novelistic love—and genius—for the horizontal, which represents the dogged leaping forward of the persistent human soul, mired in time, intermingled with space; Miriam represents the ecstatic verticalities of the Gothic arch which can overpower the horizontal persistence of the will-to-the-beyond. Given this opposition, it is inevitable that their "lad and girl love" culminates in "The Test on Miriam," in which she fails to minister to his passion for ongoing life, leaving him with the wish that "he were sexless or dead."

Anna's exasperation with *any* overt symbolization leads her to repudiate the architectonic metaphors that make such abstractions—and abstract relations—possible. She represents the dithyrambic aspect of Laurentian creativity that Anaïs Nin described in the "unprofessional study" she made of him:

> It is no mere sexual phenomenon, but more truly *the creator's craving for a climax far bigger than the climaxes life has to offer*. It is symbolical of the creative voraciousness which is, as general instinct, unsatisfiable, because it is out of proportion with the universe, with the realities surrounding him. It is the allegory of the urge which was never meant to be answered but merely to exist, like the urge to live in spite of, and even because of the certain knowledge of death, to live in the largest possible "circuitous way towards death," in Freud's words.[17]

So importunate is Anna's instinct for life that she seems destined to have no language of self-initiative, but simply, in Nin's terms, to be a term in the allegory of her own urges. Her creative voracity seems disproportionate to her own powers as a symbolic animal. Yet even she finds expression for the inchoate promptings of the life-instinct in her scandalous "dance before the Unknown," which Lawrence typologically identifies with "the story of David, who danced before the Lord, and uncovered himself exultingly" (224). Lawrence's extravagant interpretation of this Davidian transport first appears in *Study of Thomas Hardy*. His fantasia on the "Jewish" dance cycle can serve to gloss the gestural import of this rhapsodic scene, in which the full-bellied Anna "danced exulting before her Lord, and knew no man":

> At first they are only figures. In the Jewish cycle, David, with his hand stretched forth, cannot recognize the woman, the female. He can only recognize some likeness of himself. For both he and she have not danced very far from the source where they were both one. Though she is in the gross utterly other than he, yet she is not very distinct from him. And he hails her Father, Almighty, God, Beloved, Strength, hails her in his own image. And with hand outstretched, fearful and passionate, he reaches to

her. But it is Solomon who touches her hand, with rapture and joy, and
cries out his gladness in the Song of Songs. (*P.,* 449–50)

Anna's ignorance is biblical; she "knew no man" in the sense that, like David,
she knows and celebrates only a divinity in her own likeness. The great mystical,
sensual marriage of the Song of Songs is beyond her powers of figuration. She
has no particular knowledge of or reverence for Will as a separate figure: "She
only respected him as far as he was related to herself. For what he was beyond
her, she had no care" (171). Anna does not care for what Will represents in
himself, because she would abide in a world free of representation, uncluttered
by *distinct* human imaginings. This is not to say that her fecundity is without
issue. It is only to acknowledge that she forfeits, in her rhapsodic dance in
which self is absorbed by soul, the potential language of miracle "in which
things depart from their being."

Yet such self-departures enact the beginnings of all original and originating
acts, especially linguistic ones. The Creation commences in that moment of
separation which makes life—and representation—possible. This miracle is
commemorated in the Creation panels that Will carves out of wood. He depicts
God as a "dim, large figure," but his Eve is distinctly represented as "a small
vivid, naked female shape, issuing like a flame towards the hand of God, from
the torn side of Adam." The vividness of this female figure ascending toward
the Divine contrasts to the implied pathos of the mutilated Adam. Lawrence
sublimates his own dread of the destruction that attends all birth and projects
it into the suspensefulness of Will's picture: "There was a bird on a bough
overhead, lifting its wings for flight, and a serpent wreathing up to it. It was not
finished yet" (158).

Will's vision of Creation is suspended in the indefinite present where the
ascent of the bird, poised for flight, finds its demonic counterpart in the pred-
ator ascending for the kill. Given the standard if complex iconography of this
*ecphrasis,* the menacing movement of that serpent foretells all. It confirms that
for the male visionary the story of Creation is the myth of the Fall. Will's
imagination, so attached to the old religious emblems and traditions, cannot
reconceive Creation as a metaphor that will carry him across, as metaphor is
wont to do, from the known to the unknown, from what is fallen to what is to
be resurrected. He lacks the spirit for such linguistic and conceptual trespass.
Perhaps this explains why he positions, at the far sides of his Creation panel,
"two Angels covering their faces with their wings." These angelic and monitory
figures recall the dangers of visual trespass. According to the Judaic injunction,
to see God is to die; one should not look directly on the workings of the Divine,

but only abide with Its luminous vicinity. Will's imaginative reconstruction of Creation is the work of an obedient angelism, and reveals him to be neither a poet nor a maker, but an artisan of limited instruction devoted to communicating finite pieties. Not for him is the endlessness of image- and metaphor-making that for Lawrence constitutes the authentic *poesis* of religious art. Will can neither renounce his allegiance to the anachronistic and discredited idols in whom he no longer livingly believes, nor reanimate them with the life-giving power of new utterance.

The result Lawrence is at pains to record: "In spirit he remained uncreated." Will's defeated angelism makes him prey to personal demons. His self-mistrust, which cripples his creative initiatives, transforms him into an incubus who feasts on the vital Anna, whom he holds in "silent grip of his physical will": "Was he then like the old man of the seas, impotent to move save upon the back of another life? Was he impotent, or a cripple, or a defective, or a fragment?" (229). Will sees his demonic counterpart in the unstable and uxorious life-form of the predator-parasite. Like the Old Man of the Sea, he is a creature subject to perpetual metamorphosis, unable to realize or to reveal his essential identity unless subjugated by another, a stronger, female will. For Tom Brangwen, an angel is a married, not a single, soul. But Will's marriage only intensifies his consciousness of impotence and leaves him in the spell of two incompatible idolatries: his worship of the Church, whose creeds he can no longer openly or joyously profess, but whose buildings he works devotedly to restore; and the body of his wife, his "fetish" for Absolute Beauty. He reverts to the Gothic form, which Lawrence, contra Ruskin, interprets as "always assert[ing] the broken desire of mankind in its pointed arches, escaping the rolling, absolute beauty of the round arch" (280). Lawrence sees in this spiritual reversion the Will-to-Nullity of the modern male, motivated by his dread of the Norman arch with its heroic injunction to persist doggedly into the unknown. In the novel's domestic economy, Will's capitulation to Gothic mysticism leaves Anna free to rule, supreme in her female mysteries. Her matriarchy is a bit slovenly, but she is strict in compelling spiritual obedience: "She forced him to the spirit of her laws, whilst leaving him to the letter of his own" (251). And the letter, left to the idolatrous Will, killeth.

## URSULA, OR THE RESTORATION OF THE HIEROGLYPH

It is Ursula who inherits this familial division between letter and spirit and whose epic appointment is to overcome the breach between them. Several legacies promote as they impede her in performing her epic task: to witness, as she does at novel's end, the creative reformation of the world in a vast hiero-glyph "making great architecture of light and colour and the space of heaven" (548). She inherits from her grandmother the historical sense of the inclusive past, which calms her fear of the great commonplaces—birth and death—that compose the majestic background of life. From her father she derives an *archi-tectural* conception of the eternal in which the human figure appears as a unit in the Great Conclusion of the Whole. From her mother, long since immersed in the flood of fecundity, she inherits the propensity to consider life as an exegetical puzzle. Like Anna, Ursula passes her girlhood preoccupied with the questions: What does it mean? And how does it apply?

Her consciousness is the seedbed where religious nostrums are converted into true conundrums. She insists on staging the preachments of the Gospels as living enactments. Lawrence is aware of the comedy in Ursula's attempts to give the spiritual directives of Scripture immediate and concrete reference in the domain of everyday life. Yet he never condescends to his heroine; her frustra-tions are presented as those faced by anyone attempting to explicate the "inex-plicable values" of parable. One saying Ursula finds especially vexatious: "What was this relation between a needle's eye, a rich man, and heaven? What sort of needle's eye, what sort of a rich man, what sort of heaven?" (322). These, of course, are the questions an instinctive novelist would ask. The novelist is eager to know what living "sort" incarnates the general type, is curious about what concrete relations motivate human beings, what particular heaven accommo-dates or excludes them in spirit. As a religious artist, Lawrence is the most Tolstoyan of English novelists, refusing to conceal his dissatisfactions with the routine hypocrisies that underlie the pious and respectable surfaces of "official" existence.

Ursula's epic of becoming thus represents a bildungsroman in a specific and urgent sense. Her individuality is formed through her encounter with and attempted transvaluation of an inherited culture of the divine. As a modern woman emerging into self-responsibility, Ursula finds little instruction and less delight in prevailing conceptions of the holy. She is depressed by the revivalist professions of the humanity of Christ, rejecting them as the vulgar pretensions of the "impudent suburban soul" that would deny the right of anything "extra-human" to exist. Lawrence's quarrel with the language of persons extends to the theological dreariness he ascribes to the evangelical confinement of salva-tion to the personal case: "Jesus died for *me*, He suffered for me" (319). Truly it is no paradox to assert that Ursula must lose her faith in order to gain religion.

To gain religion, in its primary sense of *religare*, "to bind together," is to form a bond. Religion predicates a relationship, as Lawrence well knew. For Ursula, the religious sense awakens through the bond known as First Love. Lawrence, like Hardy, sees First Love as one of the idolatries of human culture. But where Hardy sees Darwinian laws of sexual selection working in opposition to spiritual evolution, Lawrence remains the unreconstructed Romantic for whom Nature and Spirit are one. It is only mental consciousness, he asserts, that divides and alienates them. Ursula herself speaks, in the initial stages of the spiritual crisis that will result in First Love, of the essential congruence between vision and voice, between what the spirit apprehends and what the body can perform: "There *were* words spoken by the vision; and words must have a week-day meaning, since words were weekday stuff. Let them speak now: let them bespeak themselves in weekday terms. The vision would translate itself into weekday terms" (329). The *would* here is vital; it is uttered not in the optative or conditional, but in the declarative mood—the mood of all true believers. Lawrence's religion professes the inevitability as well as necessity of this linguistic conversion, in which the language of the Sabbath is translated into the idiom of common reality, the proper speech for man or woman alive. We should recognize in this translation the inflections of true myth.

Thomas Mann, in his poignant essay "Freud and the Future," refers to the life of myth, the "life, so to speak, in quotation," as a kind of celebration "in that it is a making present of the past, it becomes a religious act, the performance by a celebrant of a prescribed procedure."[18] Lawrence has a companionable sense of the mythopoeic as a religious act of re-creation, although he is antinomian about prescriptions of ritual procedure, preferring less stylized reenactments. For Mann the Egyptian Cleopatra manifests her "mythical ego" when she puts to her breast an asp, "familiar of Ishtar, the Egyptian Isis, who is represented in a garment of scales." Lawrence's mythopoeic beings are less self-conscious adapters of the past to present contingencies. We know Lawrence has moved into this inspired mode when he begins to speak in what I will call "relaxed quotation." His language of quickened consciousness is not a solemn, verbatim repetition of an original act or ritual speech, but a relaxed recital of biblical precedents that accompanies and clarifies his own demotic stammerings. *The Rainbow* abounds in such extemporary performances, yet none is more faithful to the spirit of Lawrence's angelism than his prophetic election of Genesis 6 to describe life in "the essential days": "There were giants in the earth in those days; and also after that, when the sons of God came in unto the daughters of men, and they bare children to them, the same became mighty men which were of old, men of renown." In this novel, as in *Women in Love,* ceremonial marriage provides Lawrence with the myth answering to the spiritual problem he insisted to be *the* problem of today (his emphasis, not mine), the establishment of a new relation between men and women.

This myth is slowly translated until, in Lawrence's telling metaphysical idiom, "it took presence upon itself" in the person of Anton Skrebensky, Ursula's First Love. I specify person, because Skrebensky is a false idol and no true angel. But the Brangwens, eager for angelic company, do not see through his impersonations. Ursula inwardly hails him, in the thrill of first encounter, as the angel who will conduct her to "the illimitable endless space for self-realization and delight for ever" (489). Her mother and father, those tireless if unsuspecting allegorists, welcome his visitation, recalling the time when three angels "stood in Abraham's doorway, and greeted him, and stayed and ate with him, leaving his household enriched for ever when they went" (337). Skrebensky is too slight a figure to shoulder this allegorical burden. The angels who visited Abraham's threshold prepared the way of the Lord and his double message: the annunciation of Isaac's birth to the barren Sarah, and the promised destruction of Sodom. Skrebensky does herald imminent destruction, but he is a false prophet of new life. His role in the novel is to activate a complex historical, not religious, allegory. Skrebensky's spiritual vagrancy launches him on a modern odyssey: his tour of duty in the Boer War; his return home, not to avenge but to reinforce the cultural hegemony of a bullying and life-weary rationalism which proclaims, "Beyond our light and our order there is nothing." Lawrence, like Conrad, would expose the vanity of "our sheltering conceptions of light and order," as Marlow nervously describes the imperious—and imperial— structures of modern enterprise. But for Lawrence the heart of darkness conceals no horror, only "the dark, shadow-shapes of the angels whom the light fenced out, as it fenced out the more familiar beasts of darkness" (488).

Skrebensky could have claimed that darkness with a "flash of the sword of angels," but he determines instead "to screen himself from the darkness, the challenge of his own soul" and marry, at novel's close, the daughter of his commanding officer. In Ursula's love for Skrebensky we see the same ambiguity that Lawrence attributed to Hardy's *Laodicean*—"all the way through a *prédilection d'artiste* for the aristocrat, and all the way through a moral condemnation of him." Lawrence saw in this double attitude "the root of Hardy's pessimism" (*P.,* 435), but he himself proves unwilling to despond in kind. He seeks, like Ursula at novel's end, the "man [who] should come from the Infinite," a new heavenly hero—or angel. But it is hard for the Old Adam to yield his place to the New. This knowledge surfaces as the feeling which underlies Ursula's "poignant, almost passionate appreciation" for her First Love, an appreciation that complicates but never clouds her final judgment of him: "He seemed added up, finished." Lawrence must *narratively* dismiss Skrebensky as a Laodicean, a figure of neutrality destined to remain "the eternal audience, the chorus, the spectator at the drama; in his own life he would have no drama" (378).

Thus Skrebensky, like all the men in *The Rainbow,* are left in spirit uncreated. They appear doomed to repeat and perpetuate the servilities of the Old Adam. Perhaps this explains why Ursula turns to the New Woman to usher her into the "space of illimitable self-realization." Ursula's lesbian relation with her teacher, Winifred Inger, may be considered First Love in its scandalous form. The consequence of this episode of fascination is not Sorrow the Undesired, but, as the chapter title brands it, "Shame."[19] Arguably, the source of shame lies within Lawrence himself (Kate Millett has made this argument) for so characterizing Ursula's attachment and representing it as a fatal and perverted consequence of feminism. And surely the most disturbing assertion Lawrence makes in this chapter is the sentence, standing in isolation, "Winifred Inger was also interested in the Women's Movement" (390). Occupying a paragraph to itself, is this nugget supposed to be regarded as an indigestible morsel or food for thought?

Let me suggest, for discussion's sake, that Winifred's politics provide the occasion to mull over the ideological pabulum of the day. Lawrence the teller, the angelic Lawrence, preaches an antimaterialist creed that reductively associates lesbian loves or orgasmic politics to the feminist agitation for equal rights, especially for enfranchisement. This antifeminism is consistent with his invective against democratic liberalism, which seeks, Lawrence objects, material equality, the equality of dirt. But Lawrence's tale casts Winifred in a more complex and interesting social drama. In Winifred's assertive athleticism, and in her rather determined sylvan pursuits and seductions, Lawrence sees the lineaments of Diana, goddess of lunar distance and chaste removes. Out of this contradiction we can see a more prescient dialectic at work.

Lawrence objects to Winifred most forcefully, and less irrationally, when he criticizes her worship of the idols of modern society—mechanism and money. He denounces her as an educative disaster—a legitimate objection in a bildungsroman. She teaches Ursula that scientism, rationalism, and materialism are the gateway into the modern, the "man's world." Winifred, like Lord Chatterley, is a modern personality, whose allure is undeniable and whose fate is decided. Her marriage to Tom Brangwen, the industrialist, merely confirms her kinship with the man's world of sterile mechanism. Moreover, this marriage represents a detour into "Zolaesque tragedy" (395) that the Brangwen chronicle could have pursued, indeed was in all likelihood destined to assume, had not Ursula resisted the persuasions and idolatries of a god-despairing people in a godforsaken time. Perhaps all times appear to be godforsaken to those who must live through them, but only the novel is generically charged with documenting this feeling. (The epic, as a memorial form, rarely abandons its faith that the first of times were the best of times.) Finally, then, the worst that is said of Winifred, the worst that *should* be said of her, is that, through the contagion of her tutelage, "Ursula could not help dreaming of Moloch" (389).

That Ursula remains, until the very end of the novel, susceptible to that dream is evinced in her plans to marry Skrebensky even after she tastes the bitterness of ecstasy. The ethos of the bourgeois materialist novel, which Zola's naturalistic tragedies ironically, that is faithfully, translate, is expounded in Ursula's final letter to Skrebensky, the "last letter" with which she intends to document her life "before God at the Judgment Day." In this letter, Ursula renounces her spiritual desires as the "conceited foolishness" of an arrogant visionary and vows to become Skrebensky's devoted and contented wife. This letter, like the false pregnancy which precipitates it, results in an abortive spiritual issue. Ursula undergoes a true conversion when she perceives the rainbow as the true emblem of her human destiny. That hieroglyph redeems the literalism of her "dead" letter with a promissory vision "that new, clean, naked bodies would issue to a new germination, a new growth" (548).

This "new knowledge of eternity in the flux of Time" (545) is uttered in a very ancient language. Lawrence's poetic account of Ursula's saving vision is mythically shadowed by the figures of two noble riders—Plato's horseman in *Phaedrus* and Paul, the convert-apostle. Ursula's life is literally redirected through her encounter with wayward horses, who communicate, as they encircle her, the agony of suppressed instinct: "pressing forever till they went mad, running against the wall of time and never bursting free." In Plato's allegory of the soul, horses stood for the passions, which reason must master and guide. Lawrence's antirationalism liberates those horses from the confining walls of allegory into the energized field of poetic existence: "In a sort of lightning of knowledge their movement travelled through her, the quiver and strain and thrust of their powerful flanks, and they burst before her and drew on, beyond" (540). These horses are educative, leading Ursula to the beyond which she both desires and dreads. Lawrence reveres them as natural hieroglyphs that incarnate the Creative Source in living and wondrous forms. The lightning of knowledge that travels through Ursula, like the lightning that struck down Paul on the road to Damascus, shatters her prosaic and persecutory consciousness. This lightning leaves her stunned "like a stone, unconscious, unchanging, unchangeable, whilst everything rolled by in transience . . . sunk to the bottom of all change" (543). Lawrence may also be recalling here the more gentle slumber that sealed the Wordsworthian spirit and whirled it round with rocks and stones and trees. The knowledge communicated to her in her wakefulness is, however, novelistic, not lyrical. It is the knowledge that illumines Dorothea's morning vision of "the largeness of the world and the manifold waking of men to labour and endurance" as she enters her own crisis in *Middlemarch*. Ursula echoes and translates Dorothea's vision of "involuntary, palpitating life" as she, in a similar mood of life-weariness, sits by her window and observes "the people go by in the street below, colliers, women, children, walking each in the husk of an old fruition, but visible through the husk, the swelling and the heaving contour of the new germination" (548). The heaving contours of horses, the heaving contours of men, women, and children shedding the husk of an old fruition—these are the vivid hieroglyphs of Lawrence's religious art. Through them Lawrence's god answers the human prayer for a new germination in the involuntary, palpitating life of the world.

*The Rainbow,* in reviving the incarnational language which makes Creation—and persons—new again, becomes Lawrence's paean to the female command over "the lips and mind of the world speaking and giving utterance." But Lawrence's admission that Genesis was "the great assertion of the female" was by no means an unqualified or always happy attestation. "Cunning and according to female suggestion," Lawrence darkly warns us, "is the story of the Creation: that Eve was born from the single body of Adam, without intervention of sex, both issuing from one flesh, as a child at birth seems to issue from the flesh of its mother" (*P.,* 452). The female cunning of this story Lawrence ascribes to the subtleties of the womanly "Jewish temper," preoccupied with "self-feeling, in realization of the age." In such interpretative fantasias, Lawrence's sexual and racial mythologies reveal themselves as demonized accounts of textual and cultural history. Lawrence did not see this in writing *The Rainbow* or its precursor work, *Study of Thomas Hardy*. It was only as he came to write the continuing history of his age that he wrestled with his own angel—the figure of male assertion. *Women in Love* aspires to give voice to the male assertion of the New Testament that would "deny the age and refuse sensation, seeking ever to make transformation, desiring to be an instrument of change, to *register relationships*" (*P.,* 452; emphasis added). To register relationships is the work of all true religions and the reason one writes—ideally, the reason one reads—novels.

*Women in Love* begins as a religious novel which would register new relationships—mystic marriage and *blutbrüdershaft*—in opposition to the spirit of its age. It soon becomes a strife epic in which Laurentian angelism does battle with the diabolism of the times. But it concludes as a Judgment Book that subjects the First Loves of Male Assertion to the Wrath of the Last Days.

# SIX

# *WOMEN IN LOVE:*
# LAWRENCE'S JUDGMENT
# BOOK

# LIFE-MOTIVES

I T WAS FRIEDA LAWRENCE who thought the sequel to *The Rainbow* should be titled *Dies Irae,* the Days of Wrath. Lawrence preferred the less apocalyptically charged *Women in Love.* Frieda's suggestion preserved for Lawrence's proposed "double" novel the grace of symmetry: Genesis and Apocalypse, the total history of Creation recapitulated and reinterpreted in modern times. *The Rainbow* was a novel chronicling the creation of the first woman in "the Essential Days." *Women in Love* recounts the fate of the last men in the Final Days: the death of Gerald Crich, Nietzschean captain of industry; and the eclipse, whether temporary or terminal, of Rupert Birkin, the artist as social prophet and sage.

But fateful symmetry was what Lawrence was determined to avoid: "Shall keep the title *Women in Love,*" he wrote to Catherine Carswell. "The book frightens me: it is so end-of-the-world. But it is, it must be, the beginning of a new world too." [1] The "must" in this assertion is not only indicative, but imperative. It conveys Lawrence's prophetic intention to articulate a new dispensation in the collapse of the old. The god Lawrence preaches is the Kosmocrator and Kosmodynamos whose creations, like the earth's ever-renewable architecture, subsist within and through the flux of time. Lawrence proposes a curious term for this essentially *novelistic* temporality when he heralds, in *Fantasia of the Unconscious,* the "next future," an odd and apparently redundant locution that foresees the future as what succeeds the present but remains unconditioned by it.

The final title *Women in Love* anticipates this nonapocalyptic futurity, and seems to entrust it to the cosmic agency of Love. That Lawrence's Love, like Dante's "L'Amor che move il sole el l'altre stelle," is actually a First Love, that is, an activating force in his poetic cosmology rather than a socializing emotion in his psychology, explains the contradiction that riddles his intimations of the yet-to-be: the unknown appears to us in the light of reminiscence. As novelist and polemicist, Lawrence always insists, as he does in *Fantasia of the Unconscious,* that he is merely "trying to stammer out the first terms of a forgotten knowledge." In discussing the substance of Laurentian remembrance, I want to distinguish between what Lawrence recollects in tranquillity and what he is compelled to remember as a historian of modern times. The former comprises the essence of Laurentian prophecy, which always involves the recovery of first terms; the latter comprises his memory of *generic* codes, which qualifies and subdues his visionary dream with its reminders of the destined end. This split between the prophetic and the apocalyptic, between first and final terms, rends his novels in two and ultimately thwarts Lawrence's desire for "wholeness." Yet the pathos in his frustration is what, often to our great discomfort, confirms Lawrence as our most prescient novelist of that debacle—modern love.

Ideally, prophecy enters the novel to enunciate what Lawrence, in the foreword to *Women in Love,* calls "our true fate": "The creative, spontaneous soul sends forth its promptings of desire and aspiration in us. These promptings are our true fate, which is our business to fulfill. A fate dictated from outside, from theory or from circumstance, is a false fate." [2] The business of the novelist is to perform the work of Eros. Eros is divine desire, the motive-force for all genuine creation and fateful relationship. Lawrence's quarrel with the great "metaphysical realists," Hardy and Tolstoy, is that they misrepresented the human struggle toward fulfillment as essentially a social conflict. In the novels of classical realism, "transgression against the social code is made to bring destruction, as though the social code worked our irrevocable fate" (P., 420). Hardy's novels endlessly depict this same tragedy, "the tragedy of those who, more or less pioneers, have died in the wilderness, whither they had escaped for free action, after having left the walled security, and the comparative imprisonment, of the established convention" (P., 411).

The walled city designates the space of self-development mapped by the established conventions of the realist novel. Within its protective but also imprisoning confines, the novelistic individual is either subjected to a religious or biological determinism, or tyrannized by the practical and moral coercions of the social state, which controls the material "means" but never the actual ends of existence. Lawrence honored Hardy's pioneers for attempting to create a life beyond the walled city that enclosed but could not contain their desire: "They are people each with a real, vital, potential self, even the apparently wishy-washy heroines of the earlier books, and this self suddenly bursts the shell of manner and convention and commonplace opinion, and acts independently, absurdly, without mental knowledge or acquiescence" (P., 410). If one were to record all the creative intuitions these characters give rise to "it would fill the Judgment Book." Such a book, assuming it could ever be written, would offer us a full accounting of life novelistically rendered. It would weigh the reasonable claims of the relatively secure City (compounded of manner and convention and commonplace opinion) against the unreasoning impulses of the profligate Wilderness. A younger Lawrence might have ruled for the City of Reason as the paradigm for novelistic society. "Sapientia Urbs Conditur" was the epigraph to his first book of poems. But the Lawrence of mature deliberation advises:

"Never was anything less true. The city is founded on a passionate unreason." [3]
Passionate unreason emanates from the experience of the Wilderness; it designates the creative prodigalities as well as "the waste enormity of Nature" (*P.*,
419). Waste, Blakean excess, is the principle that rules in nature and authorizes
what Lawrence insists is the "greater morality" of an unfathomed Creation.

In Lawrence's Judgment Book, *Women in Love,* this greater morality is the
standard to which the novel's modern love stories must answer. Birkin's passion
for Ursula and his love for Gerald, which represent Lawrence's radical revisions of First Love, do not develop and cannot be understood within the
"walled security" of established narrative or social conventions. As we shall see,
Ursula and Birkin experience First Love as a mythopoeic return to the beginning of the world. For them, the new dispensations of First Love revive "the
old magic of the Book of Genesis, where the sons of God saw the daughters of
men, that they were fair." But the love between Birkin and Gerald inaugurates
a new era in human development. It is not a reembodiment of the original
male-female loves that prevailed in the first days, but the prototype for a new
mode of relationship—men united in purpose and in love.

The nature—and the morality—of these First Loves cannot be represented or judged according to the established conventions of the realistic novel.
Hence the unsettling, *deep* embarrassments in reading or teaching a Lawrence
novel. Before the great seriousness of his pronouncements on Eros and its creative mysteries, Lawrence will allow us neither the dignity of polite refusal nor
the impudence of outright mockery. These are the reflexes of those who, like
Gudrun, proudly proclaim themselves "modern" and greet all excess with with-
ering irony. Gudrun is the ironic artist who has no imagination, or stomach, for
the spontaneity of eternity:

> In vain she fluttered the leaves of books, or made statuettes in clay. She
> knew she was not *really* reading. She was not *really* working. She was
> watching the fingers twitch across the eternal, mechanical, monotonous
> clock-face of time. She never really lived, she only watched. Indeed, she
> was like a little, twelve-hour clock, vis-à-vis with the enormous clock of
> eternity—there she was, like Dignity and Impudence, or Impudence and
> Dignity. (575)

Dignity and Impudence alternate in the ticktack of ironic response, yes and no,
no and yes, monotonous as time. Lawrence detects the futility of such decorous
but mechanical impostures, in which no genuine activity—no real reading, no
real making—takes place.

The only *good* form is the spontaneous outburst, that is, the genuinely fateful act. Like Freud, who saw inner determinations at work in the physical and verbal accidents of everyday life, Lawrence believed in the deep meaning of the clichés with which we disguise the eruptions of passionate unreason. Through Birkin, Lawrence challenges the conventions of normal usages and recalls to us their first meanings, which time and a self-deceiving humanity have corrupted. Birkin is a kind of cranky lexicographer who calls attention to discredited adages and vulgar usages. Love, as we shall see, is the most problematical word deployed in his lexicon. Yet Love will never become a fateful experience if men and women have lost their belief in the reality of fate. Thus fate is the first term in our forgotten knowledge of love that Lawrence's novel attempts to recuperate. Birkin's first important verbal reminiscence uncovers the ancient wisdom concealed in our hackneyed phrase for the fateful but inadvertent act: "accidentally on purpose." Birkin considers the metaphysical reaches of that common expression: "A man can live by accident, and die by accident. Or can he not? Is every man's life subject to pure accident, is it only the race, the genus, the species, that has a universal reference? Or is it not true, is there no such thing as pure accident? Has *everything* that happens a universal significance?" (77). Birkin believes that "It all hung together, in the deepest sense." In having Birkin assert this belief, Lawrence would seem to be committing his own novel to the most exacting criterion: everything he records in his Judgment Book must possess universal significance. The fortuitous has no place in his world-descriptions and life-accountings. All narrative matter must be consumed and incorporated into the true Fate—or Life-Motive—to which it refers.

By insisting on the universal significance of everything that happens, Lawrence makes us aware, as perhaps no other English novelist does, how the novel can be such a *temporizing* form in capitulating to the determinisms of the age. The "traditional" novel is only too ready, Lawrence implies, to evoke external and mechanical cause—usually in the guise of coincidence, blind chance, or "the logic of events"—to account for the form human life assumes in its telling. Lawrence's vitalistic irrationalism inspires him to propose that the moral faculty originates in the "spontaneous life-motive" that asserts itself "in defiance of all scientific law, in defiance even of reason."[4] Birkin promotes this view through his deliberately insouciant model for good form: "Anybody who is anything can just be himself and do as he likes." Doing as one likes, expressed in such an unqualified and general way, was precisely what Arnold objected to in English culture. Doing as one likes, he insisted, really amounted to a "worship of machinery." The "really blessed thing," Arnold famously argued, "is to like what right reason ordains, and to follow her authority."[5] Lawrence treats right reason as an oxymoron; reason, not instinct, produces the machinery of static ideas and fixed responses. The only right and good form is to obey a life-urge that reason attempts to subdue or mislead.

Gerald, always suspicious, yet always interested in Birkin's ideas, asks whether "being himself" is an aphorism or a cliché. In face Laurentian usage hovers between the two, as if to remind us that current clichés once carried the authority and potency of true aphorisms. Being oneself, perhaps *the* cliché of modern psychology, becomes an original expression in the first "complete truth" that Birkin utters: "It takes two people to make a murder: a murderer and a murderee. And a murderee is a man who is murderable. And a man who is murderable is a man who in a profound if hidden lust desires to be murdered."[6] It takes two people to make a murder, just as it takes two people to make a marriage. Murder, like love, designates the presence of a profound if hidden lust for relationship; hence the demonstrative import of Birkin's later encounter with Hermione, when he simply *refuses* to let himself be killed. Lawrence strategically invokes Gerald's "accidental" killing of his brother as confirming this insight. Gerald finds his type in Cain, the first recognizably "modern" individual who cannot love, or rather, cannot assert relationship except through killing. Murder is his ritual, just as the marriage of the sons of God and the daughters of men is the ritual of Creation.

This opposition between "the power spirit" of conscious volition and the spontaneous promptings of Eros inspires Lawrence's prophecy, but also rends it, perhaps irreparably. Lawrence is torn between his New Testamentary genius for proclaiming the redemptive power of mystic marriage and his apocalyptic insight into how Eros, a cosmological force, is converted into temporal power. This dialectical conversion of love into its opposite explains how a novel that began as a gospel of Love became the greatest strife epic of modernity. It also may suggest reasons why a novel that begins with the question of what women want concludes with an elegy of male desire.

Freud's question—or lament—"What do women want?" is the ironic riddle posed in the opening chapter, "Sisters."[7] It is important to note that this question was initially presented as a *settled* point in the prologue originally drafted for the novel. There Lawrence focused on Birkin's obsession with the male body, "whilst he studied the women as *sisters,* knowing their meaning and intents" (emphasis added): "It was the men's physique which held the passion and mystery to him. The women he seemed to be kin to, he looked for the soul in them."[8] Women will appear in *Women in Love* as sisters, but they are no longer represented as Birkin's spiritual kin. If writers shed sicknesses in books, as Lawrence claimed,[9] it is Lawrence's own soulfulness that *Women in Love* exorcises. The novel consciously disavows the knowledge of the female soul acquired in the writing of *The Rainbow*. It restores to women their mystery and freedom as novelistic subjects whose life-motives cannot, as the prologue mistakenly implied, be foreknown.

This indeterminacy in turn shadows the opening discussion between Gudrun and Ursula about their marriage "prospects." To marry or not to marry— that is the question that conventionally defines the fateful choice facing novelistic heroines. But never has the choice seemed so divorced from any real desire, and never have the differing outcomes of such decisions been formulated in less urgent, yet frightening, alternatives: Gudrun ironically insisting that marriage, whatever the desire or the fitness of the individuals, is "bound to be an experience of some sort," and Ursula, in her first display of apocalyptic thinking, suggesting that marriage is "more likely the end of experience" (53). No actual desire motivates this decision to marry or not, which has become, so Lawrence avers, a purely formal and mechanical one for modern women.

The marriage question is not just linked to the modernist crisis of anomie but actually precipitates it. Nietzsche asserts in *Twilight of the Idols* that "modern" marriage and its supporting mythology of Romantic love reflect the decadence in the modern's "valuating instinct," a decadence so pronounced that the modern "*instinctively prefer[s]* that which leads to dissolution, that which hastens the end." The objection to modern marriage lies not in marriage but in modernity, which has lost the beneficial instincts "out of which institutions grow, out of which the *future* grows": "The rationale of marriage lay in its indissolubility in principle: it thereby acquired an accent which could *make itself heard* against the accidents of feeling, passion, and the moment."[10] For Lawrence, whose idea of mystic marriage is conceived in opposition to modern vagaries of passion and feeling, marriage is also the final test of the instinct for life. Marriage, he claimed, is the sphinx riddle of modern times. "Solve it or be torn to pieces" is the decree.

Failure to solve the riddle of marriage entails the ritual penalty known as *sparagmos,* the dismemberment of the sacred body. But the modern individual endures *sparagmos* as a mechanical disintegration unattended by the consolations of Dionysian rites. Modern attitudes toward marriage fragment the unitary fullness of being into subjective particles that reflect "points of view" rather than comprehensive cosmologies. It is over the marriage question that Ursula and Gudrun begin taking "last stands" before they need to do so, a symptom of their fall into the fragmented world of modernity: " 'When it comes to the point, one isn't even tempted—oh, if I were tempted, I'd marry like a shot.——I'm only tempted *not* to.' The faces of both sisters suddenly lit up with amusement. 'Isn't it an amazing thing,' cried Gudrun, 'how strong the temptation is, not to!' They both laughed, looking at each other. In their hearts they were frightened" (54).

The exchange of secret looks, "whilst each sister vaguely considered her fate," communicates more than the malaise of diminished desire; it introduces into the novel's emergent sexual dialectic a primary female negativity before any external forces of prohibition or interdiction have been called into play. This negativity, registered in the sisters' denial of their own possible future, is essentially temporal. It signals a collapse of the time needed for the self's unfolding into the compacted and airless space of irony (Gudrun) or anomie (Ursula). As a figure for their social destiny, marriage appears to them in its apocalyptic form as the dead end, rather than in its prophetic form as the end which marks their new beginning.

The following chapter, "Shortlands" (the manor of the Crich dynasty), considers the problem of the future according to the "valuating instincts" or life-motives of the male will. Lawrence conceived of the female principle as a "will-to-inertia." Hence the radicalness of his opening chapter, where two women think against their instincts (indeed against the instincts of the conventional novel) in doubting the perdurability of marriage. Lawrence identified the male principle with the will-to-motion, the will that expresses itself in work, the creation of new life-forms. Man works, writes Lawrence in his *Study of Thomas Hardy,* because the source of his life is overfull and thus "presses for utterance" (*P.,* 422). "*Weltschmerz* and other unlocalized pains" signify the pressures within man to "produce" himself. Work therefore constitutes both an inherent passion, a craving "to produce, to create, to be as God," and a perpetual mimesis, for in craving to be as God, man can only repeat and reproduce "the movement life made in its initial passage, the movement life still makes, and will continue to make, as a habit, the movement already made so unthinkably often that rather than a movement it has become a state, a condition of all life; it has become matter, or the force of gravity, or cohesion, or heat, or light. These old, old habits of life man rejoices to rediscover in all their detail" (*P.,* 429).

Work entails a conscious reminiscence of those generative movements that have congealed into immemorial "habits" we identify as conditions of nature: matter, gravity, cohesion, heat, light. The purpose of work is thus constituted by its basic form as *repetition,* "the repetition of some one of those rediscovered movements, the enacting of some part imitated from life, the attaining of a similar result as life attained." The motive of labor should be consonant with the meaning of work: "to bring all life into the human consciousness" (*P.,* 439). It is in this sense that work can be construed simultaneously as an archaic reminiscence and as a prophecy of fulfilled humanity.

The mystic harmony between knowledge and life that obtains in the truly creative work is never realized in *Women in Love.* Lawrence's philosophy of work, unfolded in his criticism of Hardy, is expressed in his own novel by its demonic opposite: the mechanical philosophy justifying the "life-work" of Gerald Crich. Gerald's "career" dramatizes this peculiarly modern tragedy of the anarchic Dionysian spirit trying to express itself in the Apollonian (degraded) forms of industrial production. Gerald reminds Ursula "of Dionysus, because his hair was really yellow, his figure so full and laughing" (159). Ursula's allusion anticipates the male fate he must reenact: the modern god dying in the Nordic rite of ice annihilation. Gerald is the tragic hero as industrial magnate, driven by a peculiarly modern perversion of the will-to-power to subjugate the world with "the sword of mechanical necessity" (298). (Lawrence is "remembering" here the root of Gerald's name in *ger,* 'spear,' and *waldan,* 'to rule.') But Gerald's rule over inert matter, though systematic, is predicated on two faulty—and fatal—acts of translation. He mistakes the mystic word "harmony" for the practical word "organization" and conceives of the godhead as pure mechanism:

> He found his eternal and his infinite in the pure machine-principle of perfect coordination into one pure, complex, infinitely repeated motion, like the spinning of a wheel; but a productive spinning, as the revolving of the universe may be called a productive spinning, a productive repetition through eternity, to infinity. And this is the God-motion, this productive repetition ad infinitum. And Gerald was the God of the machine. Deus ex Machina. (301)

The echo of Blake's Satanic Mills resounds in Lawrence's parody of the analytics that makes the godhead immanent in the world's material motions. Lawrence appropriates Blake's critique in his own jeremiad against the "pure orders" valorized by rationalist metaphysics, the ideology whose historical products—the Krupp Mills, German militarism, and "the sick Man of Europe"—are fabled in the family chronicle of the Crich dynasty, from its sick and dying patriarch, Thomas Crich, to its Bismarckian savior, Gerald Crich. In fact, this historical dimension of the novel is so obvious that, like the Great War, its informing presence can, as Lawrence said, merely be taken for granted.

## THE TOTEMIC IDOL

"Sisters" and "Shortlands" recall the perennial concerns of the novel: marriage and work, the private and public destinies apportioned to novelistic persons. Most novelists might be content to adjudicate among these different life-motives, but Lawrence holds his novel accountable to life-motivation. The artic-ulation of this judgment is the burden of his visionary utterances, which for Lawrence justifies the incursion of prophecy into the novel, a form generally inhospitable to such vatic outbursts. The law court, not the pulpit, is the tradi-tional symbol for the communal space where novelistic judgment is rendered.[11]

But Lawrence's prophecy is conditioned by his pedagogic, not his political, instincts. Birkin's first sustained attack on sentimental and moribund "modern" ideas is dramatized not as a courtroom, but as a classroom experience. In "Class-Room," the physician also ministers to himself. Birkin tries to free him-self from his sickly attachment to Hermione, who, as a lover and demonic double, mimics his ideas on spontaneous desire in her dithyrambic odes to animal joy. Her ecstatic transports are derided as the "worst and last form of intellectualism," the convulsions of a will that can only experience the "animal-istic" nature of the body as a mental abstraction. Hermione is a modern Cassan-dra,[12] or rather, a Cassandra for the modern. Yet unlike those of the ancient prophetess, Hermione's agonies are not caused by the ironic reception of her predictions. Her pathos is measured by the ironic distance between her words and the reality she incarnates. Hermione is also identified with the Lady of Shalott, another cursed female visionary whose will-bound imagination con-demns her to a mirror world of shadows that will never materialize: "You've got that mirror, your own fixed will, your immortal understanding, your own tight conscious world, and there is nothing beyond it" (91).

Birkin's struggle with Hermione, whose rhetoric shadows Birkin's in the vampirish form of unconscious parody and conscious mockery, and who reflects his fear of self-mirroring, is thus part of the larger struggle the novel seeks to portray: the "struggle for verbal consciousness," as Lawrence identifies it in his foreword. Only the verbalizing "instinct" possesses the eruptive force needed to reclaim the past and to project a future in one totalizing movement. The ceaseless promptings of desire *must* find their way into language where they can be materialized into living forms, or else they will languish in the mind. Law-rence's famous manifesto announcing the replacement of "the old stable ego of the character" also proclaims the need for such a *materializing* language;

> There is another ego according to whose action the individual is unrecog-
> nizable, and passes through, as it were, allotropic states which it needs a

deeper sense than any we've been used to exercise, to discover all states of
the same single radically-unchanged element. (Like as diamond and coal
are the same pure single element of carbon. The ordinary novel would
trace the history of the diamond—but I say "diamond, what! This is carbon." And my diamond might be coal or soot, and my theme is carbon.)[13]

To chronicle this allotropic development, Lawrence appropriates an archaic language that posited the existence of multiple states, the language of totemism.
Totemism is the atavistic language by which the constituent element that collec-
tively compose the given themes of any culture find their living expression.[14]
Totemism provides a serviceable nomenclature for an otherwise "unrecogniz-
able" and therefore potentially *unrepresentable* Laurentian ego because, as Birkin implies in the chapter titled "Totem," totemic objects convey the complete
truth of a "state" without vitiating or compromising it under the morally static
signs of analytic language.[15]

Lawrence, of course, read widely in the burgeoning anthropological literature (Frazer, Jessie Weston, Tylor, Jane Harrison) that helped inspire the pancultural myths of modernist works such as *Ulysses* and *The Waste Land* or *Totem
and Taboo* (1913). His particular interest in totemism may have been sparked
by totemism's privileged position in the anthropological descriptions of primitive cultures. According to Frazer's *Totemism and Exogamy,* religion itself
emerged out of the disruption and decay of totemism. Totemism survives as an
elemental remainder and reminder of older social forms in the later phase of
religious evolution.[16] Totemism's capacity to survive as an "archaic reminiscence" of the collective mind thus accounts for its pancultural and panhistorical
vitality. As Frazer observes, "There is nothing in the institution itself incompatible with the pastoral, agricultural, even the commercial and industrial modes
of life, since in point of fact it remains to this day in vogue among hunters,
fishers, farmers, traders, weavers, leather-makers, and stone-masons, not to
mention the less reputable professions of quackery, fortune-telling, and rob-
bery."[17]

The real appeal of totemism for Lawrence, whatever its diversionary interest as a patron institution for quacks and fortune-tellers, is that it constitutes a
system of relationships—animalistic, spiritual, and social—that honors the law
of difference, primarily through the mediating institution of exogamy. Lawrence's criticism of the modern democratic "isms" (Fabianism, Liberalism, socialism, and communism) is that each system advocates a social state based on
the utopian goal of material and spiritual equality. Speaking through the bitter

declamations of Birkin, Lawrence maintains that social life ought to reflect rather than frustrate the original purpose of life—differentiation:

> We are all abstractly or mathematically equal, if you like. Every man has hunger and thirst, two eyes, one nose, and two legs. We're all the same in point of number. But spiritually, there is pure difference and neither equality nor inequality counts. It is upon these two bits of knowledge that you must found a state . . . One man isn't any better than another, not because they are equal, but because they are intrinsically *other,* that there is no term of comparison. (161)

Equality is a theoretical construct abstracted out of the data of material necessity. Thus Birkin banishes it to the realm of number, wherein its truth and utility, if any, are to be found. In the essay "Democracy," Lawrence converts the primal fact of Otherness into the first term of his "metaphysics of presence": "Our life, our being depends upon the incalculable issue from the central Mystery into indefinable *presence*. This sounds in itself an abstraction. But not so. It is rather the perfect absence of abstraction. The central Mystery is no generalized abstraction. It is each man's primal original soul or self, within him" (*P.*, 714).

Lawrence unapologetically propounds a metaphysics of presence which demands a language purified of any false "term of comparison." Only in this way can Lawrence hope to preserve the inviolability of the "central Mystery" in his prophetic communication of it. Yet how is the absolute law of otherness to be fulfilled (or even monitored) in the verbal and social contacts of individuals and yet retain its ontological status as "the undefinable"? This problem Birkin himself encounters in a rather playful conversation with Ursula about the "nature" of daisies.

> "You know that a daisy is a company of florets, a concourse, become individual. Don't the botanists put it highest in the line of development? I believe they do."
>
> "The compositae, yes, I think so," said Ursula, who was never very sure of anything. Things she knew perfectly well, at one moment, seemed to become doubtful the next.
>
> "Explain it so, then," he said. "The daisy is a perfect little democracy, so it's the highest of flowers, hence its charm."
>
> "No," she cried, "no—never. It isn't democratic."

"No," she admitted. "It's the golden mob of the proletariat, sur-
rounded by a showy white fence of the idle rich."

"How hateful—your hateful social orders!" she cried.

"Quite! It's a daisy—we'll leave it alone." (192)

The ease with which Birkin can postulate the terms of comparison between the
composite structure of the daisy and that of democracy, thus transforming the
daisy into an emblem of the class divisions segregating the proletariat from the
idle rich, testifies to the seductive indiscriminations of analogical language. Resisting the temptations of false resemblance is part of the struggle for verbal
consciousness that the novel recounts. Birkin must forbear seeking explanations
in the concave mirror of false analogy. Herein lies the deference and delicacy of
his verbal gesture: "It's a daisy—we'll leave it alone." The concession is slight,
even comic, but Birkin honors the uniqueness of the daisy as the absolute *other*.

Lawrence's rhetoric of essential if undefinable difference found inspiration
in the naturalistic language of totemism. Totemism establishes a classificatory
system of relationships predicated on the imaginary brotherhood of resemblances in difference.[18] Totemic language externalizes the "primal, original soul
within"; it signifies the living realities issuing from the depths of the central
mystery and posits their organic relationships. The authority of this totemic
identity justifies Lawrence's banishment of the old "stable ego" hypostatized in
the novelistic cult of "personality." This *linguistic* project involves Birkin, as a
metaphysician of presence, in deadly battle with Gudrun, that formidable
apostle of Mind. Gudrun regards the living being "as a complete figure, like a
character in a book, or a subject in a picture, or a marionette in a theatre, a
finished creation." When she sees Gerald for the first time, the novel, adopting
her mode of perception, lapses into the language typical of "old" narrative
representations. Gerald is described in terms of externals, "a fair sun-tanned
type, rather above middle height, well-made, and almost exaggeratedly well-
dressed. But about him also was the strange, guarded look, the unconscious
glisten, as if he did not belong to the same creation as the people about
him" (61).

Gudrun can express the unconscious glisten that identifies Gerald as *another*, not the *same* creation as the people about him, only by invoking his
totemic reality: " 'His totem is the wolf,' she repeated to herself. 'His mother is
an old, unbroken wolf.' And then she experienced a keen paroxysm, a transport,
as if she had made some incredible discovery, known to nobody else on earth"
(61). Gudrun's "paroxysm" seems to be the result of a violent redoubling of

language upon itself, like the kinetic recoil of a discharging gun. Gudrun uses language as a murderous weapon, to fix or kill off life. Yet her "powerful apprehension" of Gerald's essence does consist in her conscious acts of metaphor making, that is, through her intellectual will to connect the known with the unknown. "His totem is the wolf" is rather a kind of double metaphor, the first part, totem, assimilating even as it traverses the second part, wolf. Totemistically, Gerald is that ancestral and universal reality struggling to express itself through him. The totemic depths of Gerald's individuality are brought to the narrative surface through a process of charged language that does not bother to discriminate between generative forces and their individual manifestations. His language aims to destroy or incapacitate that aspect of the verbal consciousness, best represented in the "mind" of Gudrun, which habitually employs language to encircle, complete, and fix the real. Only this totemic language can represent to consciousness those elemental beings and objects worthy of its love.

As the novel nears its conclusion, the battle between Gudrun's rhetoric and Birkin's vision intensifies. They compete for mastery over the novelistic spaces they occupy. Each espouses a vision of the "true fate" of modern men and women. Gudrun, fashioner of miniatures, respecter of the old virtues and corrupting privileges of the dead letter *I,* acts out of "a desire for the reduction process in oneself." Her totem is the dung beetle, the insect sacred to Egyptian death cults. Her fascination with "the process of active corruption" results in Baudelairean "fleurs du mal," dark marsh-flowers that contrast so tellingly with Birkin's pristine, inviolate daisies. Birkin, then, is a Hardyesque "pioneer" who journeys into the fruitful wastes seeking his destiny in what he calls "mystic marriage." Gudrun is the "Glücksritter," the Eternal Feminine degraded into the whore of Fortune, whose vehicle is the wheel of mechanical transformation.

## FIRST LOVE, LAST RITES

Birkin's uncertain prophecy of creative Eros is powerfully dramatized in "Moony," Lawrence's most controlled and condensed narrative meditation on modern love purged of its Meredithian "sickly cant." Birkin is shown obsessively disfiguring the image of the moon reflected in the surface of a pond. He does not see this lunar reflection as a natural icon for Mutability, but as a demonized image of Cybele, the "accursed Syria Dea" of Asiatic mother cults. He throws stone after stone into the motionless pond, turning it into "a battlefield of broken lights and shadows," a field of "white fragments" that mirrors his own obsession with disintegrative processes. Yet the moon's image proves indestructible and inviolable—the "scattered fragments" course their way back to the still center: "He saw the moon regathering itself insidiously, saw the heart of the rose intertwining vigorously and blindly, calling back the scattered fragments, winning home the fragments, in a pulse and in effort of return" (324). *Sparagmos* to *nostos:* the winning home of fragments is the consummation devoutly wished by modern narratives, from Joyce's *Ulysses* to Beckett's vagrant fictions of disintegration.

Winning home is what Birkin sees as "the remaining way" open to those weary of contemplating the modern mysteries of dissolution:

> There was another way, the way of freedom. There was the paradisal entry into pure, single being, the individual soul taking precedence over love and desire for union, stronger than any pangs of emotion, a lovely state of free proud-singleness, which accepted the obligation of the permanent connection with others, and with the others, submits to the yoke and leash of love, but never forfeits its own proud individual singleness, even while it loves and yields. (331–32)

Love, perhaps the most overused word in the vocabulary of the novel, must be either rejected as obsolete or deprived of its idolatrous power to subject the "free proud-singleness" of the creative individual. Birkin, however, remains unsure whether his vision represents "only an idea, or . . . the interpretation of a profound yearning" (329). Love must be experienced as a "travelling together," an exploratory way, never a final destination.

The "love" story of Birkin and Ursula embedded in and illuminating the dark heart of *Women in Love* represents Lawrence's attempt to render the epic exploration of the as-yet-unknown. That exploration is the true subject of Laurentian prophecy, which foresees the consummative moment of First Love as the return or winning home of paradise. This is the paradisal dream actualized, if only temporarily, in "Excurse," when Birkin makes his fateful proposal of star-marriage. The chapter opens with Birkin's decision to renounce the tutelage of luck as a vulgar minister of destiny. He refuses to accept that life is "a series of accidents—like a picaresque novel" (383). "Excurse" thus becomes one of Lawrence's most successful fictional representations of a "generic" self-overcoming. The picaresque, the narrative form which images human destiny as a series of accidents and their historical, social, and economic determinations, is repudiated as a fiction validating a "false fate." Through this repudiation, the promise of *The Rainbow* is realized: Ursula's "new knowledge of eternity in the flux of time" is fulfilled in her *internally* apprehended knowledge of "the inevi-

tability and beauty of fate, fate which one asks for, which one accepts in full"
(400).

Ursula's new knowledge is announced in the language of what I have earlier
called relaxed quotation, the language reserved for Laurentian mythmaking and
lovemaking. Her excurse concludes in a linguistic reminiscence that recalls "the
old magic of the Book of Genesis, where the sons of God saw the daughters of
men, that they were fair." Through this recollection she simultaneously discovers in "the straight downflow" of Birkin's thighs the strange reality of the redeemed body: "It was here she discovered him one of the sons of God such as
were in the beginning of the world, not a man, something other, something
more." It is easy to mock Lawrence for imaging that woman regains paradise
through the transfigured loins, but it is hard to fault the life-motive that inspires
his dreaming of something other, something more than our present understanding of human life. We can provisionally identify this "something other,
something more" with those generative powers which we endow with divinity,
personifying them as strange inhuman gods who preside over the human beginning of the world. In Ursula's recollection or "quotation" of these mythic originals, the creative source is re-uttered in the fulfilled present; ancient gods are
reembodied in the mystic body of the beloved. Ursula's own reality is dissolved
and transfigured through the cadences of such mythic quotation. She becomes
a "paradisal flower . . . beyond womanhood," a radiant "figure" of a true *human*
fate, a "fate which one asks for," not the untoward destiny one struggles against,
like a character in a picaresque novel. Lawrence, often berated for the mystical
pastorialism that infuses his sexual passages, offers here a vital instance of that
"good form" of doing—or imagining—as one likes. Through such spontaneous and imaginative assertions he traces his way back to paradise.

Authors, however, can only point the way. Characters (and readers) are free
to follow or to fall, to lapse into old and stubborn modes of refusal. Thus despite
her access to such a revelatory language, Ursula does not fully accede to the
conditions of her newfound life of free proud singleness in star-equilibrium.
The reason is partly that Lawrence prefers to leave his characters in uncertainty
and partly that Ursula remains for Lawrence totemically bound to her essence
as Magna Mater, the Great Mother who insists on pressing for a reactionary and
limited kind of love, love as ecstatic fusion. Like all of Lawrence's early heroines,
from Mrs. Morel to Anna "Victrix" Brangwen, Ursula has a predilection for a
consuming romance whose central episode is the idyll of a sexual paradise
regained. Generically, romance is the narrative form that seeks to cancel out
the differences separating love and its objects. For Lawrence, it is *the* female

form of imaginative desire, born out of the female will to absorb the "Other" in the all-comprehending womb. The Great Mother would reclaim all individualized life into the undifferentiated Source, drawing all articulated meanings and distinctions into herself. For Ursula, who might be won over by love's (and Birkin's) excursionary nature, intercourse remains the act of homecoming, the winning home of the errant male.

Birkin's suspicions that the Magna Mater's lust for "unspeakable intimacies" (343) lurks behind every female's urge to "mate" leave him dissatisfied with mystic marriage as the controlling metaphor for his transvaluing vision of life. Because marriage is disposed, by the sheer force of institutional inertia and by the reactionary demands of the "feminine" will, to enforce a unity where none should exist, Birkin advocates a complementary relation of *Blutbrüderschaft*.[19] The truly revolutionary vision of *Women in Love,* its well-conceived threat to the conventional attitudes toward human relationships propagated by the novel of bourgeois realism, is in expanding the idea of spiritual mating to encompass a male-to-male relation, a broader and less interested relation than the "egoïsme à deux" or "hunting in couples" (439) that characterizes modern marriages.

"Bloodbrotherhood" is authorized both by Birkin's personal desire for a male relationship and by the more utilitarian need to populate the "new world" of his visions with as yet undefined human constellations. But beneath Birkin's ideological justification for such a male rite, there abides the epic striving condensed and displaced in the obsessions of Birkin's *Salvator Mundi* complex: his classical yearning for the *virtú* embodied in the Homeric figure of Gerald Crich. Gerald is that preeminent Laurentian idol: the elemental male. He is prefigured in the less refined person of Baxter Dawes, Paul Morel's rival in *Sons and Lovers.* In the sexual battle between Paul and Baxter, one that rehearses the gladiatorial combat of the later novel, this instinctual desire is first named as a legitimate, but perhaps unlasting, male fate:

> He [Paul] was pure instinct, without reason or feeling. His body, hard and wonderful in itself, cleaved against the struggling body of the other man; not a muscle in him relaxed. He was quite unconscious, only his body had taken upon itself to kill this other man. For himself, he had neither feeling nor reason. He lay pressed hard against his adversary, his body adjusting itself to its one pure purpose of choking the other man, resisting exactly at the right moment, with exactly the right amount of strength, the struggles of the other, silent, intent, unchanging, gradually pressing its

knuckles deeper, feeling the struggles of the other body become wilder
and more frenzied. Tighter and tighter grew his body, like a screw that is
gradually increasing in pressure, till something breaks.

Then suddenly he relaxed, full of wonder and misgiving. (*Sons and
Lovers,* 366)

The pure instinct mobilized in this death-struggle surely refers to Paul's primary
but repressed desire for the father whom he consciously repudiates out of
loyalty to his mother. Paul recovers the ravaged but virile body of his father
through this violence, thus relieving the accumulated tension of constant
repressions and repeated rejections.

These mixed emotions of wonder (at allowing instinct to break through
the restricting walls of conscious intention) and misgiving (suspecting the nature of such instinctual attachments) survive in Birkin's gladiatorial wrestling
with Gerald. Here the instinctual passion released is not paternal but fraternal:

Both were white and clear, but Gerald flushed smart red where he was
touched, and Birkin remained white and tense. He seemed to penetrate
into Gerald's more solid, more diffuse bulk, to interfuse his body through
the body of the other, as if to bring it subtly into subjection, always seizing
with some rapid necromantic foreknowledge every motion of the other
flesh, converting and counteracting it, playing upon the limbs and trunk of
Gerald like some hard wind. It was as if Birkin's whole physical intelligence interpenetrated into Gerald's body, as if his fine, sublimated energy
entered into the flesh of the fuller man, like some potency, casting a fine
net, a prison, through the muscles into the very depths of Gerald's physical being. (453)

It is hard to say what kind of triumph this interpenetration of male bodies
represents. Birkin's physical intelligence becomes arrested on the threshold of
"necromantic foreknowledge," a ghoulish phrase that links the "fine sublimated
energy" of his clairvoyance to *nekros,* the body of death. For all of Birkin's
furious struggle to convert and counteract Gerald's physicality, it is essentially a
dead man he embraces. Laurentian prophecy thus sadly identifies itself, at the
height of its exciting power, as a communion with, as well as a struggle against,
the body of death.

For Birkin's hard wind, cognate with the mighty breath of the Kosmocrator, cannot countervail the apocalyptic whirlwind of Gerald's own dangerous
resolve—to go to Gudrun, "persistently, like a wind, straight forwards, as if to

his fate" (424). Crisis, as Frank Kermode reminds us, citing the pun of St. John, comprises both judgment and separation.[20] The death of his father provokes such a crisis for Gerald, a crisis which resolves itself in his decision to separate himself from the "one center" authorized and inhabited by his father—"the unseen, raw grave": "No, he had nothing to stay here for." But even as he enters Gudrun's bedroom seeking comfort in love, he tracks in the cold clay of his father's grave. Death and love become dialectically wedded, composing the signs that dictate Gerald's true fate. Whatever Birkin might do to counteract or contravene this death-impulse is, finally, unavailing, and it is unavailing precisely for the reasons Birkin himself had foretold: Gerald is the murderee with a lust to be murdered. He will find his true mate in Gudrun, the husband-slayer.[21]

In a letter to John Middleton Murry, Lawrence describes the limits of his own millennial vision of a world populated with the new men and women of his imaginings: "I think that one day—before so very long—we shall come together again, this time on a living earth, not in the world of destructive going apart. I believe we shall do things together, and be happy. But we can't dictate the terms, nor the times. It has to come to pass in us. Yet one has the hope, that is the reality."[22] The Götterdämmerung conclusion to the novel confirms Lawrence's intuition that neither the terms nor the times ordained for the world's "destructive going apart" can be predicted by the regenerate will of the prophet or dictated by the corrupt will of insane "ecstatics" like Gudrun and Loerke. Birkin's vision thus acquires an ambiguous status in the novel's already tortuous eschatology. He may express the hope for, not the imminence of, a new creative order. This hope diminishes as the novel relentlessly moves toward its last days, whose end terms are provided in the ironic "love story" of Gudrun and Gerald.

The destinies of Gerald and Gudrun constitute, as Lawrence said of Dostoyevski's novels, "great parables . . . but false art."[23] Their love story represents, that is, the moribund form of older (tragic) narratives whose formal integrity conformed to a deterministic notion of historical causality. This formalism appears in an early exchange between Gudrun and Gerald: "You have struck the first blow," Gerald reminds Gudrun, to which she responds with "confident assurance," "And I shall strike the last." That Gudrun's threat sounds like a prediction is a sign of her (and the reader's) confidence in the symmetry intrinsic to the resolutions of the classical novel. Lawrence's own analysis of Dostoyevski's "parables" helps illuminate his unwilling incorporation of this "false" yet inevitable formalism into the last stages of *Women in Love*. Writing again to Murry, who was working on a study of Dostoyevski, Lawrence observes: "The

Christian ecstasy leads to imbecility (the Idiot). The sensual ecstasy leads to universal murder: for mind, the acme of sensual ecstasy lies in *devouring* the other, even in the pleasures of love, it is a devouring, like a tiger drinking blood (Rogozhin). But the full sensual ecstasy is never reached except by Rogozhin in murdering Nastasya. It is nipped in the last stages by the *will,* the social will." [24]

This Dostoyevskian insight shadows Lawrence's representation of Thomas Crich's sentimental Christianity and Gudrun's demonic sensuality. Christian ecstasy, which Thomas Crich seeks through his self-abnegating charities and his sentimental, "democratic" politics, leads to his final imbecility and the slow stupor of lingering death. Sensual ecstasy is the special lust of Gudrun, whose face betrays the insane will of the "demoniacal ecstatic" (49), and whose love affair with Gerald, like her nostalgic fascination with the underworld of his mines, grows out of her desire to experience "perfect voluptuous finality" (560). Her affair with Gerald must culminate, as the Dostoyevskian parable instructs, in sensually gratifying murder.

Lawrence's unwilling but not inadvertent accommodation of Dostoyevski's spiritual determinism to resolve his visionary narrative is also reflected in the larger structural configurations of the novel. *Women in Love* begins with an unstable triangle—Hermione, Ursula, and Birkin—that Birkin attempts to replace with the transforming relationship comprehended in mystic marriage. But as the novel moves toward the Continent and into its Götterdämmerung phase, the generic imperative to observe certain novelistic symmetries begins to reassert itself. The novel's initial sexual triangle reappears in the parodic and demonic trinity of Loerke, Gudrun, and Gerald. A more dispiriting symmetry permits Birkin's vision of male love to be echoed in Loerke's relation to Leitner, an alliance that demystifies Birkin's mystic sense of *Blutbrüderschaft* in the perversions of "ecstatic" and exploitive homosexuality.

To discredit the determinism that is overwhelming his narrative, Lawrence has Gudrun mock the conventional explanation that the violence called forth in the final stages of her battle with Gerald is due to the tensions and jealousies traditionally associated with the "eternal" love triangle: " 'A pretty little sample of the eternal triangle!' And she turned ironically away, because she knew that the fight had been between Gerald and herself and that the presence of the third party was a mere contingency—an inevitable contingency perhaps, but a contingency none the less. But let them have it as an example of the eternal triangle, the trinity of hate. It would be simpler for them" (578). Gudrun's scathing dismissal of the idea that her triangular entanglements with Gerald and Loerke compose a trinity of hate is based on a quibble about the meaning and importance of "contingencies." But what does she, or even Lawrence, mean by the self-contradictory assertion that Loerke's presence operates as an "inevitable contingency"? How can a contingency be both accidental and foreseeable, the product of both chance and necessity? What is important to Gudrun's self-interpretation is not her claim that her battle with Gerald represents a singular death-struggle between two insane wills. What makes Gudrun triumphant is the power of her dismissive irony, her tonal mastery over the reality of the last facts and violent ends of *Dies Irae.*

In *Women in Love,* Gudrun's ironic vision of love and death overwhelms the imagination of the artist of life, Rupert Birkin. Birkin tries to inaugurate a reign of freedom, the new time of the transcendent individual who lives in close contact with the inexhaustible life source. Gudrun, with Loerke in attendance as her demonic consort, inaugurates the totalitarian regime of terror, the nightmare of history and a servile historicism, the coming era of real social hatred. She is the mad prophetess who presides over the apocalyptic terrors that proclaim the end of the world as a ceaseless duration. *Dies Irae* for Gudrun takes the form of a perpetual *chronos,* to paraphrase Kermode's formulation of the modernist's "intemporal agony."[25] Gudrun's is a peculiarly "modern" madness, not the classical and even pathos-ridden madness of Hermione, for she can neither envision nor hope for deliverance. She can only persist in fashioning the totalitarian, apocalyptic fantasies she plays out with Loerke, the "final craftsman" of "the last series of subtleties," who "did not deceive himself in the last issue":

> As for the future, that they never mentioned except one laughed out some mocking dream of the destruction of the world by a ridiculous catastrophe of man's invention: a man invented such a perfect explosive that it blew the earth in two, and the two halves set off in different directions through space, to the dismay of the inhabitants: or else the people of the world divided into two halves, and each half decided *it* was perfect and right, the other half was wrong and must be destroyed; so another end of the world. (551)

Gudrun and Loerke translate the central rite of modernity—*sparagmos*—into global and genocidal terms: the earth torn in two. In their last series of subtleties, Loerke and Gudrun conceive a ghastly parody of Plato's myth of the origin of sexual love. In Plato's *Symposium* Aristophanes recounts Zeus's punitive division of the original hermaphroditic body into halves, who thereafter seek to reunite through love. Gudrun and Loerke imagine mankind split in two and thereafter seeking to exterminate the ideologically corrupt other. Their millennial ecstasies find consummation in this obscene prophecy of universal murder.

Gudrun's myth of finality is registered in the cold, life-betraying voice of irony: "Everything turned to irony with her: the last flavour of everything was ironical" (511). Kierkegaard claimed that irony was "in the strictest sense a mastered moment" and saw in the birth of ironic consciousness "the absolute beginning of the personal life." [26] For Lawrence, irony is the last rites of the living dead. That the creative moment could in any way be limited to and defined by the needs and desires, the dignities—and impudence—of the personal life is repugnant to his metaphysical and rhetorical doctrines of an absolute individuality. For Lawrence, language should inhere in the reality it denominates, in the new utterances it struggles to deliver over to verbal consciousness. Irony, the conscious displacement of meaning from its vehicles of expression, irony as the deliberate estrangement of essence and phenomena, is the last betrayal of the creative Source.

Gerald's death vindicates Gudrun's status as the ironic artist of modernity. It is Gudrun who regards Gerald's death as an inevitable contingency attending the Final Days, a necessary but "barren tragedy" without meaning or significance, but hers is the view of cold irony. It is at this point that Birkin returns to the novel that he has abandoned (and that has abandoned him) to contest Gudrun's ironic reading of Gerald's death. He mourns the fallen hero and retreats, not behind the frigid dignities of irony, but into the enclosed and emotionally charged spaces of elegy: "I didn't want it to be like this" (581). Ursula, to her horror, hears the accent of nostalgia in Birkin's valedictory lament and cannot help thinking of the Kaiser's "Ich habe es nicht gewollt." In exposing the historical retreat implicit in Birkin's elegiac meditations, Ursula argues for the "realities" honored in the resolutions of the classical novel, and in so doing interprets Birkin's grief as a perversion, a refusal to accept the fate decreed by those impersonal forces that constitute the Real.

> "You can't have two kinds of love. Why should you!"
> "It seems as if I can't," he said. "Yet I wanted it."
> "You can't have it, because it's false, impossible," she said.
> "I don't believe that," he answered. (583)

*Women in Love* represents and advances the modernist crisis of separation and judgment. Its Götterdämmerung finale envisions the last symmetries in the form of an impasse and an argument. Birkin's perverse insistence that his desire to "save" Gerald was not a false nor a barren hope, but a living expression of his heart's desire, his true fate, is contrasted with Gudrun's grim, ironic view of necessity. His quarrel with Gudrun over the meaning of history is perhaps less threatening to his metaphysic than his argument with Ursula over the visionary possibility of *Blutbrüderschaft,* men wedded in purpose and in love. Both the historical impasse and the emotional argument remain unresolved, their outcomes temporarily suspended by a narrative moratorium dictated by Birkin's grief and Lawrence's own need to reimagine how the creative mystery will "carry on the embodiment of creation" after mankind is exterminated—or annihilates itself. The novel opens itself up to the future only by insisting on a kind of blank space in time, empty yet still capable of being filled with new utterances, "miraculous unborn species" (580).

In an essay on modern painting, Lawrence pictured Cézanne's struggle with the visual clichés that composed the tainted inheritance of pictorial form. His analysis illuminates and corresponds to Lawrence's own transvaluing critique of novelistic conventions: "Then again, in other pictures he seems to be saying: Landscape is not like this and not like this and not like this and not . . . etc.— and every *not* is a little blank space in the canvas, defined by the remains of an assertion. Sometimes Cézanne builds up a landscape essentially out of omissions. He puts fringes on the complicated vacuum of the cliché, so to speak, and offers us that. It is interesting in a *repudiative* fashion but it is not the new thing" (*P.,* 581).[27] *Women in Love,* despite its efforts to imagine and realize a "new thing," comes to rest on the fringe of the complicated vacuum of novelistic cliché. Lawrence keeps positing that Life is not like this and not like this and not . . . etc., but it remains questionable whether, at novel's end, we are left with the remains of his series of assertions or with a genuinely "new thing." My defense of Lawrence has consisted in the claim that his style is not of interest in a "repudiative fashion," that, in fact, Lawrence understands repudiation to be the most vitiating when it is not the most murderous of modern reflexes. Nowhere is the struggle against repudiation more passionate and more futile than in *Women in Love.* But he found himself overmastered by the ironic demon of his own creation—Gudrun, that chthonic demon who rules the modern underworld with Rhadamanthine strictness. *Women in Love* is her Judgment Book. It publishes the decrees of a vengeful Providence that Lawrence could neither ignore nor accept.

SEVEN

# JOYCE'S
# ENDEARING FORM

## THE SCANDAL OF FIRST LOVE

NOWHERE IS THE FATEFULNESS of First Love more faithfully observed than in *Ulysses*. On Bloomsday, commemorating Joyce's first
outing with Nora, First Love flowers into the epic of modernity. It is
of course a scandalous observance, this attributing to a private anniversary the
attention epical narratives traditionally reserve for world-decisive events. But
to take this view is to mistake Bloomsday for an ordinary day instead of remarking it as the extraordinary occasion that was to change modern literature's very
conception of the "eventful." It would not be too fantastic to regard Bloomsday
as the dawn of that day long anticipated by Proust's Marcel during his vigils in
the Champs-Élysée, a day "on which time starts afresh, casting aside the heritage of the past, declining its legacy of sorrows." [1] The last word of *Ulysses, Yes,*
is Joyce's greeting to that new era, one born out of the belief that the order of
the world is not "ineluctable" but, on the contrary, subject to a perpetual creation.

We know, of course, that love, like art, does not create the world but re-
creates it. Molly's *Yes*, which heralds the dawn of an unrevealed future, also
recalls her first ecstatic consent to love, when she was a flower of the mountain.
Her vocative *Yes* is voiced in response to a reality not only beyond but within
her. In the creative surge of her final lines, "the awful deepdown torrents" of
procreative nature surmount every external barrier to their vital and impetuous
force. In such upheavals First Love asserts its authority over history, and justifies
Turgenev's claim that First Love is like a "revolution" in which "the regular and
established order of life is in an instant smashed to fragments."

Unlike Proust's *Remembrance*, Joyce's *Ulysses* and Lawrence's *Women in
Love* recognize the apocalyptism of First Love as an enduring feeling, rather
than a fugitive mood or ephemeral, early phase of its development. *Ulysses*, like
*Women in Love*, aspires to a "new assertion" of reality which subjects the old
orders of life to a revolutionary liquidation and not, as in Proust, to a monu-
mental reconstruction. It is, then, in these two epical representations of modern
culture, and not in Proust, that we may observe how the visionary aspirations
of First Love to remake the world are increasingly pressured by modern history
into assuming rabidly eschatological postures. Joyce himself conceived of the
composition of *Ulysses* as "the progress of a sandblast," by which "each successive episode, dealing with some province of artistic culture (rhetoric or music
or dialectic), leaves behind it a burnt up field." [2]

But Joyce's "scorched-earth policy" differs markedly from the impolitics of

Lawrence's angelic prophecies and apocalyptic fantasias. For Joyce appreciated, as Lawrence could not, the low humor as well as the divine comedy of the world.[3] Joyce's broad comedic sense explains why the end-of-the world fantasies that overwhelm *Women in Love* can be staged as carnival entertainments in *Ulysses*. Gudrun's demoniac dream of the clockwork mechanism, which images the psychosis of the modern industrial state, finds its symbolic counterpart in the hallucinatory theatrics of the Walpurgisnacht of "Circe." In "Circe" the body and its repertoire of customary behaviors is represented in its most dissolute and graceless attitudes: the locomotor ataxia of uncoordinated reflexes, promiscuous and brutish fantasies, drunken aggression, and sottish abjection.

Yet Joyce presents the diabolic revels in which modern culture celebrates its own death-drive as an essentially comic spectacle of disintegrating life. He could forswear the tragic furor of Lawrence's denunciations because he believed, as Lawrence could not, that modern history was a nightmare from which we might eventually awake. Molly's insomnia, unlike Gudrun's tormented nights, testifies that the night might once again become the time of creative reveries. As the rest of the modern world sleeps, Molly-Penelope is at work on her web, interweaving passional reminiscences into a tapestry "that would do your heart good to see": "rivers and lakes and flowers all sorts of shapes and smells and colours springing up even out of the ditches primroses and violets". . . . (642–43). Gudrun's figures for modernity are Baudelairean *fleurs du mal,* bred in corruption. Molly's apocalyptism is projected in her vision of a redeemed Nature that can as effortlessly coax primroses and violets from rank ditches as it can adorn the earth with flowers of the mountain, of which the most spectacular specimen and prototype is Molly herself.

Lawrence, who shares such paradisal longings, mistrusts, as we have already seen, such utopian naturalism as the cunning suggestion of "female art." Female art is epitomized in the Book of Genesis, whose account of Creation, according to Lawrence, is immersed in "self-feeling" and pure sensation. Lawrence himself embraced the New Testamentary mode of "male assertion" that would "deny the age and refuse sensation, seeking ever to make transformation . . . to register relationships" (*P.,* 452). His prophecy is directed against Moloch, the god who presides over the modern culture of mechanicalness, of bodily recoil and instinctual repudiation, the Death-in-Life against which the creative Spirit strives. Although angelic Lawrence preached that the promptings of the passional self alone represent the "true fate" of the individual, *Women in Love* records a different Judgment. Modern history defeats desire in *Women in Love* and consolidates its victory by banishing Birkin's dream of a First Love, whose expressive form is Edenic pastoral, to the emotionally charged but spiritually impotent realm of elegy—the imaginative space, not of an ongoing, "novelistic" future, but of historical retreat.

Joycean prophecy is less militant and agonistic. The Joycean body is the first material site—and in modern culture, potentially the last as well—of the sacramental infusions of procreative grace. *Ulysses,* emboldened by an adulterous woman's genius for confusing her last with her first lover, closes its chronicle of the day—and ends its meditation on the epochal and cosmological cycles that shape the course of human history—in a sexual idyll: Molly Bloom's memory of her first kiss under the Moorish wall, a memory which is at the same time an anticipation of that imminent *jouissance* that reinvigorates the will-to-futurity: "Yes, I will Yes."

How are we to explain this difference except to remark that it is not Lawrence, outcast still for the *kerygma* of his dark forebodings and idiosyncratic sexual mythologizing, but Joyce who exhibits "the scandal of the intrinsic"? And where is this scandal more in evidence than in Joyce's audacious "dating" of his epical narrative on 16 June, a day whose personal and revolutionary "significance" belongs to Joyce alone? Joyce's biographer Richard Ellmann regards 16 June as "an eloquent though indirect tribute to Nora," which marks "the day upon which he entered into relation with the world around him and left behind the loneliness he had felt since his mother's death." [4] Nora's biographer, Brenda Maddox, surmises that a more intimate moment is commemorated by Bloomsday. On that memorable day of 16 June when Joyce first walked with her, Nora, with skillful embraces, "made a man" of him. [5]

Thus we observe on Bloomsday the impressive counterexample of the "scandal of the extrinsic," with its "salutary reminder," as Frederic Jameson insists, of the "determination of consciousness by social being." [6] Joyce's Jesuitical education had given him a different sense of the way the temporal and spiritual orders coexist. We should not dismiss as accidental figure Joyce's writing to Nora that he experienced her sexual touch as "a kind of sacrament" that filled him "with an amazed joy." A sacrament, the Catholic catechism propounds, is the outward sign of inward grace. In Nora he beheld the incarnation of his youthful dream-girl, "a girl fashioned into a curious grave beauty by the culture of generations before her, the woman for whom I wrote poems like 'Gentle Lady' or 'Thou leanest to the shell of night.' "[7] The sacred power of profane touch not only ushered "the strange lonely boy" into the world of adult relations. Through its sacramental agency Joyce felt himself visited by the "grace" of tradition, the culture of generations incarnated in the "warm impulsive life-giving love of [Nora's] rich nature."

The politics of identifying his working-class lover with Dante's "gentle lady" suggests more than Joyce's ingenuity in transforming an aristocratic culture of love into proletarian romance. It discloses to us Joyce's ambivalence toward the cultus of sexual idealism with its legends of beatified womanhood. In *Portrait,* he will have Stephen mock his own helpless reversion to "the spiritual-heroic refrigerating apparatus, invented and patented in all countries by Dante Alighieri,"[8] when, on the brink of his own impending exile from Ireland, Stephen encounters Emma, the young girl whose image he had sought to capture in an image of profane joy. Stephen "modernizes" the figure of Dante by characterizing the Florentine pilgrim as a literary entrepreneur who devised and patented the literary "apparatus" that preserves the erotic image by chilling it. Yet it is by no means clear whether Stephen is satirizing the idealizing aesthetics of Dante's poetic system or mocking the ironic nature of his own modern attitudes. In conversing with Emma, he catches himself performing a "revolutionary gesture," a histrionic imposture that leaves him feeling "sorry and mean." He begins talking rapidly of his plans and discovers, in the aftermath of their friendly exchange, the horizon of a new feeling: "I liked her and it seems a new feeling to me. Then, in that case, all the rest, all that I thought I thought and all that I thought I felt I felt, all the rest before now, in fact . . . O, give it up, old chap! Sleep it off!" (252).

The warmth of this new feeling is sufficient to thaw, if only momentarily, Stephen's habitually cold, ironic posture. This new sensation discloses the apocalyptism of First Love, capable of expunging all that Stephen thought he thought and felt he felt. Stephen renounces the future promised by First Love to pursue his own proud vision of artistic vocation. Yet I do not think it has been sufficiently remarked that Stephen's intention to "forge in the smithy of my soul the uncreated conscience of my race" commits him to an emotional and artistic archaism. He envisions his literary future as a *reversion* to a pretechnological, indeed idyllic, time when poet and artisan were complementary figures engaged in the work of *poesis,* of making. Yet *Portrait* has depicted Stephen's "modern" soul not as a smithy, but as a heroic refrigerating apparatus that is prone, perhaps doomed, to convert any warm impulsive feeling into "the cold indifferent knowledge of himself." The revolutionary impulse to recreate the world to reflect the compass of the soul's desire can only originate in the "new feeling" that abolishes "all that I thought I thought and all that I felt I felt."

There is no way to experience this apocalyptic feeling, to enter into this new and transfigured world, except through the grace of First Love. Only after passing through its portals do errors appear as volitional, and coarse contingency submit to the refining soulcraft of art. We need only return to the famous incident of Joyce's hysterical jealousy when Vincent Cosgrave maliciously claimed to have shared Nora's sexual favors to appreciate that for Joyce the grace of sexual touch is bestowed exclusively on the *firstcomer.* Joyce imagines himself a public spectacle and questions the paternity of Giorgio, his firstborn. Joyce is quickly disabused of his suspicions, and his deep sexual chagrin is transformed into a less anxious mood of exhortation and penitence. To Nora he writes:

> Do you know what a pearl is and what an opal is? My soul when you came sauntering to me first through those sweet summer evenings was beautiful but with the pale passionless beauty of a pearl. Your love has passed through me and now I feel my mind something like an opal, that is, full of strange uncertain hues and colours, of warm lights and quick shadows and of broken music.[9]

Stephen Dedalus, who has never known First Love except as an inchoate desire for the insubstantial image of his soul's creation, looks to the creatures of the air for his spiritual similitudes. But Joyce, mastered by love, retrospectively interprets his "new life" with Nora as a kind of minerological romance. O rocks, Molly might object, suspecting, even as she is intrigued by, the hermetic metaphors by which men seek to figure their love. But Joyce, ever alert to the grace of spiritual metamorphosis, attributes to First Love the power to effect a radical change in identity. Before the life-altering encounter with First Love, his soul possessed the lustrous beauty of a poetically sealed narcissism, whose iridescence, like the pearl's, issues from within. First Love, which for Joyce, so jealous of precedence, is both absolute and true, shatters the integrity of the pearl, pale and passionless in its impermeability. His spiritual type is henceforth the opal, whose beauty consists in the impassioned *consonantia* of its fragmented, quicksilver lights. The opal, whose luster is shadowed by doubt and distrust, emits a more modern aura than the pearl. Its *integritas* or wholeness is attended by that *claritas* or radiance of which Stephen speaks in *Portrait,* a luminosity conducing to "that cardiac condition which the Italian physiologist Luigi Galvani, using a phrase almost as beautiful as Shelley's called the enchantment of the heart" (213). A peculiarly modern enchantment, we might say, like Swann's enthrallment with the heart-wrenching phrase from Venteuil's sonata. Joyce's enchantment with the broken music emblematic of his love is, however, more productive than that of Swann, the artist manqué. Its fitful and fugitive harmony, as "The Dead" and *Ulysses* attest, is the prelude to that creative initiative that would alter the emotional tonalities as well as the verbal cadences of modern literature.

This, then, was Joyce's complex appropriation of First Love, the erotic culture of generations interpreted as a myth of soul-creation. It was a myth that posed the mystery of mortal life and spiritual existence not as a "natural" morphology, the soul "unfolding itself" in successive stages of flux and reflux, but as a symbolic birth into the common life of men and women. Artistic consciousness, unlike the political or the psychological unconscious, may symbolically apprehend, even date, its own beginning. For Joyce, his beginning is with Nora. It is she who marks the end of his artistic tutelage—"the life which I have poured a stream of my youth upon." From the perspective of his "new life," the old life of youthful rebellion appears, "now that I am wiser and more controllable," as "safe": "It would ask no questions, expect nothing from me but a few moments of my life, leaving the rest free, and would promise me pleasure in return. I thought of all this and without regret I rejected it. It was useless for me; it could not give me what I wanted."[10] What Joyce rejects is the bohemian culture of his youth—"the life of the boulevard," with its vague pleasures both licit ("chattering, crushing little fabrics of pastry") and illicit ("descending from carriages with a busy stir of garments soft as the voice of the adulterer"). To persist in such a life was worse than "safe," that is, bereft of those sudden intensities and mysterious beckonings that compel the soul out of its lethargy and summon it to that focused expenditure of imaginative energy we call heroism. It was artistically, as it was spiritually, useless. It could neither arrest his attention nor inflame his imagination. At best, it would consume a few moments of his time, leaving him to contemplate, at his leisure, an empty (because unproductive) freedom. What Joyce celebrates is a love that would sanctify as it would occupy his life. Through the mystical agency of sexual touch, First Love discloses to Joyce its utopian vocation: to deliver the spirit from its own renegade isolationism, the erotic and social apostasy of life without joy.

The scandal of the extrinsic does intrude, however, on the joyous entry into his new life. It persists as an affect, "a final sense of sorrow and degradation—sorrow because I saw in you an extraordinary, melancholy tenderness which had chosen that sacrament as a compromise, and degradation because I understood that in your eyes I was inferior to a convention of our present society." Sorrow, as we have seen in Hardy's Tess and Joyce's Gretta Conroy, is the Undesired, the unwanted, yet cherished, child of First Love. It is born out of the degradation First Love must endure, in seeing its Love either sacrificed or condemned by the conventions of society. Joyce was not so much exempt from these conventions as determined to divest them of the mantle of *ultimate* spiritual authority. His renegade "subjectivism" was first confirmed in his youthful, profound contact with the genius of Ibsen.

As *Stephen Hero* makes clear, Joyce identified with the proper name, Ibsen, and not with the constellation of modern attitudes and social doctrines known as Ibsenism. The Ibsen of Ibsenism is the name that papal scribes consigned to the Index, the "atheistic" Ibsen of religious apostasy and cultural heresy. But the Ibsen of Joyce's unreconstructed romanticism is the inspiriting model of that "sincere and boylike bravery, of disillusioned pride, of minute and wilful energy" that transcends parochial controversies. It is the Ibsen of world-epochs, a name that epitomizes even as it transforms the spirit of his age. "Here," writes Joyce, "and not in Shakespeare or Goethe was the successor to the first poet of the Europeans, here, as only to such purpose in Dante, a human personality had been found united with an artistic manner which was itself almost a natural phenomenon: and the spirit of the time united one more readily with the Norwegian than with the Florentine."[11] Artistic consciousness, according to Joyce, partakes of and is accountable to the order of natural rather than social phenomena. It is only through the mediating agency of "the spirit of the age" that the heroic artist participates in the social and political controversies of the historical moment. Joyce's understanding of the relation between social being and artistic consciousness is most succinctly formulated in a memorable maxim from *Stephen Hero: Love gives and freedom takes.* The Love that gives and the Freedom that takes might unite inner disposition to outer circumstance, a union which, in social as in artistic life, would be realized in the complete reciprocity known as give-and-take.

Perhaps no critic has celebrated the apocalyptic originality and messianic charisma of Joyce's artistic manner with the wistfulness of Harold Bloom (who wittily acknowledges the oddity of one's writing an introduction to a volume of Joyce criticism on 16 June, particularly if one's name is Bloom). Commenting on the relationships figured in Stephen's interpretation of Hamlet, Bloom the critic praises Bloom the messiah:

> Stephen as the Prince does not convince me; Poldy as the ghost of the dead king, as Shakespeare/Joyce, is rather more troublesome. One wishes the ghost could be exorcised, leaving us with the fine trinity of Shakespeare/Poldy/Joyce, with Poldy as the transitional figure reconciling forerunner and latecomer, a sort of Messiah perhaps. Shakespeare is the original Testament or old aesthetic law, while Joyce is the belated Testament or

new aesthetic dispensation. Poldy is the inter-Testamentary figure, apoc-
ryphal and apocalyptic, and yet overwhelmingly a representation of life in
the here and now.[12]

The critic who dreams of the day literary critics "will learn to read not only
Hamlet and the Inferno as written by Joyce, but Don Quixote as well, with the
divine Sancho as an Irish Jew!" confesses a wish to exorcise the troublesome
ghost of the dead father in order to canonize this dream trinity: forerunner and
latecomer reconciled in the man of the here and now, through whom the future
plunges into the past.

Bloom's is indeed a fine trinity, but not an endearing one. It elides the
divine charity of works that manifest Love by incarnating it. The sacred texts
and saintly figures of Bloom's pantheon give to these incarnations feminine
forms and female names: Beatrice, Dulcinea, Molly. The endearing forms of
these literary bodies have no place in Bloom's testamentary model, which conforms to the dictates of what Lawrence understood as the gospel of male assertion. But, as we shall see, *Ulysses,* which begins by interpreting literature as a
displaced theological quest for an author-father, concludes with the "scripture"
foretold in Samuel Butler's interpretative fantasia—a female authorship of the
*Odyssey.* To use one of the words Bloom (Harold) has donated to our understanding of modern consciousness, the authoress of *Ulysses* reveals herself belatedly, in her retrospective rearrangement of the "old" and decidedly "male"
dispensation. But this only confirms my (female) assertion that First Love is a
modern invention, an imaginative and emotional solution to the crisis of belatedness, by which originality is recuperated by re-presenting the feelings of the
first time.

Crucially, Bloom omits in his admittedly brief synopsis of Stephen's artistic
theory the "novelistic" or life-affecting details of erotic entanglement that Stephen conscientiously includes in characterizing his cultural idols: "We have
shrewridden Shakespeare and henpecked Socrates. Even the allwise Stagyrite
was bitted, bridled and mounted by a light of love." Male assertion is humbled
in the encounter with Eros, which instructs the instructors in the limits of their
knowledge of and their power over life. We need only return to Stephen's "reading" of Shakespeare's artistic life to remind ourselves how his account is primarily a retelling of Shakespeare's life as the *new* life, the affective and aesthetic
dispensation inaugurated by First Love. In Stephen's critical biography, *Hamlet*
serves as the paradigmatic, but hardly the inaugural, occasion of Shakespeare's
new life. Stephen considers *Venus and Adonis* the text that symbolically reenacts

the birth of Shakespeare's artistic vocation, one that mythifies the Stratford wench as the tutelary goddess of Shakespeare's life-odyssey. What's in a name? Everything, to those skilled enough to read the signatures of all things. The figure who presides over Shakespeare's amatory and artistic destiny is Ann Hathaway. Her name is a prophetic admonition of the limits of the male Will, for according to Stephen's slightly abashed pun, "if others have their will, Ann hath a way." Ann, like Gretta Conroy, eludes the grasp of an irony that administers to—and secretly flatters—the masculine will to absolute self-mastery. By virtue of her being first in time, she retains the first place in the bard's troubled affections. Ann's pleasure in having her own sexual way, concludes Stephen, is the source of the obsessive motifs and the emotional ambivalences that riddle the tragedies and afflict the late romances: the figure of the adulterous queen-mother; the theme of the false, of the usurping or adulterous brother; the reunion with the lost child—Marina, child of storm; Miranda, a wonder; Perdita, the living symbol of the lost mother. "Will any man love the daughter if he has not loved the mother?" Stephen pointedly asks (161).

Ann not only has a way, she *is* the way, being all in all to Shakespeare: "She saw him into and out of the world. She took his first embraces. She bore his children and she laid pennies on his eyes to keep his eyelids closed when he lay on his deathbed" (156). To First Love and its embraces are attributed maieutic powers which extend throughout an entire life and culminate in the birth-unto-death. Earlier, in "Proteus," the chapter in which Stephen tries to fathom the materiality of artistic images, he contemplates the tidal rhythms of the sea, our great sweet mother and handmaid to the moon, as emblematic of the ineluctable cycles of human life. The sea, in a series of metonymic associations, is symbolically apprehended as the uterine "bed" of procreation: "Bridebed, childbed, bed of death, ghostcandled. Omni caro ad te veniet." All flesh emerges and returns to the "allwombing tomb"—the body of the Mother. Stephen articulates the entelechy of human desire in all its mutations and vicissitudes: First Love is the form of forms, whose first and decisive incarnation is *amor matris*, subjective and objective genitive, the one true thing in life.

Given the emotional succor and theoretical lucidity of this model, why does Stephen hesitate? Hesitate, that is, to authorize the identity-realizing power of First Love? Why does he seek an alternative model in the nonbiological institution of apostolic succession, even as he declares that for the man of genius it is his own image that provides "the standard of all experience, material and moral" (161)? The answer may be gleaned in Stephen's attempts to explain why Shakespeare, a lord of language and author of *Romeo and Juliet,* sent a lordling to woo for him: "Why? Belief in himself has been untimely killed. He was overborne in a cornfield first (a ryefield I should say) and he will never be a victor in his own eyes after nor play victoriously the game of laugh and lie down. Assumed dongiovannism will not save him. No later undoing will undo the first undoing" (161). For Stephen, superb dialectician and well-schooled Aristotelian, the fatefulness of the first time is incontrovertible and irreversible. No later undoing will undo the first undoing. The aesthetic triumphs or sexual "victories" of his subsequent life will be but imaginative ruses "to hide him from himself." For the lord of language, victory can assume only one existential and economic form: to make loss his gain. The artist cannot renege on his debts to the first time and its life-determining consequences. He may not, like Don Giovanni, compose lists in a vain attempt to account for his irregular erotic commerce with women. The rock of Joycean realism is founded on a concrete acknowledgment of the first undoing and its legacy of debts and obligations. The recognition and discharging of these sexual debts is the formative act of the "heroic naturalism"[13] that Joyce shares with Wordsworth, our main poet of first affections.

## THE ART OF THE ORDINARY

We might begin to examine how Joyce's heroic naturalism is dependent on the myth of First Love by recalling the erotic maxim that characterizes the sexual and affective life of Joyce's modern "characters": "With all the talk of the world about it people make its only the first time after that is just the ordinary do it and think no more about it." We should immediately recognize the idiosyncratic but observant naturalism of Molly, who, as we shall see, is not only the Muse, but the primary "authoress" of Joyce's modern odyssey. In the ordinariness she both satirizes and desires, we find the scandal of *Ulysses* epitomized. The critical heritage of *Ulysses* is organized around this fascination with the "ultimate" significance of this ordinary day. For T. S. Eliot, the day was epochal by virtue of Joyce's "mythic method," which, "by manipulating a continuous parallel between antiquity and contemporaneity," made "the modern world possible for art."[14] For Lawrence, it was a day often wasted in observation of trivial, even brutish sensation: " 'Did I feel a twinge in my little toe, or didn't I?' asks every character of Mr. Joyce."[15] But the testamentary vocation of *Ulysses* as simultaneously a realistic and a messianic text may actually consort with what Cynthia Ozick deems the fundamental disposition of art in "first noticing, and then sanctifying the Ordinary." "Art," she maintains, "is making the Ordinary into the Extraordinary. It is the impairment of the distinction between the Ordinary and the Extraordinary." This impairment of the distinction between ordinary and extraordinary yields a new understanding of time in its more benign manifestation as "what is expected":

> The Ordinary lets us live out our humanity; it doesn't scare us, it doesn't excite us, it doesn't distract us—it brings us the safe return of the school bus every day, it lets us eat one meal after another, put one foot in front of the other. In short, it is equal to the earth's provisions; it grants us life, continuity, the leisure to recognize who and what we are, and who and what our fellows are, these creatures who live out their everydayness side by side with us in their own unextraordinary ways. Ordinariness can be defined as a breathing-space: the breathing-space between getting born and dying, perhaps; or else the breathing-space between rapture and rapture; or, more usually, the breathing-space between one disaster and the next.[16]

When we credit the novel with being concerned with "ordinary" life or ordinary men and women, surely it is in the sense Ozick defines. The novel, in its expansiveness, typically grants us the leisure as well as the breadth of observation necessary to recognize who and what we are, who and what our fellow creatures might be. The naturalism of *Ulysses,* a text fanatically devoted to tracking down who, what and where everyone might be in Dublin on 16 June, evinces this respect for the ordinary as the breathing-space between rapture and rapture, or one disaster and the next.

Moreover, the novel, which represents the complex natural and social *ecology* of human life, is the literary form best suited, indeed generically obligated, to examine how we succeed or fail in living according to the earth's provisions. Those who hold to the morality of supply-side economics have never read novels. In the novel's complex economy, human demand, in both the economic and the Lacanian sense, is constantly forced to adjust to fluctuations in the "supply" of social provisions (happiness, work, status) or historical opportunities (peace, war, scientific discoveries, the creation of new markets, etc.). A vision of how this economy determines the ordinary existence of particular men and women is what, in fact, the novel may be said to provide. First love is an exemplary instance of this novelistic movement through the world of everydayness precisely because it impairs the distinction between the ordinariness of human mating—by which, of course, society ensures its own continuance—and the extraordinary resonance of the first time. It provides us with the extraordinary occasion on which it is possible for freedom to be wrested out of necessity. Or, failing that, the novel will set to work in showing us how necessity, *what is to be expected,* can be seen as the ordinary, the appropriate and designated, domain in which our freedom is to be found.

Ordinariness can quickly collapse, however, into triviality, the "heaviness" of life of which Lukács so eloquently speaks in attributing the "metaphysics" of the novel to the modern feeling of transcendental homelessness. In the course of its wanderings, the heart, burdened by feeling too far from heaven and too close to the earth, constricts. A kind of narrative angina sets in for the characters and indeed for many readers of *Ulysses.* The expansive dilations of the sympathetic heart contract under the sheer weight of contingent, "realistic" detail that threatens to obscure the lucid trajectory of the novel's Odyssean paradigm: exile, wandering, and return. Such anxiety attacks indicate, even as they diagnose, a dwindling capacity to draw inspiration in dailiness. In such moments, the ordinary does not dispense the blessing of the expected. Rather, as Lukács notes, it enforces our imaginative bondage to the "sheer brutal materiality" of a purely contingent existence.[17] For Bloom, the innate heaviness of life, which augurs the shared destiny of all earthly bodies, is a matter of simple demonstration: "Law of falling bodies: per second per pecond. They all fall to the ground. The earth. Its the force of gravity of the earth is the weight" (59). A sauntering female form soon distracts or lightens this somewhat homely phenomenology. Fortunately, Eros and Physis are not on a collision course, but on a parallactic course. They will eventually unite in the celebrated identification of Molly with Gea-Tellus.

But that mythic confluence of erotic and terrestrial motion is achieved only in the *nostos* of "Ithaca," where all wandering and falling are subsumed into the diurnal rotation of earthly bodies. Bloom's beginnings are rather distanced from this restitutive end. "Calypso" introduces to us a "hero" rather complacently observant of the sexual and social regime of his ordinary but alienated life. Still, a rather extraordinary consciousness of the mythic analogues to his routine bondage accompanies Bloom as he hurries out to fetch pork kidneys for his morning meal—the first of many mundane errands that will consume his day. During this tentative sally, preparatory to his exilic departure from 7 Eccles Street, Bloom glimpses a prospectus for Agendath Netaim, planters' company, soliciting funds for the cultivation of orange plantations in Turkey. As a commercial sign, this ad disseminates the fiction that colonialism represents a civilizing infusion of Western capital and technology into less advanced—or economically depleted—Eastern nations. But Joyce makes clear that this commercial venture attracts Bloom's notice as an ideological rather than economic investment, whose inducement is the ecological promise of reclamation and reforestation of a barren land.

For Bloom, toiling in the enforced labor of the diaspora, this appeal to reclaim the wasteland is rightly perceived as a mirage, but one against whose ideological horizons he might yet glimpse a forsaken but still attainable destiny. Bloom, as suspicious of as he is susceptible to utopian fantasy, good-naturedly demurs: "Nothing doing. Still an idea behind it." Bloom's imagination is salvational, but not millenarian. He can only build a new world out of the old by salvaging the detritus of modern commercial life—its "throwaway" literature of propaganda posters, ads, ambulatory signs, and leaflets—and reassigning to them their original symbolic value as motivating, as well as motivated, cultural icons. Agendath Netaim, north of the melon fields of Jaffa, prototype of the promised land, of Flowerville, of the New Bloomusalem, will find its ordinary, if eccentric incarnation in Bloom's glimpse of the melon fields—Molly's backside.

Yet this symbolic condensation of the utopian signifiers for a redeemed homeland in the contours of Molly's buttocks completes rather than institutes the novel's own ideological refashioning of a "natural" and thoroughly human environment. Moreover, as Molly justly complains, Bloom projects his utopian dream on the one feature of the woman's body that allows him to forget her individuality—the woman's bottom "where we havent 1 atom of any kind of expression in us all of us the same 2 lumps of lard" (639). Bloom conveniently images "all habitable lands and islands explored or unexplored (the land of the midnight sun, the islands of the blessed, the island of Greece, the land of promise)" on the one bodily site "insusceptible of moods of impression or of contrarieties of expression" (604)—that is, the one bodily feature from which all signs of female expression and female demand are effaced.

Molly is right to protest the use of her body as the mute signifier of male desire. In Bloom's defense, he is understandably weary ("He rests. He has travelled") when he has his "tentative revelation" of Molly's plump melonous hemispheres "redolent of milk and honey." Earlier in the day, less tired and more alert, he entertains a more skeptical attitude toward his sexualized utopian fantasies. Agendath Netaim has lulled him into a soul-comforting reverie about the divine dispensation that rules the world and provides us with our daily bread "on earth as it is in heaven." But as a cloud eclipses the sun, his mind reverts to more demystified images of his homeland:

No, not like that. A barren land, bare waste. Vulcanic lake, the dead sea: no fish, weedless, sunk deep in the earth. No wind could lift the waves, grey metal, poisonous foggy waters. Brimstone they called it raining down: the cities of the plain: Sodom, Gomorrah, Edom. All dead names. A dead sea in a dead land, grey and old. Old now. It bore the oldest, the first race. A bent hag crossed from Cassidy's, clutching a naggin bottle by the neck. The oldest people. Wandered far away over all the earth, captivity to captivity, multiplying, dying, being born everywhere. It lay there now. Now it could bear no more. Dead: an old woman's: the grey sunken cunt of the world.

Desolation. (50)

Bloom's metaphysical skepticism quickly devolves into a grave mood of unqualified, unrelenting negativity that interferes with his customary, "ordinary" delight in the concrete richness of daily existence. Present reality intrudes in the unlovely, unassuring form of a bent hag, whose crossing back from Cassidy's is tracked as a mythical exodus back to "the grey sunken cunt of the world." An aged female body weighed down by the accumulated miseries of a personal (and unknowable) past becomes the ambulatory emblem of the general historical collapse of the "omphalos," locus of racial myths of origination. Through this emblematic representation, history is endowed with the force of gravity. Time comes to denote not only a measurement of movement, but the weight the ordinary days and years of human life amass in their passage. Time is weighty enough to reduce even the cyclic patterns of generation—being born and dying—to a demoralizing redundancy: captivity to captivity. In this redundancy we can apprehend the inveterate "drag" of a soulless realism that projects the brute materiality of the world. This grave vision of historical entropy exerts an inertial pull on Bloom's vital perceptions, which become bogged down in the morass of a single word: desolation.

Desolation is the linguistic precipitate of an entropic vision of history. Its semantic density is sufficient to warrant a paragraph to itself. In its etymological sedimentation, Joyce excavates the double sense of modern desolation as both a cultural devastation and a psychological isolation. There is no distinction in being first in a desolate land, where one feels oneself to be solus. Nor is the mythical origin of the world, its first place, exempt from this vastation. With the gods' desertion, the omphalos becomes the "grey sunken cunt of the world," blasted and infertile, at once a travesty and a reproach to the male dream of replenishing the world with his imaginative provisions, the seeds of his creative labors. With his reliable genius for correlating psychological mood with narrative event, Joyce shows us Bloom at the start of his day obsessed with the lore of lost or wasted beginnings rather than entranced and motivated by a dream of desired ends.

Bloom's depression issues out of his awareness of his own belatedness as a latecomer in an irreversible human diaspora. He is mystified by the atavistic ethos of epic, which, as Bakhtin has remarked, celebrates the prestige of first or "peak" times and founding fathers.[18] Here the novel's Homeric infrastructure, represented in this instance by the most reified of epic elements—the catalogue (specifically designated as a catalogue of dead names)—mimics the architechtonics of the mausoleum. Even the most purely conventional evocations of these dead but mighty names is sufficient to blight whatever hopes Bloom may modestly entertain as heir to the heroic tradition, the tradition not of war and plunder, but of Odyssean migration and Quixotic revivalism. He struggles throughout the day to preserve a more novelistic consciousness of the here and now, of time as the medium of becoming and history as a breathing-space to be filled with more ordinary expectations of what he, as a good, an all-round man, is reasonably due.

What restores Bloom's spiritual buoyancy is the summons of recall to a female domain. Bloom, keen on a more reinvigorating regimen, vows to resume Sandow's exercises, and hurries home, seeking company: "Be near her ample bedwarmed flesh. Yes, Yes." *Yes,* of course, is Molly's word, her spiritual signature. "Yes. Yes" is not an emphatic redundancy, but a motivated repetition, comprehending at once affirmation and assent. This affirming and renewing repetition encapsulates the stately plump entelechy of *Ulysses* itself as the triumphant assertion of the artistic will over what T. S. Eliot called "the immense panorama of futility and anarchy which is contemporary history."[19] Affirmation is the expressive gesture of the spirit, but only the will can assent or demur in the ongoing creation of the world.

In Molly's lexicon, *Yes* corresponds, says Joyce in his famous letter to Budgen, to the cunt, the bodily point of male entry and female *jouissance.*[20] Philippe Sollers has remarked on the curious sexual politics of this identification. The curiosity consists in the conventional supposition that this *Yes* represents an authentic female utterance recorded, as it were, rather than imagined, by a male writer. For Sollers, then, *Yes* is Joyce's countersign to the imputed impossibility of a male writing of a female *monologue intérieur,* an impossibility incarnated in his wife's proper name: NOra.[21]

But we should also remark how, in the Joycean lexicon, the female word of affirmation is also performative, her gesture of reply. In *Portrait* Stephen felt summoned by the world's "spell of arms and voices, white arms of roads, their promise of close embraces . . . held out to say: we are alone, Come." But this anthropomorphic vision of the world as the site of unimaginable intimacies belongs to "exultant and terrible youth." The novel—and that, after all, is Stephen's "world"—is, as Lukács insists, the art form of virile maturity. The novel reveals the enchantments of romance as the seductions of a siren song, with its delusive compensations for our transcendental homelessness. Joycean *nostos* images an immanent homeland—a woman's recumbent body, symbolic of the earth's provisions that beckon the artist with the seductive promise: "We are alone, Come."

*Yes,* then, is first of all an answer to this summons, an affirmative reply to the call of nature and the first injunction of Genesis—Be fruitful and multiply. What riddle is more ordinary than the riddle of what makes us say, as Molly does, yes, as well him as another? That makes us choose the first time from so many available times, and select the one from the many to whom we might respond in kind? How many extraordinary answers to that question has the novel, in the course of its history, offered us? Molly's pragmatic view of sex— "do it and think no more about it"—is actually a utopian prescription that would signal the end of narrative in any ordinary sense of that term. *Ulysses* ends with such a moment, which remains, despite any critical attempts at de-mystification, as the most "gratifying" closure in modern narrative. Molly's *Yes* gratifies not because it represents an obstacle overcome or an impossibility denied, but because it voices an answer immanent, and hence always repeatable, in human experience. Her concluding *Yes* is the sustained grace note of sexual excitation in which the reminiscence of the first time and the anticipation of the next time are fatefully suspended. Molly's last word, a repetition of her first words, gives her "coda" the appearance of an overture. In Molly's chosen moment of closure without foreclosure, talk could abate and words might cease in the blessed "ordinariness" of sexual exchange.

The grammar that governs the expression of this creative exchange is disclosed in "Ithaca." The catechizer obligingly, if somewhat academically, parses for us the first entelechy in relating how Bloom, as a "conscious reactor against the void of incertitude," justifies his own personal sentiments regarding "every natural act . . . executed in natured nature by natural creatures in accordance with his, her and their natured natures, of dissimilar similarity": "the natural grammatical transition by inversion involving no alteration of sense of an aorist preterite proposition (parsed as masculine subject, monosyllabic onomatopoeic transitive verb with direct feminine object) from the active voice into its correlative aorist preterite proposition (parsed as feminine subject, auxiliary verb and quasimonosyllabic onomatopoetic past participle with complementary masculine agent) in the passive voice" (604). Any practicing critic of narrative for whom "character" is reducible to its assigned role as narrative agent might envy the catechizer's virtuosity in depicting character—indeed gender itself— as a sublimation of sexual agency. Others of less theoretical, more empirical, even licentious, disposition might urge, like Molly, "Tell us in plain words." So we might comply by translating the natural act as "He fucked her; she was fucked by him."

Actuality, the grace of entelechy, here suffers no ultimate loss of sense, should we be willing to perform the necessary translation into the plain Saxon idiom. Indeed, Fritz Zenn, commenting on the "righting" of *Ulysses,* advises that we should think less about the "signified" of conjugal sex and more about the signifier in its work of conjugation:

> Joyce elaborately and deviously works in the conjugation of a verb around which some of the offstage action of *Ulysses* turns. From hints such as these many critics have concentrated, perhaps rightly, on conjugal relations and, perhaps less rightly, on conjugal imperatives. Here the emphasis is on conjugation itself, one of many names for a dynamic process. *Ulysses* refuses to stay put. Once we know what it *is* we are sure to be wrong.[22]

Zenn would like to translate the discussion of the "natured nature" of human conjugation out of the realm of cognitive and ethical controversy—what are the rights and wrongs of conjugal relations?—into a purely verbal realm where the vexations of determining reality and ascribing value are dissolved in the "dynamic process" of narrative signification. This translation would be fine if we could in good faith ignore the time-determining agency of the aorist, which, as grammarians, we cannot in good conscience do. The aorist preterite specifies an action without indicating whether that action is completed, continued, or repeated. It designates the past in its aspect as an open and ongoing time which encroaches on the present moment. This temporal indeterminacy directs the course of Bloom's nocturnal reflection on the "natured nature" of sexual inter- course. Bloom begins by acknowledging "the preordained frangibility of the hymen" and concludes by contemplating "the futility of triumph or protest or vindication: the inanity of extolled virtue: the lethargy of nescient matter: the apathy of the stars" (604). The first time, symbolized by the preordained fran- gibility of the hymen, leads, ineluctably it would seem, to a cosmological as well as ethical anomie. "Natured nature"—the "continued product of seminators by generation"—persists, comically eluding any regulation by ethical codes, unmindful of the apathy of the stars. Sex is the one dynamic process that insists, contrary to Zenn, on what it *is*. We would be foolish, if not wrong, to refuse natured nature its *ordinary* rights, rights which are quite different from the rules of verbal conjugation. It is, then, the voice of natured nature that speaks in Molly's monologue, a voice cheerfully, willfully amoral and nonmetaphysical in regarding the first time as "more than inevitable, irreparable" (603). The tense of First Love is the aorist preterite, the tense that corresponds to our sense that the feelings of First Love are never definitely experienced, but persist in our present consciousness.

The first sexual conjugation, then, is the definitive one. After the irreparability of the first time, and only after, may conjugation, in Zenn's sense, be said to commence. After the first conjugation, as Molly puts it, one can play, repeat, transgress at will and, if one chooses, think no more about it. Molly's fond attachment to that initial conjugation helps explain the otherwise notorious discrepancy between her stated preference for deed over word and her loquacious monologue. Molly, it appears, inveterately talks about nothing but the world as the domain of sexual advertisement and display. It is the organizing "topic" of her monologue, through which the "ordinariness" of her life makes itself sensible, if not intelligible, to her. But it is also her topic in the sense that Vico intends when he reminds us that "topics have the function of making minds inventive, as criticism has of making them exact."[23] We will later consider Molly's exacting criticism of the first time, but now we might applaud the inventiveness that allows her to pursue the fugitive image of her First Lover, Mulvey, through all his subsequent incarnations, from the imaginary Miguel della Flores (whom she invents) to the inimitable Master Poldy (whom she loves). Without the first time there is no topic, no extraordinary inception of a life-chronicle (and, needless to say, no subject for nocturnal reminiscences on the rights and imperatives of conjugal relations). In Joyce's terms: no entelechy; no transformation of potentiality into actuality, of word into deed, of speech into action.

Hence the significance of the Joycean quest for the "first entelechy," the form of forms that endows the Word with the material agency of Deed. In "Circe," Stephen proposes that the "first entelechy" is constituted by human "gesture." Gesture, he hazards, "not music, not odour, [is] a universal language, the gift of tongues rendering visible not the lay sense but the first entelechy, the structural rhythm" (353). "Circe" itself opens by activating mute gesture into a structural rhythm of call and answer.

*The Call*

Wait, my love, and I'll be with you.

*The Answer*

Round behind the stable.

(A deafmute idiot with goggle eyes, his shapeless mouth dribbling, jerks past, shaken in Saint Vitus' dance. A chain of children's hands imprisons him.) [350]

In the domain of "Circe," which is ruled by dreams and runs by contraries, the structural rhythm reverts to an atavistic model: the brute animality of sexual exchange. Atavistic, too, is the personification of gesture, by which words not only signify but enact their "meaning." Masculine and feminine cannot be parsed except as active or passive agencies of libidinal conjugations. The human figures of this opening tableau attest to this de-individualizing, dehumanizing play of entelechy, just as the deaf-mute proleptically makes a mockery of Stephen's pentecostal ideal. The mute is bereft of the gift of tongues. Not only is he incapable of sending or receiving signals, but he is afflicted by the locomotor ataxia that seems the specific syndrome of the city dweller and of the urban body politic. In the face of this psychotic reversion, gestures speak for themselves, or rather, call and answer to themselves. Love loves to love love, as the derisive refrain from "Cyclops" puts it.

"Come up, Kinch, come up you fearful Jesuit," parodically anticipates the entelechy of call and answer. Buck, of course, is mocking Stephen's renunciation of a religious for an aesthetic vocation, but the deeper blasphemy is directed against the "idea" of Stephen's accession to manhood. If Stephen is symbolically assigned the narrative role of heir, an essential part of his birthright is to develop into a mature sexual and "civil" body endowed with inalienable sexual and political dignities and rights. As Joyce wrote to Carlo Linati, he conceived of each adventure as "so to say one person although it is composed of persons— as Aquinas relates of the angelic hosts." [24] The person of "Telemachus" is, we might say, an unembodied one. This is suggested in the schema, which assigns no bodily organ to its initial three chapters. That Stephen can only reply to Buck in mute resentment is due less to his sullen grievances against the usurper who steals from him the provisions of his life than to his general anomie as an indeterminate body. The "Telemachiad" presents its hero in utero—all potentiality, yet to be fully embodied. He must be "summoned" into life, as language is coaxed into articulation in "Oxen of the Sun," by the midwife's cry: "Hoopsa! Hoopsa! Hoopsa, boy!" Stephen, if he is to experience his symbolic birth, must respond to the maieutic cry of First Love, whose beckonings he has so far resisted, fearing them to be the seductions of a siren, rather than the solicitations of the life-conferring mother-midwife-wife.

## THE GRACE OF ALACRITY

*Ulysses* separates its men from its boys, its fathers from its sons, according to a specific criterion: promptness in answering the female summons of recall. There is nothing innately moral about this discrimination, since errant as well as steadfast men may reply. What Joyce first opposes in his representations of modern Dublin life is not errant or aberrant action, but moral paralysis. When Simon Dedalus, delinquent father, requests a drink, the sweet siren is prompt to provide—"With the greatest alacrity, miss douce agreed":

> With grace of alacrity toward the mirror gilt Cantrell and Cochrane's she turned herself. With grace she tapped a measure of gold whisky from her crystal keg. Forth from the skirt of his coat Mr Dedalus brought pouch and pipe. Alacrity she served. He blew through the flue two husky fifenotes. (215)

The grace of alacrity is diffused, as we would expect in Joyce, through the sexual panoply of Miss Douce's crystal keg and Dedalus's musical pipe. But it primarily manifests itself in the female's prompt ministrations, which enlivens (*alacer*—"to make lively") all that comes within her reach. That this signaling of call and answer occurs in "Sirens" further complicates the matter. We thus know this entelechy to be misplaced and divagatory, an enticement to sexual wandering that might not just postpone, but end, all thoughts of return.

In assimilating musical models to his linguistic notations, Joyce departed, as he wrote to a mystified Harriet Weaver, from the book's "initial style." Hence the formal fatefulness of its fugal form, by which Joyce expressed not only the affective impulse but the constituent form and language of sexual flight. In 1922 Ezra Pound situated *Ulysses* among "that large class of novels in sonata form, that is to say, in the form: theme, counter-theme, recapitulation, development, finale."[25] But "Sirens" suggests that Joyce arranged, albeit retrospectively, the diverse motifs of this chapter and the work as a whole according to a more "novelistic" or "dialogic" musical patterning—the fugue. The structure of the fugue accords with the novelistic ethos of multivoiced narration, competing or cooperating "subjects" insistent on their own expressiveness but bound by the rules of imitative and interactive counterpoint. These rules are fairly strict, which would seem, although only at first consideration, to distance them from the cacophony known as life. Yet as an emotive form and certainly as an expressive register, the fugue provides Joyce with an existential metaphor for sexual flight and erotic dalliance. The fugal form also discloses the structural rhythm of human exchange, which, up to this point, has been intoned primarily in the minor key of desolation.

As Roland Barthes proposed in *S/Z,* the form of the fugue shares a demonstrable affinity with the novelistic "scoring" of those "enigmas" whose formal articulation, suspended disclosure, and delayed resolution constitute the "hermeneutism" of narrative. "The development of an enigma," writes Barthes, "is really like that of a fugue; both contain a *subject,* subject to *exposition,* a *development* (embodied in retards, ambiguities, and diversions by which the discourse prolongs the mystery), a *stretto* (a tightened section where scraps of answers come and go) and a conclusion."[26] But fugal, like novelistic, development is capable of even more complicated modulations than Barthes' summary indicates. The "Voice of Truth" appears in the fugue as multivalent and dialogic. At its inception, a short theme called the subject is presented by the first voice, which is subsequently repeated by the second voice. This reprise is designated as an answer. Here we can detect how fugal "repetition with a difference" is isomorphic with the gestural rhythm of call and answer. The fugal rhythm imitates, then, the movement from univocalism to multivocalism, from "simple" melody to complex counterpoint. As if to deepen the enigma of its own flight toward the "truth" achieved through counterpoint, a third voice is normally introduced into the fugue, which repeats the melodic subject in a higher or lower register of the octave. Within this elaborate structure of imitative counterpoint and counterstatement, the fugue also allows for musical interludes called epidodes, which may further vary and transform the initial subject through "augmentation or diminution (lengthening or shortening of the note value), inversion (be turned upside down), or stretto (to be taken up so quickly by the different voices that answer overlaps subject)."[27]

The narrative and musical significance of the episode is formally thematized in "Sirens" as a complex exchange of calls and answers. In this chapter devoted to the erotic escapism that characterizes the libidinal life of modern Dublin, we can once again observe and respect the difference between the providential import of First Love as a spirit-manifesting occasion and the inconsequential vagaries of those sexual episodes that interrupt or divert the course of a fateful love. The episode in question involves Molly's adultery, a question posed by the accidental convergence of Bloom, who strays in fantasy, and Boylan, with whom Molly actually strays, at the Ormand Bar. Narratively, the convergence never attains the status of a dramatic encounter. Rather it languishes, as the languorous alliterative language of the chapter indicates, as a sexual interlude in a day that is moving toward more violent confrontations in "Cyclops" and "Circe," the areas, respectively, of discreditable male heroics and disreputable female sexuality. "Cyclops" is set in the all-male society of Barney Kiernan's pub, the site of incendiary nationalism and patriarchal politics. The setting of "Circe" is the brothel where the frenzied sexuality of the megalopolis is represented as a female version of Pandemonium—the "Womancity." But Ormand's is the space of "interlude" in which sex is granted a temporary reprieve from monstrous and promiscuous politics.

Yet this does not necessarily mean that "Sirens" is purely an escapist episode. For it is here, in the deliberate rests from the civic and domestic turmoil of modern life, that the submerged semitones of Dublin's erotic culture find a hearing. The sensible Bloom is the most sensitive to their sad burden. Disheartened as he is embarrassed by the presence of Boylan, he reacts to Richie Goulding's rendition of "All is lost" in painfully personal terms: "Taking my motives he twined and turned them. All most too new call is lost in all. Echo. How sweet the answer. How is that done? All is lost now. Mournful he whistled. Fall, surrender, lost" (224). Aware that both his motives and his wife have been taken from him, Bloom poignantly wonders, "How is that done?" The answer to that question will be found in Molly's sustained and sustaining coda. Bloom in this moment is simply, touchingly resigned: "Order. Yes, I remember. Lovely air. In sleep she went to him. Innocence in the moon. Brave. Don't know their danger. Still hold her back. Call name. Touch water. Jingle jaunty. Too late. She longed to go. That's why. Woman. As easy stop the sea. Yes: all is lost" (224). Molly's eagerness in signaling her sexual consent is endowed with all the foolhardy bravery of a natural phenomenon: ignorant of danger, she longs for new departures, her will as unstoppable as the sea's. Bloom's *Yes,* which anticipates Molly's affirming assent, renders the grace of female alacrity suspect. Here we observe Bloom in one of his moods of *unheroic* naturalism, ceding to things as they are the inexorability of natural phenomena that cannot be stopped or changed. The "Order" that Bloom evokes through this memory is not a human creation but the order of "natured nature."

Bloom's lapse into marital quietism is soon dispelled, however, by a new, reorienting strain of song: "The harping chords of a prelude . . . a chord, long-drawn, expectant, drew a voice away." It is Simon Dedalus's voice singing now, the voice of the derelict father who signals all the lost sons of Dublin the way back to a *first* time in which all is still to be made and nothing is yet lost:

*—When first I saw that form endearing . . .*

The affective counterpoint of this song deftly intermingles the two strains of human song—the modern melody of loss, the ancient rhapsody of love at first sight: "When first I saw that form endearing / Sorrow seemed from me to depart."

Stephen might object, nay madame, I know not seems. But against his Hamletian skepticism (and heartsickness) I would reply that the grace of alacrity is only to be found in the "seemliness" of First Love, at once a decorous and fitting consolation for our modern sorrow. This seemliness Bloom, the spiritual father, emphatically affirms:

> Good, good to hear: sorrow from them each seemed to from both depart when first they heard. When first they saw, lost Richie Poldy, mercy of beauty, heard from a person wouldn't expect it in the least, her first merciful lovesoft oftloved word.
>
> Love that is singing: love's old sweet song. (225)

Both the beauty and mercy of First Love reverberate in this resumption of love's old sweet song. First Love, foolish but brave, repeats the oft-loved word *seemingly* for the first time. In this moment, love, the word known to all men, sings its old sweet song as if it were infinitely citable in all its moments in the past, the present, and the new life to come.

To Bloom, interested auditor of the seductive strains of this song, Love discloses to him the fatefulness of the first time: "First I saw. She thanked me. Why did she me? Fate. Spanishy eyes. Under a peartree alone patio this hour in old Madrid one side in shadow Dolores shedolores. At me. Luring. Ah, alluring" (226). Though it is Bloom who first saw, it is Molly who first sang, singling Bloom out, luring him on to ask her to say yes. Molly entices Bloom with the promise of an absolute Fate, "One love. One hope." It is this hope that the air from "Martha"—"Come thou lost one . . . "revives—revives, of course, as a siren song, since Bloom is lured by the false hope of a false object, Martha, the new love who can never replace his one love, Molly. Though advised to "beware of imitations," he cannot resist, as yet, the siren call, "Come to me . . ." In the "high vast irradiation" of this musical ascent into the "high . . . effulgence symbolistic . . . of the etherial bosom," Bloom believes that omnipresent, soaring Eros has at last found him out as the transcendental goal and object of its sustained flight: "[Come] . . . to me! Siopold! Consumed." Having predicated himself as the object of this erotic and musical conjugation, Bloom then can postulate the "naturalness" of all subsequent conjugations: "All clapped. She ought to. Come. To me, to him, to her, you too, me, us" (227). This transfigured and transfiguring cry is sung or spoken, one can hardly tell, by the first entelechy of gesture, beckoning "Come to me."

Bloom, of course, realizes that he is being carried away in the idiomatic and figurative sense of that phrase. He knows that he is not the first term nor the last of all-conjugating Eros. He is quite aware of the empirical ground of these celestial soundings and even gives it a name—Musemathematics: "And you think you're listening to the etherial. But suppose you said it like: Martha, seven times nine minus x is thirtyfive thousand. Fall quite flat. It's on account of the sounds it is" (228). Musemathematics is the science of articulated sound. But while this science can analyze the material production of music, it falls quite flat in solving the riddle of the ordinary song—whence does it derive its power to move the soul to transcendent heights of extraordinary feeling? Musemathematics can analyze but never affirm, as Molly can, love as universal gesture.

For Molly, this gesture comes "naturally." Her words, like the sea, compose a liquid unity which dispenses with ordinary punctuation in the tidal flow from desire to utterance. Bloom finds the first entelechy of call and answer more difficult to perform. In thinking of his correspondence with Martha, Bloom inwardly determines to "Ask her no answ." Semantically, as typographically, Bloom forestalls the possibility of an answer by asking Martha a nonquestion. His adventure in sexual dalliance is thus fated to conclude in erotic and narrative impasse. Bloom, assessing his own stumbling efforts to delay responding to Martha's sexual alacrity, wisely admits his own folly: "It is true. Folly am I writing" (229). There is no *flow* in his utterance. Male assertion ("It is true") is sundered from its semantic and utopian function as affirmation.

It is Molly's coda, with its inventive and hilarious stretto of erotic motifs, that rescues the language of love from the folly of male writing, which asserts, but cannot affirm. As Sollers begrudgingly observes: " 'I am the flesh that eternally affirms' is Molly's password, an inversion of the Faustian 'I am the Spirit who always denies.' "²⁸ Molly, of course, is the silent object and desired end of the novel's attempts to conjugate and affirm the fatefulness of the first time. Her silence throughout the long Ulyssean day constitutes the actual "scandal" perpetrated by the novel's intrinsic politics of male assertion. Her voice muted throughout the narrative, Molly "speaks" in the early morning hours that follow the exhausting and futile travails of male odyssey. At last the heroine is heard, ending the scandal of her muteness and, more important, restoring to *Ulysses* the cadences of a more "natural" speech.

Viewed in this light, the narrative progress from "Telemachus" (young narrative) to "Eumeus" (mature narrative) and "Ithaca," where male assertiveness achieves its most systematic and encyclopedic expression, recounts the history of patriarchal discourse as an estrangement from "natural relations." "Penelope" is the coda that returns to the first principles of human speech and its symbolic institutions by reinstituting the entelechy of call and answer. The difference between Bloom's "no answ[er]" and Molly's "The answer is yes" marks the truly radical difference between a male discourse propagating the "symbolic" law of the prohibitive father, and a female discourse of "imaginary" reciprocity which originates in the figure of the responsive and ministering mother. In *A Lover's Discourse,* Barthes recognizes "No Answer" as one of the more desolate "figures" (which Barthes understands and deploys in its original sense as "the body's gesture caught in action" rather than an inert and abstract rhetorical trope) in the image-repertoire of amorous discourse: "The gratifying Mother shows me the Mirror, the Image, and says to me: 'That's you.' But the silent Mother does not tell me what I am: I am no longer established, I drift painfully, without existence." [29] In Molly's amorous discourse, *Ulysses* averts the desolation of drifting painfully, without existence. Stephen's Wildean epigram associating Irish art with the cracked looking-glass of a servant, we should appreciate by now, is an image resonant of an earlier infantile dependency, one more positively figured in the child seeking a mirror in the attentive mother. It remains for Molly, mute throughout the day, to reintegrate that shattered maternal mirror which alone confers identity, integrity, and direction to the "lost" and dissociated soul of modernity. It is she, novelistic genius and not silent Muse, who teaches us the gift and grace of tongues in her maternal lullaby—love's old sweet song.

Her idiosyncratic rendition of love's old sweet song is the "clou" of the book, as Joyce insisted to Budgen.[30] It is at once the nail that rivets the book into place and the "feature attraction" (as the colloquial sense of "clou" implies) for which the novel has longed. Her "coda" puts an end to the "flight" from nature and from social reality that is *Ulysses* up to her monologue. But it is also the prelude to a fugal dialogism by which the novel, harmonizing the human voice with the music of natured nature, may properly be said to fulfill its mission of being equal to the earth's provisions. It is she who realizes Bloom's dream of a life fitting for men and women—"I mean Love, the opposite of hatred." Molly, Dublin's chanteuse, is the body swayed to the music of Love's old sweet song and its oft-loved words. In this Yeatsian rhapsody who cares— or dares—to distinguish the singer from the song?

## THE AUTHORESS OF ULYSSES

To "induce Stephen to deduce that originality, though producing its own reward, does not invariably conduce to success," Bloom adduces a peculiarly droll example of the kind of carnival entertainment he would provide in the New Bloomusalem he had fantasized in "Circe": "an illuminated showcart, drawn by a beast of burden, in which two smartly dressed girls were to be seated engaged in writing" (560). Originality can be envisioned, and, one might adduce, the originality of *Ulysses* can be proved, only in the spectacle of female writing.

As we might expect, Stephen and Bloom conjure up two completely different scenes of female authorship. Bloom, even though he realizes that all tales of circus life are demoralizing, imagines, according to the gregarious impulses of his own nature, writing as a festive activity. His authoress is subject to public display, her writing an occasion for communal entertainment. Stephen, the *isolato,* stages the scene of writing as a romantic closet drama:

> Solitary hotel in mountain pass. Autumn. Twilight. Fire lit. In dark corner young man seated. Young woman enters. Restless. Solitary. She sits. She goes to window. She stands. She sits. Twilight. She thinks. On solitary hotel paper she writes. She thinks. She writes. She sighs. Wheels and hoofs. She hurries out. He comes from his dark corner. He seizes solitary paper. He holds it towards fire. Twilight. He reads. Solitary. (560)

The high Romantic "demon" of solitariness, the affective legacy of Stephen's youthful Byronism, invests this scene redolent of sexual intrigue and betrayal with its telltale mood of desolation. Stephen's desolation, unlike Bloom's, is not an emotional reaction to historical entropy. It is a desolation wrought by figuring woman as the abandoning rather than the abandoned one. The death of the mother, the actual traumatic legacy of the dispossessed son, lingers in this paranoid fantasy of female defection. Stephen, caught in the antinovelistic "repetition compulsions" of this scenario, can only reproduce the text of suspected sexual treachery in a series of uninflected, repetitive signatures of place: "Queen's Hotel, Queen's Hotel . . ." Joyce's heroic naturalism and epic effects depend on his validating the formal principle of metempsychosis, the reincarnation of the heroic tradition, as a repetition with a difference. What Stephen reveals is the anxiety that threatens to undermine this recasting of ancient epos into modern terms: the anxiety about repeating oneself. "Said that before" is a common refrain of Bloom throughout the day, and only Joyce's virtuosity in transposing his literary paradigms into interesting and startling arrangements prevents such lapses into sterile repetition. But there is no combinatorial, as there is no amatory, magic in Stephen's isolating passion that forecloses any possibility of the novelistic exchange.

Bloom, more attentive to the details by which commonplaces assume extraordinary, fateful particularity, immediately recognizes the Queen's Hotel as the place where his father, Rudolph, took his own life. For the first time, however, this "homonymity" is attributed neither to Stephen's "information" nor to his artistic "intuition," but to coincidence. It is one of the few genuinely non-paranoid moments in the novel, which typically regards coincidences with suspicion, seeing in them "shadows of coming events" or evidence of the "determinism" that undermines human freedom. That this particular affect should result from the imagination of a feminine writing is neither incidental nor fortuitous. It suggests how events might be interwoven into a web of life, rather than diachronically and synchronically arranged in a pattern of paranoid mappings.

And yet there is a further, allegorical dimension to this staging of female writing within the symbolic precincts of the Queen's Hotel. For in this convergence of Stephen's representation, which restages the infantile fear of female abandonment, and Bloom's memory of his father's suicide, the "catastrophe" that haunts Homer's *Odyssey*—the death of Agamemnon on his return to Clytemnestra's domain—is displaced onto a mythic-literary plane: the death of the father in the mother's or queen's house. Stephen's peculiarly Orestean reading of *Hamlet,* which is his primary model for solving the riddle of artistic gestation, is imaginatively consummated on the premises of female hegemony. But it is precisely his male paranoia of female hegemony in life and in art that is exposed as a debased myth contrived by a true paranoia. It is the projection of a mind at once beside itself and enclosed within itself, with no salutary, corrective contacts with the First Entelechy of human life: *amor matris,* the one true thing in life. The loving Mother alone accepts what Barthes bemoans as the "injustices" of communication: "One who would continue speaking lightly, tenderly, without being answered," Barthes avers, "would acquire a great mastery: the mastery of the Mother." [31] This is the mastery afforded Molly by her investiture as Gea-Tellus, the great earth-mother, who, in speaking last, knows that she can expect no answer, except the one she herself provides.

The structure of *Ulysses* does not fully comport, then, with patriarchal models of succession. Ultimately the originality of *Ulysses* can be adduced in Joyce's own eccentric but original apprehension of the mastery of a "feminine" writing. "Calypso," we might recall, concluded with Bloom's costive fantasy of a collaborative venture between Molly and himself: "Might manage of sketch. By Mr. and Mrs. L. M. Bloom. Time I used to try jotting down on my cuff when what she said dressing" (56). Bloom's literary pretensions are limited to the sketch. Molly has more epic ambitions. She contemplates a larger composition—"the works of Master Poldy" (621).

Female literateness is, of course, a comic topos in *Ulysses*. Molly experiments with writing as a purely alphabetic gesture: "In disoccupied moments she had more than once covered a sheet of paper with signs and hieroglyphics which she stated were Greek and Irish and Hebrew characters" (562). The markings of language flow, intermingle, are consonant, simply by virtue of her authorial assertion. I do not take seriously—that is, I take comically—the catechizer's insistence that Molly's facility in cursive writing is a symptom of her deficient mental development. Indeed, the structure of *Ulysses,* which posits "false analogies" between ancient archetypes and contemporary personages, may be criticized as partaking of the same "original deficiencies" attributed to Molly's mode of cerebration: "Unusual polysyllables of foreign origin she interpreted phonetically or by false analogy or by both: metempsychoses (met him pike hoses), alias (a mendacious person mentioned in sacred scripture)" (562). Phonetic interpretation is deficient, but it is not corrupt. It is precisely the deficiency of a certain line of reasoning that confers upon it the prestige of a *first* apprehension, which enjoys both a chronological and a cognitive priority. Molly, like the unconscious or Vico's first peoples, regards words as coequal with the ideas and things they signify. Her first reported question in the novel introduces the interpretive "error" that discloses the "mythic method" of the novel—metempsychosis. This is one of many phonetic errors that Joyce converts into a portal for discovery. Molly's ingenuity is in animating the concept of metempsychosis so that it becomes a lively sexual rebus whose decipherment would yield a figure for the novel itself. "Met him" suggests the potential for amorous encounter, "pike hoses" the "local color" of period costuming. Here we have an episode in the making, one that intuits a novelistic potentiality (the manner and fashions of human encounter) within the mythos of reincarnation.

Molly's narrative methods of accounting the provisions and recounting the local color of human life, while unconventional, are impeccable in satisfying that exacting creditor—Real Experience:

> What compensated in the false balance of her intelligence for these and
> such deficiencies of judgment regarding persons, places and things?
> The false apparent parallelism of all perpendicular arms of all bal-

ances, proved true by construction. The counterbalance of her proficiency of judgment regarding one person, proved true by experience. (562)

The enigma of *Ulysses*'s "mythic method" is resolved by the imaginative false apparent parallelism by which Joyce puts forth his most outrageous claim: that a "Jewgreek is greekjew." "Ba! It is because it is. Woman's reason" (411) mocks the derisive voice of Lynch's talking cap. But it is only "woman's reason" that can traverse the interval between origin and end, self and reality, and demonstrate, through its imaginative tautologies (it is because it is), the novelistic "solution" of doubles: God, the sun, Shakespeare, a commercial traveler are all Odyssean figures, each one of which "having itself traversed in reality itself becomes that self" (412). Essence and existence, archetype and figure coincide in the tautological assertions of woman's reason.

Male assertion, with its reputed superior intelligence and skeptical empiricism, can react to incertitude only by producing a sequence of infinitely regressing terms. However eager to return to the first, the inceptive term, male ratiocination arrives, in the course of its obsessive, unstoppable flight toward the origin, at nullity: "dividends and divisors ever diminishing without actual division till, if the progress were carried far enough, nought nowhere was never reached" (574). Infinite regress, infinite progress. This is movement, but not in Aristotle's form-actualizing sense. No entelechy can emerge from this restless search for ever-receding origins or unattainable ends.

Molly does not deliberately *tamper* with sequences. She only, to cite the catechizer's description, "with care repeated, with greater difficulty remembered, forgot with ease, with misgiving remembered, rerepeated with error" the fateful history of her erotic, social, and fantasy life. Throughout her monologue, Molly shows herself to be exquisitely sensitive to the onset of the first. She begins by remarking the breaking of a precedent and the possible inauguration of a new martial order: "Yes because he never did a thing like that before" (608). What is new is that Bloom has asked to get his breakfast in bed. An ordinary request, but one made extraordinary by the promise not so much of role reversal, but of reciprocity, what Bloom calls "mutual equality." First me, then you—a diurnal alternation might become the new regime in the Bloom household. We need not indulge this fantasy to appreciate its importance, even as a possibility. For Bloom's call for reciprocal and reversed order reinstates, in principle if not in eventual practice, the first entelechy, the structural rhythm. He has asked for a change, in this and in many customary arrangements, throughout the day. Now it is Molly's turn to reply.

Her answer is, unsurprisingly, elliptical, but that is not to say that it is evasive. No stranger to the *taedium vitae* of modernity, her mind revolves in a curvilinear orbit whose midpoint, as Diane Tolomeo has demonstrated, discloses a vision of "a new paradise, the new world which is born from love." [32] More precisely, Molly's paradisal vision is evoked by the promise of a love letter, which alone might compensate a woman who feels she has "no chances at all in this place":

> I could write the answer in bed to let him imagine me short just a few words not those long crossed letters Atty Dillon used to write to the fellow that was something in the four courts that jilted her after out of the ladies letterwriter when I told her to say a few simple words he could twist how he liked not acting with precipat precip itancy with equal candour the greatest earthly happiness answer to a gentleman's proposal affirmatively my goodness theres nothing else its all very fine for them but as for being a woman as soon as youre old they might as well throw you out in the bottom of the ashpit. (624)

The "greatest earthly happiness" is the pleasure of saying yes. Molly may have difficulty saying "precipitancy," but her stammering quickly yields to the mellifluous grace of alacrity, of quick and solicitous reply. She does not postulate, as Barthes says of the Marquise de Merteuil, a *correspondence,* i.e., a tactical enterprise to defend positions, make conquests. That, presumably, is Bloom's strategy with Martha Clifford. Molly, rather, is downright insistent that love letters correspond to a natural, if ideal, human relation: men and women brought together, however precipitantly, on the simple but firm ground of equal candor.

A man might write promising such natural relations, but "as for being a woman," Molly suspects that his pledge, like the aging female body, is too easily discarded. Thus Molly's vision of paradise regained rapidly declines into an imaginative "descent into hell"—the ashpit, mass grave of female bodies past their procreative time, the pit where all unanswered or unfulfilled letters are consigned. It is the mythological site of feminine destiny which corresponds to "the grey sunken cunt of the world." Tolomeo has described how this precipitous descent into hell is quickly reversed and incorporated into a larger "octagonal" cycle of reascent and renewal. What she omits in her schematic parsing of Molly's eight sentences is the pivotal memory that converts descent into reascent—Molly's remembrance of the first time: "Mulveys was the first."

Molly's recovery involves a simple imaginative conversion of a woman's last end to her first time. Molly's simplicity validates even as it engenders the amorous and writerly utopia she desires. Philosophy, as Stephen reminds us in "Eumeus," speaks of simple substances as uncorrupted and potentially immortal. Molly's monologue, whose substance Joyce identified with immortal "Weib," attains the mystical estate envisioned in "Little Gidding"—"A Condition of complete simplicity / Costing not less than everything."

For T. S. Eliot such spiritual simplicity was annunciatory of "the dawning of this Love and the voice of this Calling." Molly's incantatory coda invokes the same transcendent bliss *beyond the reach of irony* in which essence and phenomenon inhere and "the fire and the rose are one." Molly's affirmations are almost inconceivable after the savage ironies of *Ulysses,* which is why, I suspect, critics have been embarrassed by her effusions. Yet I believe it is indisputable that her triumph represents the most heartening victory of nonironic narration in modern literature. It is a triumph whose simplicity costs not less than everything in returning us to our first consciousness of the world. Molly's monologue resounds to the simplicity that Vico attributed to humanity in its "first" nature and first poetic fables.

> Irony certainly could not have begun until the period of reflection, which wears the mask of truth. Here emerges a great principle of human institutions, confirming the origin of poetry disclosed in this work: that since the first men of the gentile world had the simplicity of children, who are truthful by nature, the first fables could not feign anything false; they must therefore have been, as they have been defined above, true narrations.[33]

Molly is a feigner, but not a prevaricator. She cannot feign anything false, though she abounds in fantasies and inventions. Her true narration, a belated development in a long day of male culture, returns us to the limpid and fluid simplicity of a plain style, the great principle of human institutions. It is the language of female Flesh, "perfectly sane full amoral fertilisable untrustworthy engaging shrewd limited prudent indifferent,"[34] that actualizes the rhetorical polis of Joycean desire—the dream of female governance.

This dream is dreamed in the dawn hours after the novel itself awakens from the nightmare of its patriarchal narrations. In "Eumeus," Bloom, after a day spent encountering the myriad cultural and civic forms of male assertion, passes on to Stephen, as a kind of patrimony, his reflections on the life of men and women, the life that all novels are bound to represent. Bloom begins by stipulating that "every country, they say, our own distressful included, has the government it deserves." Wishing to disseminate "a little goodwill all round,"

Bloom advises Stephen, "It's all very fine to boast of mutual superiority but what about mutual equality. I resent violence and intolerance in any shape or form. It never reaches anything or stops anything. A revolution must come on the due instalments plan." (525). Patriarchy, we might say, is the government (most) men deserve. Bloom is the egalitarian who disavows the fiction of paternity and its sexual ideology of mutual superiority as a civic and narrative catastrophe. Male assertiveness, which ideologically flowers in the social Darwinism that works for the "destruction of the fittest," is repudiated as antinarrative. It has neither goal nor purpose, being incapable of reaching anywhere or stopping anything. Bloom adheres to the narratable politics of change in "due instalments." The citizen destined to inhabit this new society must be the new womanly man, who has declined the legacy of patriarchy.

Bloom leaves us in no doubt that the political and narrative catastrophe of modern life biologically originates in the male body with its hormonal impulses of self-assertiveness: "All those wretched quarrels, in his humble opinion, stirring up bad blood, from some bump of combativeness or gland of some kind, erroneously supposed to be about a punctilio of honour and a flag, were very largely a question of the money question which was at the back of everything greed and jealousy, people never knowing when to stop" (526). Male endocrinology, combative and acquisitive, has no narrative destiny. Theoretically, patriarchy is an interminable as well as legal fiction, stopping nowhere, achieving nothing. Its entelechy is comprised in a sequence of endless quests for new lands, new markets, or new women to conquer. Patriarchy traffics in money, the symbolic counter whose function is to acquire, but never to institute.

Molly in her monologue shows herself in conjugal agreement with Bloom, sharing his aversion to male politics. But she revises his program for a sexual revolution by proposing a new regime of female governance: "I dont care what anybody says itd be much better for the world to be governed by the women in it you wouldnt see women going and killing one another and slaughtering when do you ever see women rolling around drunk like they do or gambling every penny they have and losing it on horses yes because a woman whatever she does she knows where to stop" (640). Women, unlike men, know where to stop. Molly is not being disingenuous in making this claim. Though her own thoughts flow associatively and without regard for normal punctuation, she has a genius for knowing where to stop.

But we might go further and contend that Molly knows not only where to stop, but how to end. Without Molly's affirmation, Joyce's errant male epic could not end. It could only stop. Or rather it could only halt on the brink of that mythic dot at the conclusion of "Ithaca," the final period of the male narrative, that invites us to enter into a genuine, if restful, delusion. For reality is not mythically transfigured, but deliberately flouted in the catechizer's claim that Bloom has gone to the dark bed where there is a square round egg, Sinbad the Sailor's roc's auks egg, in the night of Darkinbad the Brightdayler. If one believes that the problem of the "quadrature of the circle" could be so easily solved, then one quite as easily believes in the actual existence of the fabulous roc's egg. Neither can be accredited as actual, and it is precisely to reality that Joyce's heroic naturalism holds itself accountable. Thus, for all of Bloom's late-night inventory-taking, it is Molly who proves herself equal to that final accounting of all persons, places, and things, the very stock of the novel's provisions, by which the novel discharges its debts to reality. If its debts to reality remain outstanding, the novel cannot end honorably, but only, as "Ithaca" does, sentimentally—that is, enjoying the reality of ending without acknowledging the immense debtorship for the thing done.

It is not, I believe, outrageous to speak of Molly's "honor," however temporizing it may sometimes appear. Samuel Butler's argument for the female authorship of the *Odyssey* rests in good part on his observation that the writer shows "a markedly greater both knowledge and interest when dealing with women, but she makes it plain that she is exceedingly jealous for the honour of her sex, and by consequence inexorable in her severity against those women who have disgraced it." [35] It is such jealous concern for female honor that prompts Butler to consider whether the authoress has deliberately "whitewashed" the character and conduct of Penelope:

> It is known that scandalous versions of Penelope's conduct are current among the ancients; indeed they seem to have prevailed before the completion of the Epic cycle, for in the *Telegony,* which is believed to have come next in chronological order after the "Odyssey," we find that when Ulysses had killed the suitors he did not go on living with Penelope, but settled in Thesprotia, and married Callidice, the queen of the country. He must, therefore, have divorced Penelope and could hardly have done this if he accepted the Odyssean version of her conduct. [36]

Butler, in his large-hearted way (for he is clearly fond of his authoress), indulges her whitewashing of Penelope's character and the chronological lapses meant to silence all speculation about her fidelity: "If this is so, I for one, shall think none the worse of her." Molly's reputation has fared worse than most, but that is because her sexual transactions have been computed, we might say, according to the double standards regulating the patriarchal exchange of women. Her final *Yes* may be said to liquidate that system and return us to the more primal economy of "natured nature" in which demand-and-supply is reckoned according to the simple exchange of call and answer: "then I asked him with my eyes to ask again yes and then he asked me would I yes to say yes." Molly both acknowledges and acquits her debt through the simple expedient—and guile—of asking that the question be asked again so that she may give the answer, the only answer, which it is in her nature to give and her destiny to supply. In this new, female economy, there is an answer to every question, a reply to every summons.

If we are lucky, and in *Ulysses* we are, the answer will be yes. When Emma Woodhouse is entreated by the man first in her interest and affections to give an answer, the narrative observes a discreet but hardly ambiguous silence: "What did she say—Just what she ought, of course. A lady always does." [37] Between Austen's witty reserve, which renders female assent as an elegant formality, and Molly's *Yes,* the very nature of female tautology has been altered to include the apocalyptic (not orgiastic) tremors, the procreative grace of First Love. Molly's *Yes,* at once introit and benediction to the life-ritual of sexual exchange, is the apocalyptic tautology which so intoxicates Barthes, that "preposterous state in which are to be found, all values being confounded, the glorious end of the logical operation, the obscenity of stupidity, and the explosions of the Nietzschean *yes.*" [38] But it would be patronizing to say that "Penelope" mimics the climax of Nietzsche's Dionysian *yes.* Molly's affirmation is neither explosive nor eruptive. Her *jouissance* is registered in the final surge of her monologue, excitedly dilating to the sexual rhythm of call and answer, prolonging the joy of female initiative: "first I put my arms around him yes and drew him down to me so he could feel my breasts all perfume yes and his heart was going like mad and I said Yes I will Yes." Perhaps there is more art than honor in this pledge that shrewdly and prudently surmounts, though it does not obliterate, the betrayals and sorrows that have intervened between the first and the present time. Molly's *Yes* marks the end, as Eliot says, "where we start from." In this respect, Bloom is the wise fool who does not know his own wife. For Molly's will is, in fact, not unstoppable like the sea. Whatever she does, Molly, like a supreme artist, knows where to stop.

EIGHT

# BECKETT'S
# AFFECTIONS

"M E . . . TO PLAY." The audacity of Hamm's first words in *Endgame* lies
in the exhibitionistic genius of that "me." Hamm commands the histrionic rhetoric of the child, for whom the pronoun *I* is a usage of
belated and difficult acquisition. The child, in its unreconstructed narcissism,
imperfectly comprehends the idea of an "I" at once independent of and an-
swerable to a "you." Its grammatical notion of self is centered in the grandiose
egotism of a "me" to whom everything belongs and to whom everything must
refer. Beckett's art, which aspires to the condition of uninterrupted monologue,
is haunted by the memory of the child's shadowplay. His expressiveness reverberates to that peculiar tone, at once puerile and futile, by which the child
solicits the attention of an otherwise inattentive world. It is the tone first
rehearsed in *Murphy,* "the tone of an exhibitionist for his last words on
earth" (39).

No one will dispute, I trust, the testamentary quality of Beckett's acerbic
pronouncements on a life he seems only too eager to conclude. Some, however,
may quarrel with my attempt to locate the motive force of Beckett's strange
pronominal and human conjugations in an exasperated exhibitionism. Yet surely
only a thwarted exhibitionist would play and replay the self's disarticulation as
the most absorbing spectacle in his dramatic repertoire. Only an aggrieved
exhibitionist, feeling the full impact of such shocks to self-integrity, would be
capable of the syntactic suspense of Beckettian soliloquy, in which each word is
hoarded, contemplated, rehearsed, and ultimately delivered as if it might potentially *be* the last word, thus arousing, if not always rewarding, our spectatorial
attention. By its dissolution of dramatized action into dramatic saying, Beckett's
art at once fulfills and mocks the exhibitionist's dream of existing in a state of
pure representation. Beckett's creativity can be said to originate in an inspired
reading of *esse est percipi* as the formula expressing a dramatic verity rather than
a philosophical truth.[1]

Even Beckett's cynical derelicts must honor the magical properties of that
formula. The most degenerate and downcast of his characters are *conspicuous* in
their dereliction, for reasons most succinctly put by Malone in *Malone Dies:*
"One calls attention to oneself as best as one can. It's human." That one's
distinct humanity is first asserted and confirmed through such exhibitionistic
gestures is the major insight of Heinz Kohut, the ego-psychologist whose work
seeks to demonstrate the value of a positive narcissism. Kohut has discerned a
deep and abiding connection between the narcissistic-exhibitionistic impulses

of early childhood and the creative powers of adult life. He considers exhibitionism to be "a principal narcissistic dimension of all drives . . . the expression of a narcissistic emphasis on the aim of the drive (upon the self as the performer) rather than on its objects." The ideational *content* of such exhibitionistic-narcissistic performances Kohut identifies as the "grandiose fantasy." This fantasy, Kohut goes on to explain, is neutral in itself:

> Whether it contributes to health or disease, to the success of the individual or to his downfall, depends on the degree of its deinstinctualization and the extent of its integration into the realistic purposes of the ego. Take, for instance, Freud's statement that "a man who has been the indisputable favorite of his mother keeps for life the feeling of a conqueror, that confidence of success that often induces real success." Here Freud obviously speaks about the results of adaptively valuable narcissistic fantasies which provide lasting support to the personality.[2]

We have, of course, no such success story to interpret in Beckett's artistic biography. Beckett seems to offer us the poignant counterexample of the child whose grandiose exhibitionistic impulses went a-begging. We read in him the sad history of the emotional foundling who failed to find the maternal mirror to confirm the narcissistic pleasure in his own performances. Thus Hamm concludes his hour on the stage by discarding all props—his gaff, his dog, his whistle—yet clings, to the last, to his handkerchief, symbol of this narcissistic injury: "Old stancher!" he intones, "you remain." Hamm's final tableau commemorates two world-catastrophes: the destruction of the child's pre-oedipal paradise and the vastation of a postapocalyptic world.

To describe the extent and nature of this self- and world-vastation is to comprehend Beckett's unique contribution to the modern tradition of Rue and Regret: First Love. This narrative is dispersed and retold throughout Beckett's work, but receives its most extended narrative attention in four novellas that constitute something like a First Love saga: "First Love," "The Expelled," "Calmative," and "The End."[3] Yet whether First Love proves, in its issue, to be either an emotional way-station on the route home to Mother (as in Molloy's dalliance with Loy or Lousse in *Molloy*) or a milestone event (as in "First Love"), Beckett's version is consistently told from the perspective of that risible and pitiable figure: the banished or abandoned child-man. In reconstructing the stages of his abandonment, Beckett returns to the primary affections of our first nature, a nature obscured by time and ravaged by habit. Beckett shares with Proust the fascination and dread of transitional periods in which the individual encounters and re-creates the world as a projection of his own consciousness. These periods, of which First Love is both prototype and paradigm, represent those "perilous zones in the life of the individual, dangerous, precarious, painful, mysterious and fertile," of which he speaks in *Proust,* "when for a moment the boredom of living is replaced by the suffering of being."[4]

This encounter with unmediated being excites neither joy (of discovery) nor shock (of recognition), but a strange compounding of both affects which we may call, after Beckett, ruthhilarity. *Ruthhilarity* is a neologism Beckett devised to describe the masturbatory revels of his first quiescent "anti-hero," Belacqua.[5] This word interests me not because it inaugurates or even portends (for it does neither) a Beckettian style, but because it encapsulates the mood or the constituent emotional elements of a new species of writing that we can recognize as Beckettian. In such a writing, hilarity finds its antecedent and sufficient cause in the infant's ruth over its expulsion from the amniotic dark, where, needless to say, *esse est percipi* does not yet pose an existential problem. The manchild in the womb requires only the *presence* of another (the Mother), and so is oblivious to the spectatorial, mirror world of society which will lay claim to his essential nature. The repertoire of laughs cultivated by Watt expresses, in a different register, the infant's ruth at his expulsion from that liquid world where the buoyancy rather than the visibility of being is what matters. Watt's laughter, a supreme instance of ruth leavened by mirth, is "strictly speaking . . . not laughs, but modes of ululation."[6]

In interpreting human laughter as an ambiguous cry, Beckett aligns himself with the "hypochondriac profundity," as Kierkegaard's romantic controversialist calls it, of the classical English psychologists. One of the refrains of "Diapsalmata" anxiously ponders the implications of David Hartley's observation: " 'When laughter first manifests itself in the infant, it is an incipient cry, excited by pain, or by a feeling of pain suddenly inhibited, and recurring at brief intervals.' What if everything in the world were a misunderstanding, what if laughter were really tears?"[7] Watt would never fall victim to such misunderstanding, as demonstrated by his personal predilection for the "dianoetic laugh." "It is the laugh of laughs, the *risus purus,* the laugh laughing at the laugh, the beholding, the saluting of the highest joke, in a word the laugh that laughs—silence please—at that which is unhappy. Personally of course I regret all. All, all, all" (48).

Watt's "risus purus" surely derives from the first human ululation—the birth wail, which is the prototype of all subsequent Beckettian lamentations. The *vagitus,* then, constitutes the prologue to Beckett's existential comedy and the source of all ensuing unhappiness. From then on the note of banishment, banishment from the heart, banishment from home, sounds, as Stephen Dedalus claims it sounds in Shakespearean dramaturgy, uninterruptedly. It doubles itself, reflects and repeats itself, "protasis, epitasis, catastasis, catastrophe" (174). "The Expelled" presents this protasis, the child's entry into the world, as a true hysterical formation, that is, as a traumatic reminiscence. "In a sort of vision I saw the door open and my feet come out." Malone, on the other hand, anticipates his death-catastrophe as a hysterical *premonition* that takes, predictably, the conformations of a breach birth:

> I am being given, if I may venture the expression, birth to into death, such is my impression. The feet are clear already, of the great cunt of existence. Favourable presentation I trust. My head will be the last to die. Haul in your hand. I can't. The render rent. My story ended I'll be living yet. Promising lag. That is the end of me. I shall say I no more.[8]

Typically, the Beckettian character, even as death approaches, never quite manages the proper presentation. His life takes the form of an existential redundancy, two failed births separated by a promising lag. This lag operates as the maieutic sign that he has been given "birth to into death."

Malone's impression of a promising lag accords with Freud's memorable description of birth as an "impressive caesura": "There is much more continuity between intra-uterine life and earliest infancy," Freud avers, "than the impressive caesura of the act of birth would have us believe."[9] Freud, writing partly to repudiate Otto Rank's *Trauma of Birth,* never uttered a more Beckettian sentiment, nor in a more Beckettian idiom. Freud's general claim in "Inhibitions, Symptoms and Anxiety" is that the infant's anxiety, attributable to a premental, preconscious "non-satisfaction, of a *growing tension due to need*" (emphasis in original), is the prototype for the danger *situation* that summons anxiety. Freud interpreted the infant's cries as distress signals echoing his original protest against the primordial and archetypal "anxiety-situation": separation from the body of the Mother. Freud's gift for poetic figure should not, however, blind us to the positivist spirit of his inquiry. Freud's humanism is inseparable from a scientism frankly puzzled, as Freud claims to be, by what precisely an affect *is.*[10] Freud's feeling about human feeling is mediated by his conviction that the complicated expressions of the emotional life are governed by processes subject to clinical observation and analysis. Beckett is the artist whom life affects as an ordeal to be suffered, a reality subject to tragicomic representation rather than scientific notation.

We may gauge the temperamental oddity and originality of Beckett's representation by comparing his conception of our earthly pilgrimage, a conception indebted to a deep absorption in Dante's *Divine Comedy,* to the most imposing single work of modern odyssey ever written, Joyce's *Ulysses. Ulysses* portrays a hero, Leopold Bloom, who makes his way through the world, meeting friends, strangers, but inevitably himself. His pilgrimage, like Dante's, is undertaken in the artistic faith that man and his world can be figured in harmonious, self-realizing relation. If Socrates go forth tonight, it is toward himself his steps will tend—on that proposition the Joycean identity is founded and founded irremovably, like the world, macro- and microcosm, upon the void. Bloom's final posture, bodily emblem of his remythifying destiny, is that of the manchild in the womb, "reclined laterally, left, with right and left legs flexed, the indexfinger and thumb of the right hand resting on the bridge of the nose, in the attitude depicted in a snapshot photographed by Percy Apjohn" (607). Beckett's vagrants skeptically regard the metempsychosis promised by sleep. And they are less sanguine about the ontological prospects of Aristotelian narrative, which renders character in the process of its becoming and affirms the value of both the journey and its desired end—a justified life. In fact, *Murphy* mocks the optimism of Joyce's peripatetic fiction in anticipating the impending annihilation of its titular hero as proof of a crippled Aristotelianism: "So all things limp together for the only possible" (235). The concluding wish of "First Love" is to obliterate the distinction between the cry of and the cry for new life: ". . . faint or loud, cry is cry, all that matters is that it should cease" (30). The desired end of the Beckettian quest is "the Belacqua bliss" of embryonal repose, whose ideal mimesis is closer to the aesthetic of a sonogram than to that of an Apjohn photograph.

Beckett does not bother to disguise the regressive nature of his enchantment with the amniotic idyll. Womb fantasies are the most elaborate in the Beckettian inventory, and are classically allied to his obsessive interest in rooms. Lear's unaccommodated man may serve as the *literal* embodiment of Beckett's tragic man, who retreats to his child-sanctified space hoping to avert rather than expiate "the original and eternal sin . . . the sin of having been born."[11] To expiate that sin is the appointed fate of the tragic hero, an appointment Beckettian man would as soon not keep. The Beckettian subject is "l'homme moderne," who conceives himself, as does the speaker of "First Love," as "roi sans sujets,"[12] royal pretender to a preoedipal kingdom. Thus the infantilism Beckett perceived as highly developed in Proust may also be seen to be a pronounced feature of his own artistic temperament. Beckett's affective infantilism accounts,

as it does in Proust, for an essentially tragic pessimism being rendered comically. Hugh Kenner concludes his splendid study of Beckett, the tramp philosopher, with a fine (and I suspect for Kenner, final) characterization of Beckett
as "the Comedian of the Impasse, genial to the last, the ever-receding last." [13]
The object of my *recherche* is located within a similar continuum, but reversed
as to direction. I do not seek the comedian of the impasse, genial to the last,
but the child who is the father of that man. Or rather, the manchild—Mr.
Kelly, Hamm, the Unnameable.

In his emotional afflictions, this child is a descendant, not of Sterne's ribald
melancholia, nor of Swift's satiric ferocity, but of Samuel Johnson's profound
dejection. "They can put me wherever they want," Beckett has written, "but
it's Johnson, always Johnson, who is with me. And if I follow any tradition, it is
his." [14] Beckett's most elaborate play, *Eleutheria* ("Freedom"), abandoned on his
way to *Fin de Partie,* emerged out of what Beckett called "my Johnson fantasy."
In a letter to Thomas McGreevy, Beckett remarked the emotional absurdities
of Johnson's conduct:

> It seems now quite certain that he was rather absurdly in love with her all
> the fifteen years he was at Streatham, though there is no text for the
> impotence. It becomes more interesting, the false rage to cover his retreat
> from her, then the real rage when he realizes that no retreat was neces-
> sary, and beneath all, the despair of the lover with nothing to love with,
> and much more difficult. [15]

Beckett's feeling for Johnson as a tragic figure, spiritually self-conscious and
emotionally isolated, may serve to gloss the false (that is, histrionic) rages of
Beckett's narration and its central text: the despair of the lover with nothing to
love with. In this depletion of Eros and its difficult, minimal replenishments lies
the affective reality of Beckett's art.

To comprehend the nature of Beckett's affective reality is not only to recover its Johnsonian antecedents, but to establish Beckett's identity as, psychologically, not the foundling, but the legitimate child of his age. (Beckett never
tires of reminding his readers that his creatures are legitimate, not bastard
progeny of their times.) His rueful characters typify the narcissistic personality
disorders that Kohut believes are as indigenous to the twentieth century as the
libidinal excesses of oedipal man were to fin de siècle European culture. Kohut
interestingly distinguishes between two prominent psychological types—Tragic
Man and Guilty Man. The Guilty Man inhabits the classical world of drive-
psychology: "Guilty Man lives within the pleasure principle; he attempts to

satisfy his pleasure-seeking drives." His inner life is sundered by the conflict between primordial instincts and cultural prohibitions. Tragic Man is afflicted by emotional lassitude rather than by a psychic conflict. His disorders and discontents, which are rooted in pre-oedipal disturbances, represent the dominant psychological problem of post-1900 culture. Kohut writes:

> We are asking . . . whether the disorders of the self have gained ascendancy over the conflict neuroses or, put differently, whether the disorders of the self, even if they have not increased in absolute number or relative proportion, are now more intense, cause greater suffering, are, to put it in still different terms, more significant now, in view of the shift of the leading psychological problem of Western man from the area of guilt-ridden overstimulation and conflict to that of inner emptiness, isolation, and unfulfillment.[16]

For Kohut the feeling that the self is falling apart, its world disintegrating, disguises the actual psychological reality that no self has ever been constituted.

We know from Dierdre Bair's biography that Beckett himself was fascinated by just such a possibility when he attended Jung's 1934 Tavistock lectures and there heard recounted the case history of an unhappy young girl whose incurable life-disorder Jung rather mystically attributed to her never having been really born.[17] Kohut takes a less poetic view of such self-disorders, ascribing their origin to a failure to consolidate what he calls the "nuclear self," the self "experienced by the individual as the basic one, and which is most resistant to change." In isolating this basic psychic component, Kohut attempts to rationalize the feeling, endemic to modernity, that the personality, while composed of multiple and multivalent selves, nevertheless possesses a core self, a key self, as Virginia Woolf's *Orlando* envisions it, that controls and commands them all. The nuclear self is composed of derivatives of the grandiose-exhibitionistic self and the idealized parental imago "which contains not only the individual's most enduring values and ideals but also his most deeply anchored goals, purposes and ambitions."[18] In the creative mediations of the nuclear self Kohut locates "the basis of our sense of being an independent center of initiative and perception, integrated with our most central ambitions and ideals and with our experience that our body and mind form a unity in space and continuum in time."

Kohut's conceptualization is useful generally for our study, since he identifies how the modern self may come to regard itself as a center of world-transforming initiative and perception. But his specific analysis of the role that exhibitionist impulses play in securing this confidence is of inestimable help in understanding, within the bleak confines of Beckett's despondent narratives, why the self experiences itself as coming apart in space and disintegrating in time. Kohut summarizes:

> The child that is to survive psychologically is born into an empathic-responsive human milieu (of self-objects) just as he is born into an atmosphere that contains an optimal amount of oxygen if he is to survive physically. And his nascent self "expects"—to use an inappropriately anthropomorphic but appropriately evocative term—an empathic environment to be in tune with his psychological needs-wishes with the same unquestioning certitude as the respiratory apparatus of the newborn infant may be said to "expect" oxygen to be contained in the surrounding atmosphere.[19]

I would venture that Beckett would be both appalled and delighted by the psychological assumptions and existential metaphors of this passage. It is a passage that abounds with possibility for Beckettian comic improvisation, particularly upon the notion that survival depends on assuming an empathy as unquestioningly as a newborn assumes oxygen. Expiration, not inspiration, is the reflex of Beckettian life, which does not take such expectations for granted. The rarefied atmosphere of Beckettian fiction testifies to this emotional vastation of a world emptied of self-objects. Kohut will thus help us interpret, through his postulations, how Beckett's vision of this "dehiscence of world and self coming asunder"—Beckett's idiomatic way of characterizing *the* modern topic—is intimately related to the failure to secure the affections of first love, the most important love, the love of that ideal spectator, the all-accepting Mother.

For Kohut, working within a tradition of classical Freudianism whose insights he wished to refine rather than replace, the most critical phase in the formation of the nuclear self attends the mother's initial responses to the child's grandiloquent bodily performances:

> She responds—accepting, rejecting, disregarding—to a self that, in giving and offering, seeks confirmation by the mirroring self-object. The child therefore experiences the joyful, prideful parental attitude or the parent's lack of interest, not only as the acceptance or rejection of a drive, but also—this aspect of the interaction of parent and child is often the decisive one—as the acceptance or rejection of his tentatively established, yet still vulnerable creative-productive-active self. If the mother rejects

this self just as it begins to assert itself as a center of creative-productive initiative (especially, of course, if her rejection or lack of interest is only one link in a long chain of rebuffs and disappointments emanating from her pathogenically unempathic personality) or if her inability to respond to the child's total self leads her to a fragmentation-producing preoccupation with the feces—to the detriment of the cohesion-establishing involvement with her feces-producing, learning, controlling, maturing, total child—then the child's self will be depleted and he will abandon the attempt to obtain the joys of self-assertion and will, for reassurance, turn to the pleasures he can derive from the fragments of his body-self.[20]

Kohut presents here a rather dense, even intimidating, account of how the mother's responses to the child's fecal productions and self-assertive play are decisive in determining whether the child will perceive his body-self as cohesive, assertive, and creative, or incoherent, fragmented, and depleted.

Now it may be argued that psychoanalytic literature generally is rich, perhaps cloying, in evidence of the child's need to arrest the mother's attention and secure her tender ministrations. Such literature recounts how the child's growing awareness of biological transformations is coinvolved with the fantasies which make the mother-child relationship vivid, tense, and ambivalent. To attract the mother's eye, the child exhibits its assortment of creative products, arranged in a fantastical chain of association. Its feces symbolically duplicate the supreme "gift" of life—a child. Beckett sees in these fantastical associations the absurd plot of a life-satire—"an ordure from beginning to end," as Watt's predecessor in Mr. Knott's domain vividly defines it. This unamused but enlightened gentleman leaves Watt with a "short statement" (which fills pages), the gist of which may be summarized as follows: that the world of the fathers, and of the fathers and mothers, and of their fathers and mothers, and in fact of all those who figure successively as inheritors and procreators on "the poor lousy earth," may be represented, in the infinite recessiveness of their breeding, by a single term—"an excrement"; that, moreover, the Blakean world of generation, the world of seasonal change and organic metamorphosis, April showers and autumn harvests "and every fourth year the February débâcle," may be similarly represented by a synonymous but still single term: "A turd" (47). All internal and external life-motions, whether metabolic or sexual; all times, whether seasonal, chronometric, or ritual, coincide in the same figure of Waste.

But "First Love" redeems the ferocious misanthropy of this Swiftian sentiment by exposing the comic and creative nature of the primal contiguity of waste and love. The narrator confounds his Father's House with "hothouse" (where he dreams of tending to tomatoes and seedlings) and "necessary house" (where he endures cruel sessions of "anxiety constipation," failing, that is, to give birth to waste). "It's all a muddle in my head," he finally concedes, "graves and nuptials and the different varieties of motion" (12). In an equally muddled moment, he inscribes his passion for Lulu, where it is most fitting—on "time's forgotten cowplats." The inscription, he observes, is made with "my devil's finger into the bargain, which I then sucked." It is at this point of his demonstration, perhaps inspired by the somatic memory of the infant's suck, that he tires of the name Lulu and rechristens his love Anna, which, as any student of Christian onomastics knows, is the name of the mother of the mother of Christ. The beloved of "First Love" takes her image, as Freud told us she would, from the mother. But Beckett gives this predictable tale a ruthhilarious twist by showing how the symbolic logic that makes the mother a model for all future loves is also the symbolic logic that inspires the lover to fashion his love-tokens out of the body's rejectamenta.[21]

Beckett, of course, is skilled at parodying the kind of "poor juvenile solutions, explaining nothing" proposed in psychoanalytic readings that would relate his disintegration anxiety to an anal fixation with the creative, affective properties of human waste. In "The Expelled," he offers the "psychopathological wholehogs" (the phrase appears in *Murphy*) a ruthhilarious account of the etiology of his "gait":

> This carriage is due, in my opinion, in part at least, to a certain leaning from which I have never been able to free myself completely and which left its stamp, as was only to be expected, on my impressionable years, those which govern the fabrication of character, I refer to the period which extends, as far as the eye can see, from the first totterings, behind a chair, to the third form, in which I concluded my studies. I had then the deplorable habit, having pissed in my trousers, or shat there, which I did fairly regularly early in the morning, about ten or half past ten, of persisting in going on and finishing my day as if nothing had happened. The very idea of changing my trousers, or of confiding in mother, who goodness knows asked nothing better than to help me, was unbearable, I don't know why, and till bedtime I dragged on burning and stinking between my little thighs, or sticking to my bottom, the result of my incontinence. Whence this wary way of walking, with legs stiff and wide apart, and this desperate rolling of the bust, no doubt intended to put people off the scent, to make them think I was full of gaiety and high spirits, without a

care in the world, and to lend plausibility to my explanations concerning my nether rigidity, which I ascribed to hereditary rheumatism. My youthful ardour, insofar as I had any, spent itself in this effort, I became sour and mistrustful, a little before my time, in love with hiding and the prone position. (38)

The narrator counsels no "need then for caution, we may reason on to our heart's content, the fog won't lift." Indeed it won't. But the parody itself stands as a literate trace of those first totterings that govern the fabrication of character. The mother is remembered as a benign ministrant to the toddler's incontinences, but the "goodness knows" smacks of a smarminess typical of Beckett, even, I would venture, as a toddler. His own mother, May Beckett, a woman of depressive character given to insomniac pacings, seems all too dreadfully to present herself as Melanie Klein's "Bad Mother," clearly the prototype for Kohut's clinical description of the "pathogenically unempathic personality" who deprives her child of the admiring gaze and positive mirroring that confer self-integrity and self-security to his otherwise inchoate, uncoordinated being.

The vivid brutalitics of Beckettian story may then be seen to originate in a child's troubled perception that he neither inspires nor receives from the mother—or her delegates—the "empathic responses" known as love. According to Kohut, if the child fails to secure empathic responses to his exhibitionistic performances, or if recognition is late in coming (a frustration tragicomically rendered in the perpetual postponements of *Waiting for Godot*), then he reacts with "narcissistic rage." "Destructive rage, in particular," asserts Kohut, "is always motivated by an injury to the self." [22] Outbursts of rage and desecration are the emotional epiphenomena stipulated by Beckett's repertoire of tragicomic effects: Moran's sudden paternal rages and his brutal beating of the old wayfarer in *Molloy;* Lemuel's carnage at the end of *Malone Dies;* the collective drubbing of Lucky during his extraordinary outburst—at once lyric and tirade—in *Waiting for Godot.*

Beckett himself boldly identifies these abrupt furies and bodily cruelties as "most gratifying brutalities" in the ninth of his extraordinary *Texts for Nothing.* There the contention is made that failing to inspire abuses is an outrage equal to, indeed surpassing, the outrage of having suffered them: "But the fact that I was not molested, can I have remained insensible to that?" Here we find articulated the vicious symmetry of Beckett's dramatic compositions, in which "esse est percipi" can only be played out in the sadomasochistic improvisations of the psyche's vaudeville.

Perhaps the most amazing performance is recorded in "Calmative," where the Beckettian vagrant, having just emerged from his dark woods, is haunted by thoughts "of cruelty, the kind that smiles." These thoughts are provoked by a scene offered to him as either counterpart or contrast to his own conspicuous misery. A comedian telling a funny story about a fiasco is rewarded by the shrill laughter of women: "Perhaps they had in mind the reigning penis sitting who knows by their side and from that sweet shore launched their cries of joy toward the comic vast." Excited by the phallic comedy of Aristophanic theater, the women applaud the comedian performing in the wilderness of the comic vast. It is at this point that the Beckettian storyteller reasserts his self-prerogatives:

> But it's to me this evening something has to happen, to my body as in
> myth and metamorphosis, this old body to which nothing ever happened,
> or so little, which ever met with anything, loved anything, wished for any-
> thing, in its tarnished universe, except for the mirrors to shatter, the
> plane, the curved, the magnifying, the minifying, and to vanish in the
> havoc of its images. (53)

The aggrieved exhibitionist can be heard to speak in the assertiveness, at once theatrical and childish, of that "me"—"But it's to me this evening something has to happen." Beckett's insistence on a myth, even one of negative metamorphosis, discloses the reactive and compensatory nature of his tragic affections. His feeling of impotent and unavailing love—"to my body . . . to which nothing ever happened"—retains the despondent resentment against the mother who failed to mirror the young body in all its grandiose, yet vulnerable, striving to be whole. To counteract the mother's extinguishing gaze, the child fantasizes a mythic consummation in which the maternal mirrors are *shattered* even as they shatter. In that specular reversal, the child is liberated from all imprisoning images, free to launch himself into the comic vast that preexists the mother. For what is important for the child is not whether the mother mirrors a magnified or a diminished image; it is that she mirrors a *discrete* image, and so conveys to the child both its original delight and its original sin—the delight of being whole and entire, the sin of having been born single and alone.

The title of the story indicates a "calmative" against the anguish of per-ceivedness and identifies this sedative power with the memory of the father. The father's role is to define the ambitions and establish the ideals, rather than abet the narcissistic pleasures, of the fledgling ego. The child's imaginative de-sire for a grandiose destiny figured "as in myth and metamorphosis" is traced to the father, who creates for him a bridge from the anxious world of the "realistic ego" to the fabulous world of the heroic self:

> Yes, this evening it has to be as in the story my father used to read me,
> evening after evening, when I was small, and he had all his health, to calm
> me, evening after evening, year after year it seems to me this evening,
> which I don't remember much about, except that it was the adventures of
> one Joe Breem, or Breen, the son of a lighthouse-keeper, a strong muscu-
> lar lad of fifteen, those were the words, who swam for miles in the night,
> a knife between his teeth, after a shark, I forget why, out of sheer hero-
> ism. . . . For me now the setting forth, the struggle and perhaps the re-
> turn, for the old man I am this evening, older than my father ever was,
> older than I shall ever be. (53–54)

The calmative nature of the story originally consisted in its sheer repeatability,
as if in each retelling the story became less a chronicle than a prophecy of the
child's heroic destiny. The son was soothed, and emboldened, too, by the figures
psychologists identify as "ego-ideals": the father, in full vigor of his health, the
strong muscular lad destined, out of the fullness of his nature, for heroic ex-
ploit. The calmative nature of the *memory* of Joe Breen's adventures can be
attributed to something quite different, associated as it is with the son's belated
recognition of the father's dispensation. Now the son recalls the story in order
to hear, with the spirit's inward ear, the father decree the propitious moment
for departure: "For me now the setting forth."

This story does not, needless to say, have a happy ending. A different blessing is discovered at story's end. Entering the city which promised, falsely, to be
the Heavenly one, the narrator falls into a swoon. "I didn't lose consciousness,"
he protests; "when I lose consciousness it will not be to recover it." Finding
himself, rather, "in the same blinding void as before," he recalls his heroic
prototype and remarks:

> A blessing he was not waiting for me, poor old Breem, or Breen. I said,
> The sea is east, it's west I must go, to the left of the north. But in vain I
> raised without hope my eyes to the sky to look for the Bears. For the light
> I steeped in put out the stars, assuming they were there, which I doubted,
> remembering the clouds. (68)

This moment of light-eclipsing vision extinguishes all but the hopeless imperative of departure—"it's west I must go." Heroic story and its hero are merci-
fully occupied elsewhere. Even the sky can give no direction or reflect any
solace, assuming, as it does here, the aspect of a displeased countenance. Dante
charted his course by the stars, steeped in a light that illumined the heavens. No

such love moves Beckett's sun and the other stars. This stark realization motivates the most astonishing yet self-certain declarations in Beckettian soliloquy.
It comes in *Company:* "God is love. Yes or no. No" (52).

Joe Breen is the heroic ideal rescued from the shattered dream-images of
childhood. In him we divine the destiny the son believed to be fashioned and
authorized by paternal love. Mr. Endon, ancestor to Godot, is a contemplative
idol who concentrates the essence of that eternal "No." Onto him is projected
the hopeless love the son bears for his father-figure. Mr. Endon, a higher schiz-
oid, is an idol ideally suited for someone who, like Murphy, is appalled by the
deist's clockwork god and prefers a catatonic divinity. According to his own
system, Murphy should have been content with Endon's mere presence, but
living by precepts, even one's own, is not what Beckett's ne'er-do-wells do well.
The philosophic Murphy who renounces the colossal fiasco of bourgeois society
betrays his unsuspected affiliation to the self-seeking heroes of bourgeois narrative when he insists on being perceived, if not formally recognized, as Endon's
spiritual heir.

In what seems to me to be the most affecting as well as the most evident
coincidence of Joyce's and Beckett's revisioning of our inherited fictions of
paternity, Murphy tries to provoke Mr. Endon into giving him the paternal nod.
But in the chess game he plays with Endon, Murphy, defeated by Endon's im-
perturbable genius for solitaire, is forced to retire without securing the desired
recognition. The god-search has led Murphy into contradicting his own life-
premises. He can accept Endon as a mad clockwork god who upsets the appointed rounds of the Mercyseat Hospital with his own random permutations.
But he cannot abide the idea of Endon as a Nobodaddy who withholds the
precious paternal dispensation—the nod of recognition. Murphy's filial demand underlies the aphoristic lyric addressed to Mr. Endon, his nonextensive
god: "Murphy is a speck in Mr. Endon's unseen." In this instance, as in so many,
expression fails of its reputed thaumaturgic effect. A restless Murphy seeks to
recall to mind the pictures of his past to allay the anguish of nonperceivedness.
He begins to disrobe, as if to expose some conspicuous nakedness in which *esse*
and *percipi* might at last coincide without the ego's attention-getting masquer-
ades.

> When he was naked he lay down in a tuft of soaking tuffets and tried to
> get a picture of Celia. In vain. Of his mother. In vain. Of his father (for he
> was not illegitimate). In vain. It was usual for him to fail with his mother;
> and usual, though less usual, for him to fail with a woman. But never

before had he failed with his father. He saw the clenched fists and rigid upturned face of the Child in a Giovanni Bellini Circumcision, waiting to feel the knife. He saw eyeballs being scraped, first any eyeballs, then Mr. Endon's. (251)

Murphy's train of thought, normally so divagatory, here follows an unwavering Freudian track. Murphy, all mind, first attempts to summon his "natural" mate, Celia, all body. When this fails, he attempts to recapture the image of the mother, apparently the image most resistant to voluntary memory. Such failures with the mother are common, but rare is the obliteration of the paternal imago, the ego-ideal after which the self takes its pattern. All Murphy's *distinct* human images converge in a *generic* pun where according to Freud they originate: in the symbolic sight of human sexual difference as the potential site of castration. Murphy's self-recollection involves an imaginative re-collecting of life-images that hark back to a ritual picturing of circumcision. Here the Beckettian child-man traces his destiny to Bellini's divine manchild, about to be inducted into human society. The memory trace concludes in a visionary image that echoes Buñuel's initiating shock-image in *Le Chien Andalou*—a lacerated eyeball, Buñuel's Medusa-symbol for cinematic perception. Buñuel's surreal violence mocks, even as it evokes, the castration anxiety that haunts an art dependent on the mechanics of projection, displacement, and substitution.

Beckett's surrealist image represents a similar assault on the visionary apprehension of life—in this instance, an entire life. But he stresses the alienating power of that dream image, when, as in myth and metamorphosis, the son watches a displaced version of his own castration. Endon is an indifferent god, Godot an absent god; the figure of "universal malignity" who causes all the rain to fall in *Mercier and Camier* is the actively punitive god who provokes Mercier's rather quaint curse: "As for thee, fuck thee." Camier reminds Mercier that "it's he on the contrary fucks thee. Omniomni, the all-unfuckable."[23] Omniomni, the All in All, is a Father-Figure curiously compounded, narcissistically self-contained and impermeable as Mercier and Camier are not. But Omniomni is also a sublime tautology, a redundancy fitting to express an apostolic theology in which the mystery of procreation is conceived as like engendering like. Indeed, Mercier misapprehends Camier's metaphysical allusion to "Omniomni, the all-unfuckable" as a domestic gibe and huffily retorts: "Kindly leave Mrs. Mercier outside this discussion."

Only to the Mother belongs the power of distinct conjugations and individual (at best stylish!) mediations. For the son-writer she is the source of that primary language in which things and persons are discriminated in their sub-sisting integrity against the ground in which they figure. Let us call this ground "Molloy country," the habitat whose ditches, ravines, and furrows symbolically evoke, if landscape ever did evoke, the body of the Mother. Beckett gives this maternal figure a rather morbid turn by suggesting that the maternal body is half cadaver. The return of *this* native to the mother's house bespeaks a recidi-vism that regards the mother's house as both asylum and death chamber. Yet it is also on these dilapidated maternal premises that all true writing commences.

The Mother, in Beckett's amazing reversal, is the logocentric idol who commands the secret of self-presence. Only she possesses the power of trans-forming *esse est percipi* into the equation of apotheosis, the exhibitionist's dream. Murphy initially renounces "the glorious world of discrete particles, where it would be his inestimable prerogative once again to wonder, love, hate, desire, rejoice and howl in a reasonable balanced manner, and comfort himself with the society of others in the same predicament" (177). It was from just this consideration that Murphy, while still less than a child, had set out to capture himself, not with anger but with love.

To capture himself with love—never has the positive narcissistic founda-tion of *amor intellectualis* been so lucidly declared. The particular object of Murphy's quest is scrupulously reconstructed in the famous section 6, which not only describes Murphy's mind, but issues a bulletin on his mental condition. In this bulletin, we are told that Murphy distinguishes between the experiences of the body and the experiences of the mind, but does not understand how the two experiences came to overlap:

> He was satisfied that neither followed from the other. He neither thought a kick because he felt one nor felt a kick because he thought one. Perhaps the knowledge was related to the fact of the kick as two magnitudes to a third. Perhaps there was, outside space and time, a non-mental non-physical Kick from all eternity, dimly revealed to Murphy in its correlated modes of consciousness and extensions, the kick *in intellectu* and the kick *in re*. But where then was the supreme Caress? (109)

As an enthymemic demonstration, this passage has its own appeal as a satire on the complications of Cartesian existence. But it should be pointed out that Murphy's logical attempt to correlate life of the body and life in the mind culminates in a transcendental *affect*—the rapture of "the supreme Caress." Caress is not related to kick as pure antonym, for the kick can only impress us negatively with the *force* of tactile connections. Caress answers to kick as a positive sensation elicited by bodily contact. Yet *caress* is a word that evokes an added, heightened sensation of a focused tenderness. Beckett's precision in distinguishing between a discrete sensation (the kick) and a human *contact* (the caress) confirms his prescience as a psychological novelist. Indeed, recent pediatric studies strongly suggest that touch, not mere presence, is essential to the infant's physical as well as emotional maturation.[24] That the neurochemical effects of skin-to-skin contact contribute to infant survival is another Cartesian intuition confirmed.

But how are we to interpret this intuition or to pursue this dream? Is the supreme caress a sublime Platonic sensation gesturing to us outside space and time? Does it exist only in the mind of Murphy, where its possibility is for the first and perhaps last time posited, only to be thereafter abandoned as an absurd Platonism of the heart? It is important to emphasize that Beckett's yearning for a transcendent affection involves no tepid satisfaction, but a genuine *raptos* such as Dante felt basking in the astral radiance of his Beatrice. "All life is figure and ground," asserts Neary; "but a wandering to find home," returns Murphy. The gesture that signals the transformation of alien ground into authentic homeland is not the father's welcoming embrace, but the mother's enlivening caress.

The first and the most fearful expression of this yearning for an *affective* sublimity occurs in an early short story, "Assumption," whose title alludes to the most spectacular of the religious mysteries centering on Mary. "Assumption" allegorizes the mother-child relation in the fateful—and fatal—encounter of the aspiring poet with his mother-muse. The subject of the story is a poet tormented by a "rebellious surge that aspired violently towards a realization in sound." He lives in terror of the time when the voice of this inner daimon would "be released in one splendid drunken scream and fused with cosmic discord."[28] In the obsessional rituals devised by the fledgling poet to ensure the silencing of this rebellious inner voice, we can discern the dark, defensive beginnings of Beckett's self-silencing art. He scarcely leaves his room. He wards off sleep, lest the forces of repression relax his aphonia: "He began to have a horror of unexpected pain, of sleep, of anything that might remove the involuntary inhibition." Self-barricaded, he anxiously realizes that "by damning the stream of whispers he had raised the level of the flood."

It is at this life-deciding juncture that "the Woman came to him." At first she appears to be nothing more than a hackneyed figure of a hackneyed muse: "It was the usual story, vulgarly told: admiration for his genius, sympathy with his suffering, only a woman could understand . . ." Yet as she advances into his secured space of "terrifying silent immobility," the young poet is compelled to attention: "An irruption of demons would not have scattered his intentness so utterly." Beckett would later hope to capture such intentness, established here as the primary attribute of the self-in-recoil, in the face of Buster Keaton. His scenario for *Film* describes the desired effect of the last shot of Keaton's face as an expression "impossible to describe, neither severity nor benignity, but rather acute *intentness*" (47; emphasis Beckett's). Such intentness, "Assumption" suggests and *Film* displays, can be achieved only through the effacement of all affect, whether severe or benign. As such it seems a belated and defensive reaction against the mother's habitual negative mirroring, a theory that *Film* also confirms in having Keaton remove from his room any form or object that resembles in appearance a reflecting eye or mirroring surface. This emotional and specular ascesis is the condition of Beckett's intentness, and is scarcely human. Perhaps only filmic art could realize such a derealized projection of human existence. But for the young Beckett, still vulnerable to the maternal appeal, this ascesis is hardly to be dreamt of. The poet's intense self-absorption is doomed to be sacrificed to the distracting yet desirable presence of the woman-mother-muse.

Beckett shows himself, even in this early work, to be the master of the emotional reversal and affective upheaval. The woman's invasive presence becomes, indeed will routinely become in the later Beckett, an emotionally revivifying occasion. Indeed that is the trouble with women. Beckett's irony is not French; he is no Stendhalian whose desire is for desire itself. He seeks the ablation of desire, not its resurrection, as the irony of this story's title instructs. Thus it is against his own creative instincts that the young poet finds himself beginning to appreciate the "charming shabbiness" of the woman's face. Her departures, no matter how temporary, are felt to be acts of desertion or—more accurately—evacuations of something vital and integral to himself: "When at last she went away he felt that something had gone out of him, something he could not spare, but still less could grudge, something of the desire to live, something of the unreasonable tenacity with which he shrank from dissolution." Woman is identified—without apology or apparent anxiety—with the young man's "essential animality," his self-preserving, self-affirming instinct to shrink from annihilation. Two forces thus confront each other in a soul with "nothing to spare": Eros, which affiliates and attaches, and Thanatos, which undoes and dissolves. "Assumption" resolves their conflict in an auricular catastrophe in which voice obliterates sight: "Then it happened. While the woman was contemplating the face that she had overlaid with death, she was swept aside by a great storm of sound, shaking the very house with its prolonged, triumphant vehemence, climbing in a dizzy, bubbling scale, until, dispersed, it fused into the breath of the forest and the throbbing cry of the sea" (271). The scream of sound marks the poet's ritual *sparagmos:* his dismemberment, scattering, and assumption—reabsorption, actually—into primal Nature. The storm of sound that annihilates him, like the gas explosion that blows Murphy to bits, symbolizes a carthartic release of repressed powers. But "Assumption" intrigues us by presenting us with a more intimate victimization than the cosmic scattering of Murphy's body into superfine chaos. The poet of "Assumption" nightly reenacts his Dionysian theophany ("each night he died and was God, each night revived and was torn") as a ritual preparation for his final return and reassumption into maternal Nature. The woman, who personifies Nature as a figure of life-in-death, survives the catastrophe staged in her honor and tenderly ministers to her poetic minion: "They found her caressing his wild dead hair." Here the supreme caress comes at the hands of Mother death.

## THE MATERNAL REBUKE

Let us retrace the origins of this traumatic equation between voice and death, as Beckett does in *Company,* to the memory of a maternal rebuke:

> A small boy you come out of Connolly's Stores holding your mother by the hand. You turn right and advance in silence southward along the highway. After some hundred paces you head inland and broach the long steep homeward. You make ground in silence hand in hand through the warm still summer air. It is late afternoon and after some hundred paces the sun appears above the crest of the rise. Looking up at the blue sky and then at your mother's face you break the silence asking her if it is not in reality much more distant than it appears. The sky that is. The blue sky. Receiving no answer you mentally reframe your question and some hundred paces later look up at her face again and ask her if it does not appear much less distant than in reality it is. For some reason you could never fathom this question must have angered her exceedingly. For she shook off your little hand and made you a cutting retort you have never forgotten. (10–11)

The cutting retort is reported and remembered as a traumatic memory. The child's breaking his silence is connected with his need to know his own position vis-à-vis the desired homeland—the horizon connecting seen and unseen. The matter of the retort is not given; what Beckett stresses is his bewilderment at the mother's *tone,* the apparently unprovoked anger his question elicits. The cross-purposes of Beckettian dialogue, with its hidden tensions and its undertone of explosive resentment, find their prototype and, arguably, their antecedent cause in the unfathomed reason of the mother's cold retort. In the mother's world, where silence is enjoined, a whisper can dislocate as well as a bomb. The only sound in Beckett's silent *Film* is "Sh . . . ," an admonitory (and vituperative) hush, delivered, as if to a refractory child, to the figure (Keaton or O) who flees the eye of the camera.

In *Company* the maternal rebuke is represented as a traumatic event. In *Malone Dies,* Beckett recalls the circumstantial as well as the essential matter of the maternal rebuke. In this fictional retelling of this childhood event, Beckett acknowledges the distance that separates the mother's mind and the son's. This concession contributes to the child's abjection:

> We were not often of the same mind. One day we were walking along the road, up a hill of extraordinary steepness, near home I imagine, my memory is full of steep hills, I get them confused. I said, The sky is further away than you think, is it not mama? It was without malice, I was simply thinking of the leagues that separated me from it. She replied, to me her son, It is precisely as far away as it appears to be. She was right. But at the time I was aghast. (98)

Again, the child is left aghast less at the content than at the tone of the mother's reply. This emotional reaction persists, even though the mother's response here is conceded to be a "right" answer to a question and not, as in *Company,* an incomprehensible rebuke for a childish impertinence. The child reacts to what he perceives, correctly, to be the violence of the mother's heartless exactitude: "It is precisely as far away as it appears to be." For it is not the truth that the mother declares which shocks and frightens, but the mother's malice—or, worse, indifference—in responding so flatly to the child's sense of and need for wondrous vistas. The cool astonishment of that phrase, "to me her son," suggests how the maternal reply is felt to be a *retort,* at once a negation and a disparagement of the child's complex yearning for home. The mother refuses to mirror his wonder of distances, and so intends, thinks the child, to diminish him too. She appears neither to endorse nor to enhance his destiny as a voyager in the world. Could the mother not have known the child's enchantment with horizons that separate the seen from the unseen? Could she not appreciate or sympathize with the child's immense pull skyward, that yearning for ascent that is figured in the steep hills and gentle slopes of Beckett's imaginary landscapes? Mother and son, it is clear, simply do not see eye to eye.

"The End" gives us the most sardonic version of this radical incompatibility between the maternal mind and the lyrical sensitivities of the son-poet:

> Now I was making my way through the garden. There was that strange light which follows a day of persistent rain, when the sun comes out and the sky clears too late to be of any use. The earth makes a sound as of sighs and the last drops fall from the emptied cloudless sky. A small boy stretched out his hands and looking up at the blue sky, asked his mother how such a thing was possible. Fuck off, she said. (74)

The tone of his maternal retort is vulgar, as if to offset, if not indeed to obliterate, the child's sensitivity to Nature. Those who favor the hard-knocks school of child rearing might see in this maternal retort a necessary antidote to the boy's impractical, lyrical susceptibility to his natural environment (natural environment!—so Beckett would typographically protest the immense complacency of that phrase). I read this episode as a sardonic illustration of Beckett's original ruthhilarious predicament: that nothing can minimize and yet nothing can replace the prestige of the mother who takes the reality of appearances, as she does their precision, on faith. The precision of the mother's formula— "precisely as far away as it appears to be"—deadens the child's quickening imagination. Her formula has the power to transform the romantic horizon into an empty firmament. The heart recoils from the coldness of such exactitudes, which effectively deride and so dissipate the spirit-elevating mood of all creative perception. It is the mood Beckett explicitly and somewhat sentimentally identified in his essay on Proust in the paradoxical phrase "the enchantment of reality," an enchantment only to be experienced when the heart can dream and embrace its beloved objects detached from "the sanity of a cause." [26] And it is, according to Beckett's reading of Proust, only in such moments, when we abandon our rational determinations (the sanity of a cause) and submit to our ignorance, that "our first nature . . . corresponding to a deeper instinct than the mere animal instinct of self-preservation, is laid bare." This deeper instinct desires to annihilate all temporal and spatial restrictions in a consuming and consummating sensation which unites subject and its objects in "the enchantments of reality." [27]

The Mother stands at the crossroads where these two strains of Beckettian affectivity are fated, doomed actually, to intersect in perpetual enmity: his aesthetical yearning for a mystical experience "at once imaginative and empirical, at once an evocation and a direct perception, real without being merely actual, ideal without being merely abstract, the ideal real, the essential, the extratemporal"; his defensive antisentimentalism. It is the antisentimentalist in Beckett who sees life as a cause for dianoetic laughter, a laughter that can make fun of everything and everyone *except* the one realist at whom he dares not sneer: the Mother and her cold precisions. It is to her idol that he sacrifices his grandiose-exhibitionist dreams of ideal-real perceptions on the altar of silence.

Beckett's preoccupation with the aesthetics of the inexpressible may be traced, then, not to the Father's castrating, silencing displeasure, but to the Mother's extinguishing indifference. So much is apparently confirmed in the ninth of Beckett's *Texts for Nothing,* in which the speaker asks himself "on what score I could possibly be anxious," and finds his answer: "I haven't yet been noticed even though I could scarcely have gone unperceived." This recognition is the first thing, complains the speaker, "always the same thing proposing itself to my perplexity, then disappearing, then proposing itself again, to my perplexity still unsated, or momentarily dead, of starvation." [28] The infant wail can be heard behind this controlled lament, in which the abandoned and unperceived child, still unsated, starving for the confirming maternal gaze, searches for a way to enter the graveyard where the dead Father is interred. There he might "pass out, and see the beauties of the skies, and see the stars again." The emotional power of this dream-memory does not emanate from the son's desire for the father's company, but from his yearning for a vista: the sight of the heavens, the beauties of its skies and its hidden stars. It is a yearning heightened by the artistic expectation that sustains it: "to know exactly where" this first, last, and most magnificent of nights might be contemplated would, the speaker hopes, "be a mere matter of time, and patience, and sequency of thought, and felicity of expression." This seems to me an admirable description of the novelist's life discipline, dealing in patience with the matter of time, creating sequency of thought and felicity of expression out of the "problematic patrolling, unconstrained, before the gates of the graveyard" (120). Delicate though telling is Beckett's simple juxtaposition of the confined space and extensive time of human life. He speaks of knowing *exactly* where in a *mere* matter of time, the precision of "exactly" jeopardized by the implied naiveté of that foolhardy "mere."

The foolishness of trusting to Time, the old Fornicator, as Beckett personifies it in *Murphy,* is the object lesson of Beckett's most pained recollection of the son's effort at loving accommodation, "First Love." This novella is the most brashly oedipal of Beckett's narratives, as its justly famous first line announces: "I associate, rightly or wrongly, my marriage with the death of my father, in time." The semantic and structural rigor of associating the father's death with the son's marriage (by which he recovers the mother, if only in the woman who replaces her) is compromised by the added qualification, appended as if in afterthought, "in time." Which time? is precisely the question narration must answer, and Beckett's First Lover distinguishes, as he awaits his beloved, three different times converging and coexisting in the "time" of his erotic vigil: ". . . one is the hour of the dial, and another that of changing air and sky, and another yet again the heart's" (20). Chronological time, seasonal time, the heart's time—typically, Beckett's distinctions collapse even as he attempts to articulate and discriminate among them. The narrative and sexual obsession of "First Love" with birth dates, boundary markers, and boundary states (like pregnancy) identifies it as an initiation fiction of a peculiarly vexed kind.

"First Love" indeed has been regarded as the threshold fiction that transformed Beckett from a writer of English fictions to an artificer of French prose.[29] Beckett withheld publication of the story, written in 1943, until 1970, when both his mother and the woman who occasioned the story were dead. The "coming of age" that is the explicit subject of First Love narratives involves, in Beckett's case, a complex process whose analogue is not so much ritual rebirth as formal adoption. The pathos of the linguistic self-estrangement that underwrites Beckett's adopting the French tongue is epitomized in one of Beckett's more dour aphorisms: "What goes by the name of love is banishment, with now and then a postcard from the homeland, such is my considered opinion, this evening" (15–16). Now what Beckett is immediately referring to is the felt effect, linguistically as well as psychosomatically, of an involuntary erection. In "First Love" Eros assumes his most common manifestation—an erection, where it is the supreme and comic instance of self-extension and self-loss that is purportedly the physiological condition and existential promise of sexual encounter: "One is no longer oneself, on such occasions, and it is painful to be no longer oneself, even more painful if possible than when one is. For when one is one knows what to do to be less so, whereas when one is not one is any old one irredeemably." This mordant if rather scholastic account of sex vividly underscores the potential comedy in Kohut's distinction between pleasure-seeking oedipal man and the narcissistically depleted man for whom tension is merely pain, and not the preliminary to a pleasurable discharge. To keep oneself, no matter how empty, is preferable, for Tragic Man, to laying waste what little powers one has in trying to find a new self, a new love. It is therefore not only useful but necessary to see Beckett's sexual satire as a peculiar emendation of erotoleptic narratives, which interpret sexual transport as a species of self-alienation. Here is a supreme instance of Beckett's Cartesian comedy, in which the words of the mind struggle to keep pace with the body's irrepressible and independent system of sexual signals. The sexual *entendre* is understood, but it is perceived to be another instance of Nature's semantic trickery.

In Beckett's increasing reluctance to participate in Nature's semiotic fecundities we detect the will-to-monotony, the effacement of all affect that characterizes the late style. Beckett's asceticism is implicated in his self-exile from the profligacies and fluencies of the mother tongue. Beckett seems to have dreamt of this ascesis as early as "Dream of Fair to Middling Women." In this unpublished fictional fragment, Belacqua contemplates the crystallized magic of the phrase "black diamond of pessimism":

> "Black diamond of pessimism." Belacqua thought that was a nice example, in the domain of words, of the little sparkle hid in ashes, the precious margaret and hit [sic] from many, and the thing that the conversationalist, with his contempt of the tag and the ready-made, can't give you, because the lift to the high spot is precisely from the tag and the ready-made. The same with the stylist. You couldn't experience a margarita in d'Annunzio because he denies you the pebbles and flints that reveal it. The uniform, horizontal writing, flowing without accidence, of the man with a style, never gives you the margarita. But the writing of, say, Racine or Malherbe, perpendicular, diamanté, is pitted, is it not, and sprigged with sparkles; the flints and pebbles are there, no end of humble tags and commonplaces. They have no style, they write without style, do they not, they give you the phrase, the sparkle, the precious margaret. Perhaps only the French can do it. Perhaps only the French language can give you the thing you want.[30]

We are instructed not to be too hard on Belacqua; "he was studying to be a professor." Still, even in less academic moods, Beckett will not renounce the phrase, the precious margaret that makes the artist's chthonian life worthwhile. The Beckettian phrase, like the pearl or precious margarite, exists by virtue of creative irritations. The "mature" or postmodern Beckett also writes as if the precious phrase is awarded only him who represses or renounces the romantic "uniform, horizontal writing, flowing without accidence"—the feminized discourse of a flamboyant, narcissistic, self-exuberant romanticism, the romanticism of that stylish man who loved women, D'Annunzio. The child-man must renounce the grandiose exhibitionism of his narcissistic youth and its romantic infatuations if he is to become his ego-ideal, the man without a style. It is an ideal ironically celebrated in *Company,* that autobiographical musing in which Beckett observes the characteristic "trait" of his voice, which comes to him in the dark: "Same flat tone at all times. For its affirmations. For its negations. For its interrogations. For its exclamations. For its imperations. Same flat tone. You were once. You were never. Were you ever? Oh never to have been! Be again. Same flat tone" (20). This astounding passage not only catalogues but exemplifies the affirmations (You were once), the negations (You never were), the exclamations (Oh never to have been!), and the imperations (Be again) of Beckettian soliloquy.

We should not forget, however, that the exhibitionism of Beckett's self-representations, particularly in his early work, is precisely what makes Beckett's "style" conversant with the exuberant modernism best typified in Joycean writing—the exhibitionism of promiscuous styles, profligate vocabularies. Beckett's lexicographic genius marks a further affinity with Johnson, but I want also to remark here Beckett's resemblance to another lexicographer, the author of the *Dictionary of Received Opinions.* Like Flaubert, Beckett is an assiduous, bemused (when not exasperated) taxonomist of culture. Beckett's "late style" still suffers occasional "erotoleptic" fits of expression which disrupt the controlled monotony and repressions of his flat tone. In such virtuoso performances Beckett pays homage to the specificity of the verbal world man creates for himself, an imaginatively vital world where names are invented and realities created by the sheer audacity of neologism or the rare romance of learning. Everyone who *really* reads Beckett will have committed to memory his favorite Beckettian cadenza, in which Greco-Roman magnificences and monkish jewels gleam through the deliberate reticences and repressions of the flat and faceless style.

In these moments of verbal vehemence, Beckett's exhibitionistic personality reasserts itself. Observe, for example, how the narrator of "First Love" defines his "way of loving":

> Are we to infer from this that I loved her with that intellectual love which
> drew from me such drivel, in another place? Somehow I think not. For
> had my love been of this kind would I have stooped to inscribe the letters
> of Anna in time's forgotten cowplats? To divellicate urtica *plenis manibus?*
> And felt, under my tossing head, her thighs to bounce like so many de-
> mon bolsters? Come now! (20)

The self-allusion to Murphy and his quest for intellectual love would be attention-getting enough. But, the moment being opportune for further self-displays, the narrator compounds this astonishment by producing that precious and preposterous phrase—"To divellicate urtica *plenis manibus?*" Here indeed is what we might call an uncommon expression, one calculated, as Kohut might say, to call attention to the speaker and not the content of his speechifying. The "Come now," interpreted in this spirit, seems both a colloquial put-down and the vaudevillian's come-on, beckoning us to witness yet another feat of verbal prestidigitation by which the narrator arranges, on time's forgotten cowplats, his own loving inscriptions.

Such verbal eruptions historicize Beckett's prose; they force us to recall the involuntary, erotoleptic transports of the lover of words—the more arcane and useless the word, the more precious, because so rare, so uncontaminated by common usage or the glare of habit. And from the perception that there exist occasions when only the right word will do, we derive the related perception that in such life-instances only the right person will do. This is the imperation of First Love, which mingles erotic and verbal yearnings in a rapturous apprehension of the world. For the lover, the semantic succor of the mot juste resides in rescuing the beloved image from the rubble of the commonplace. For do not the dream of First Love and the dream of an original style, in pursuing the same exhilarating course of self-expression, conclude in the same sad recognition: that the first reveals itself to be neither the first nor the last, but only a continuation of a perpetually including middle? For habit soon obliterates the startling clarity of the image, forgetfulness blurs the outlines of the invented and beloved object, and what was first and irreplaceable is in peril of becoming general and common once again.

But we still need to determine in what language *love* is a word that disguises and so facilitates the banishment the son is fated to undergo. Julia Kristeva maintains that it is the language of the *dead* father, whose corpse inspires the son with an impossible fantasy of love that "survives paternal meaning." Kristeva offers us this reconstruction of the fantasy:

> *Father* and *Death* are united, but still split and separate. *On the one hand,* Death—the ideal that provides meaning but where the word is silent; *on the other,* the paternal corpse, hence a possible though trivial communication, waste, decay, and excrement mobilizing pleasure and leisure. A verbal find seals this junction of opposites: *chamber pot,* a term that, for the son-writer, evokes Racine, Baudelaire, and Dante all at once, summarizing the sublimated obscenity that portrays him as consubstantial with his father, but only the *decayed* cadaver of his father, never leaving the black mourning of inaccessible paternal function, which itself has found refuge on the side of *Death.* [31]

In a footnote, Kristeva observes that the paternal names Beckett evokes in *Premier Amour* to establish his consubstantial sonship—Racine, Baudelaire, and

Dante—do not appear in the English version. This deliberate omission of the paternal roster once Beckett translates his story back into his mother tongue is remarkable in its own right. Indeed, one of the unwavering convictions that both sustains and irritates the Beckettian writer is his belief that the bold paternal line of succession has become a mere squiggle. In *Company* Beckett retraces, against the surreal landscape of Freudian tragicomedy, the son's inability to follow the Father's trail back to the maternal gap: "Halfway across the pasture on your beeline to the gap. The unerring feet fast. You look behind you as you could not then and see their trail. A great swerve. Withershins. Almost as if all at once the heart too heavy. In the end too heavy" (38). In a typical Beckettian compression, the feet are unerringly fast, quickened with desire but suddenly immobilized by the heart's heavy burden. The son's path begins as a beeline but retrospectively is seen to be a "great swerve."

Yet this swerve actually traces a Joycean *ricorso* in which the son's divergence from the father's path provokes a confused but potent memory of First Love: "Bloom of adulthood. Imagine a whiff of that. On your back in the dark you remember. Ah you you remember. Cloudless May day. She joins you in the little summerhouse" (38). The summerhouse, it appears, once served as the father's retreat; there he retired with his *Punch* and a cushion with "the waist of his trousers unbuttoned." In the father's precincts the body can relax and the spirit chuckle—so Beckett remembers, and remembers, too, scenes in which he first experimented in the imitative arts: "When he chuckled you tried to chuckle too. When his chuckle died yours too. That you should try to imitate his chuckle pleased and tickled him greatly and sometimes he would chuckle for no other reason than to hear you try to chuckle too" (39). This memory returns laden with all its original "calmative" promise. Recalled are the physical ease and emotional pleasures of the father-son exchanges, in game and in play. But the bloom of adulthood also carries a whiff of an errie reality and the stilled—dead still—feeling it accommodates. Beckett's memory spans the intervening years from childhood to young adulthood and recalls how as a young man he looked on his beloved only to find that she did not return his smile: "Your gaze descends to the breasts. You do not remember them so big. To the abdomen. Same impression. Dissolve to your father's straining against the unbuttoned waistband. Can it be she is with child without your having asked for as much as her hand?" (42). In the son's befuddled "can it be" the mystery of paternity and First Love declares itself. The mystery of precedence and succession is comprehended in the quick cinematic dissolve that connects the mistress's distended belly to the father's unbuttoned trousers. A similar impression will appall the son of "First Love" when he looks on his mistress's big belly:

> Look, she said, stooping over her breasts, the haloes are darkening already.
> I summoned up my remaining strength and said, Abort, abort, and they'll
> blush like new. She had drawn back the curtain for a clear view of all her
> rotundities. I saw the mountain, impassible, cavernous, secret, where from
> morning to night I'd hear nothing but the wind, the curlews, the clink
> like distant silver of the stone-cutter's hammers. (29)

The work of creation is chthonian. It transpires in the womb, the lost paradise
whose gates are forever impassable to those expelled from its cavernous, secret,
treasured world. This is as clear a view of woman's fertile rotundities as we are
likely to have, at whose edges the Beckettian laborer chips away in increasing
silence. But should he even succeed in approaching the dark interior from
which life and his own speech issue, he will make a curious discovery. It is the
discovery the lover makes during his "night of love" when he realizes the power
of the woman to *absorb* his voice:

> I was so unused to speech that my mouth would sometimes open, of its
> own accord, and vent some phrase or phrases, grammatically unexcep-
> tionable but entirely devoid if not of meaning, for on close inspection they
> would reveal one, and even several, at least of foundation. But I heard
> each word no sooner spoken. Never had my voice taken so long to reach
> me as on this occasion. I turned over on my back to see what was going
> on. She was smiling. (26)

This night of love reenacts the primal maternal rebuke. It is not the semiotic
fullness or emptiness of his speech that matters—in fact, the narrator's words
possess a meaning, even several. What marks this moment as memorable and
subject to traumatic fixation is the ambiguous female smile that suggests a
superior power to absorb, as it inspires, his voice. This moment of silence is the
foundation to which all Beckettian expressiveness must descend.

What is retrieved from this descent into the depths of human feeling and
human language is the stark formula that concludes "First Love": "But there it
is, either you love or you don't" (30). Beckett invokes Kierkegaard here to
strange effect. Kierkegaard's Either/Or entertains an opposition between the
erotic and moral, the aesthetic and ethical import of love, an opposition that
may be dialectically resolved in the "eternal present" of the First Love which is
the true love. Beckett's Either/Or enforces, through its syntactic parallelism, a
more radical antinomy. Both in its emotional and in its grammatical moods, his
either/or posits not a dialectical relation but a radical separation between loving
and not loving, a perpetual alternation between two extreme existential states:

immense fulfillment or extreme vastation. "First Love" is the text that memorializes this impasse, but cannot devise a way out.

Only in the creative poetics of the pun does the erotic impasse find a sad echo of transcendence. This is the possibility to which Celia, the streetwalker apprised of the way love is bartered in the world, returns us. Her name, as her profession, makes of her life a sad pun. Celia is both prostitute and heavenly promise, "s'il y a." It is this promise that gives Beckett's dubious metaphysics a poetic authority and human poignancy, and reminds us that Beckett's slapstick romances, for all the physical comedy of their erotic vaudeville, have at their core the formal dignity of comic topos: mésalliance, the social form of irrational mating. Murphy, all mind (as described in the book's famous section 6), loves Celia, all body (introduced to us in chapter 2 as a table of measurements). In the Beckettian lore of love, theirs is a singular and apparently inimitable instance of love requited, "the short circuit so earnestly desired by Neary, the glare of pursuit and flight extinguished" (29). Neary, Murphy's erstwhile mentor and one-time Pythagorean, can only approach this state of heartsease which he labels, successively, Apmonia, Isonomy, and Attunement. He lives in the vicinity of such celestial harmony, as his doggerel name, Neary, suggests. Only Murphy and Celia manage to complete the much-desired but rarely accomplished short circuit, Murphy, all mind, loving Celia, all body.

This attunement, a Cartesian dream come true, is also registered in Celia's name, which recalls to us the patron saint of music. Here the associations are both sacred and obscene, as witness Celia's threat to Murphy—"No more music," a phrase, the narrator informs us, "chosen with care, lest the filthy censors should lack an occasion to commit their filthy synecdoche" (76). One can resist the temptation to confuse what Celia does with what she symbolizes, yet still marvel at the poetics of Celia's name, the poetics of the pun, in which the world itself, according to Beckett, had its inception: "In the beginning was the pun." Gas—chaos—in this pun Murphy anticipates his own demise and impersonalizes it as part of the cosmological scheme. His death is ruled a case of misadventure; he is a victim of a universal pun on which Creation is irremovably founded. Who knows what other universes might exist that were created out of more propitious homonyms?

What we do know is that the universe half-perceived, half-created out of a first and abiding love might put an end to desire's endless tautologies: Yes. No. Either you love or you don't. To Celia is appointed the task of articulating the conditions of this heavenly promise. Tellingly, her description of paradise comes in the form of an elegy:

"At first I thought I had lost him because I could not take him as he was. Now I do not flatter myself."

A rest.

"I was a piece out of him that he could not go on without, no matter what I did."

A rest.

"He had to leave me to be what he was before he met me, only worse, or better, no matter what I did."

A long rest.

"I was the last exile."

"The last, if we are lucky."

"So love is wont to end, in protasis, if it be love." (234)

Celia, all body, stages the Golgotha of her love. Murphy's mind could not do without life in the body, although he was fated to leave—not abandon—her. She allegorizes herself as the last exile. But she humanizes herself in the striking melancholy of her protasis, "The last, if we are lucky." Protasis is a difficult grammatical figure. No child could master the intricacy of its subordinations, its delicate and tactful deferrals in which form and content finally meet—the conditional expressed in the conditional mood. In Celia's striking protasis, which proceeds through a series of musical and hermeneutical rests, love is brought to its wonted end—accepting the conditional in the language of the conditional. What makes Celia's vision, like her name, so heavenly, is the music trying to sound through her distinctive pauses, the promising lags that intermit her final words on love. Hers is an impressive caesura, as solemn and as irreversible as birth.

# NINE

# A DEFENSE
# OF FIRST LOVE

I N HIS ARRESTING 1921 ESSAY, "Eros, Platonic and Modern," Georg Simmel remarks "the peculiar and not particularly praiseworthy fact" that the claim of philosophy "to provide a deeper estimation of life has been left unfulfilled with respect to a number of important and problematic elements of life." "Perhaps the most neglected of all the great vital issues," Simmel continues, "has been love—as though this were an incidental matter, a mere adventure of the subjective soul, unworthy of the seriousness and rigorous objectivity of philosophical endeavor." [1] Luckily, the novel, that commodious form that treats of incidental matter with all due seriousness and makes the adventures of the subjective soul one of its vital concerns, has been diligent where philosophy may have been negligent. Indeed the novel has often accorded its deepest estimation of life to the life-affecting, spirit-manifesting power of human love. It has been the contention of this book that the modern novel, the English novel in particular, reserves its highest esteem and deepest attachment for the First Love. It is to the firstcomer that modernity delegates the task of following love "to the ultimate ideals and metaphysical potencies, to all the places where life as experienced is connected to these potencies." [2] In First Love, the subjective culture of modernity, which originates, as Simmel remarks, in "that ultimate deepening and individualization of the self-being," flowers into a mythology, one which at once imposes on the world the imprint of individual desire and confers on the lover the life-productive illusion of an incontestable priority, a profound originality.

It is a mythology whose idols, though now widely discredited by Nietzschean assaults on their validity, we might do well to honor, if not revere. We ought to respect them, as we should all vanishing relics and abandoned beliefs, because they attest to the visionary power of first things, primordial feelings. Readers schooled in the tradition of the "new life," or those newly initiated into its marvels and pleasures, may compile their own canons of First Love narratives: James's *What Maisie Knew,* Mann's "Disorder and Early Sorrow," Eudora Welty's "First Love," Harold Bradkey's "First Love," Ian McEwan's "First Love, Last Rites," and, most impressive, Gabriel García Marquez's *Love in the Time of Cholera* are but some of the many works that explicitly evoke or implicitly testify to the persistence of First Love in the modern literary imagination. Yet it is Nabokov's first novel, *Mary,* that epitomizes for me that magical endurance and perpetual newness of First Love in the modern writings of the world. Nabokov's *Mary,* drawn, as Nabokov openly confesses in his introduction, from his own youthful experiences, is the template fiction after which future Nabokovian fictions will be patterned. *Mary* resounds with all the poignant, acerbic, witty, magical expressions of Nabokovian feeling: nostalgia, imagination's wizardry in resurrecting the past in the midst of the "new life" of exile, the deep sentiment for concrete things whose veneer of immediate reality may be pierced by the clairvoyant eye ("Transparent things, through which the past shines!").[3] *Mary* recounts the experience of a Russian emigré, Lev Ganin, who is floundering in exile in Berlin. Through a chance meeting, he discovers that his first love will soon arrive in Berlin to rejoin her husband, who lives at Ganin's boardinghouse. This rather whimsical coincidence buoys Ganin's despondent spirits. He lapses into a kind of clairvoyant trance and roams the wide streets of Berlin, strangely excited by the perception that the people he passes are "no longer a reveler, a woman, or simply a passer-by, but each one a wholly isolated world, each a totality of marvels and evil." To see individuals in this way is to see them novelistically. It is to perceive the individual, not as a conventional figure for a generalized alienation, but as a totality of marvels and evil, a complete world whose isolation ends once it is represented in all its mysterious and inimitable particularity. "It is at moments like this," comments the narrator, "that everything grows fabulous, unfathomably profound, when life seems terrifying and death even worse."[4] It is moments like this, then, moments infused with "glorious dazzling recollections of past happiness—a woman's face, resurgent after many years of humdrum oblivion," that we apprehend the fabulous and metaphysical potencies that rule our existence. As Ganin stumbles his way back through "the bright labyrinth of memory," he is careful to pay strict yet fond attention to all the details, even the most trivial, that contribute to the concrete totality of the world in which he first loved: "He was a god, re-creating a world that had perished. Gradually he resurrected that world, to please the girl whom he did not dare to place in it until it was absolutely complete" (33).

It is a world, of course, only to be recaptured in imagination, never to be reinstalled and translated into the immediate present—the life of the here and now, with its own completely different world of things, attachments, and miraculous possibilities. Ganin's accession to creative individuality is not to be measured by his success or failure in resurrecting the world of his youth, which, at novel's end, he knows to be past revival. His real metamorphosis and the "secret turning point of his life" is marked by the resurgence of his power for creative perception:

> Ganin walked down the middle of the sidewalk, gently swinging his solidly packed bags, and thought how long it was since he had felt so fit, strong and ready to tackle anything. And the fact that he kept noticing everything with a fresh, loving eye—the carts driving to market, the

slender, half-unfolded leaves and the many-colored posters which a man
in an apron was sticking around a kiosk—this fact meant a secret turning
point for him, an awakening. (113)

Well-equipped with his solidly packed bags, emotionally reinvigorated by the
intact beauty of a past from which he has forever departed, Ganin is ready not
only to tackle but to love the world. His creative initiative is registered, as it
always is in Nabokov, by the freshness of his perception, the cleansing of vision
that reveals things in their vibrant integrity. In this keen attention to the concrete objects and ordinary sights that compose the human environment, Nabokov makes the modern world possible not only for art, but for prophecy: "But
then who can tell what it really is that flickers up there in the dark about the
houses—the luminous name of a product or the glow of human thought; a
sign, a summons, a question hurled into the sky and suddenly getting a jewel-
bright, enraptured answer?" (26–27). It is Nabokov's genius to divine, as Joyce
also divined, numinous signs in the world's most common, often its most garish,
things. A commercial advertisement lighting up the night sky can be as propitious a sign as "the appearance of a new star (1st magnitude) dominating both
day and night . . . about the period of Shakespeare's birth" (*Ulysses,* 575). Like
Joyce, Nabokov discerned in the everyday sights and ordinary objects of the
immanent human world a transcendent entelechy of call and answer. A neon
sign is as fitting a vehicle for hurling a question to the heavens as a prophet's
trumpet; a nighttime sky may still shine forth its astral reply. For Ganin, as for
Nabokov, the mere recollection of First Love refreshes the eye, so that it may
once more experience the rapture of the first time, when every sign seemed a
summons, every bright detail of life a numinous hieroglyph that contained its
own radiant and vivid reality.

It is this reality that First Love preserves against the enforced exiles and
heartless liquidations of history, against the brute (because imaginatively un-
transfigured) materiality of the world. Gilbert Murray's *Five Stages of Greek
Religion,* itself a work of modern imagination, quotes the "beautiful defense of
idols" by Maximus of Tyre, which states what I can only fitfully recapture: the
grace of idols, in allowing us to know, to love, and to remember—often through
laughter, more commonly beyond tears—the days that having been, can be no
more:

> God Himself, the father and fashioner of all that is, older than the Sun or
> the Sky, greater than time and eternity and all the flow of being, is un-
> namable by any lawgiver, unutterable by any voice, not to be seen by any

eye. But we, being unable to apprehend His essence, use the help of sounds and names and pictures, of beaten gold and ivory and silver, of plants and rivers, mountain-peaks and torrents, yearning for the knowledge of Him, and in our weakness naming all that is beautiful in this world after His nature—just as happens to earthly lovers. To them the most beautiful sight will be the actual lineaments of the beloved, but for remembrance's sake, they will be happy in the sight of a lyre, a little spear, a chair, perhaps, or a running-ground, or anything in the world that wakens the memory of the beloved. Why should I further examine and pass judgment about Images? Let men know what is divine . . . let them know: that is all. If a Greek is stirred to remembrance of God by the art of Pheidias, an Egyptian by paying worship to animals, another man by a river, another by fire—I have no anger by their divergences; only let them know, let them love, let them remember.[5]

The modern idols fashioned by First Love need not, then, resound as hollowly to us as they did to Nietzsche, armed with his hammer. The modern mind, conscious of the flight of divinities, confronted with the "death" of God and the silencing of his creative Word, has nonetheless retained its need, if not for God, for the godlike power Ganin feels in resurrecting his lost world and recapturing the enchantments of First Love. For, as I have been arguing, the enchantments of First Love *are,* as Beckett says, the enchantments of reality. These enchantments unite all idolaters, Greek or Egyptian, ancient or modern, in paying homage to the beauty of the world. Murray poetically intuits the profound connection between pagan idolatries and love's reliquaries. The lover, like the pagan idolater, venerates those beings and cherishes those experiences that bring us into immediate relation with the ultimate ideals and mysterious potencies of human life. Fostering this connection to the deepest and highest sources of existence is what gives First Love its religious character—and fascination. First Love discloses to us the invisible bonds or ligatures that unite us each to each. This etymological sense of the religious serves to connect the imaginations of First Love to the larger and more generous affections of the novelistic imagination, intent on keeping watch over a more common, pitied, and loved humanity. The idols fashioned out of our first and abiding affections give form to this inchoate sense of the divinity of the Beloved, to this mysterious intuition of the Other as a totality of marvels and, as Nabokov warns, evil. These idols voice our questions about the deeper meaning and ultimate significance of life, questions whose answers lie in our own hearts to provide. For though First Love asks the same questions, issues the same summons, we will each respond according to the dictates of our own heart and our own times. That is why our solution, however belated, to the riddle of First Love, to the enigma of our deepest affections and our relation to the mysterious necessities that govern our existence, will appear to us as original, as essentially ours alone. We will be true moderns, graced with discovering love's ancient secrets, as if for the first time.

APPENDIX

# HARDY'S
# PRIMAL SCENE

NO OTHER NOVELIST is as ingenious as Hardy in staging a "primal" scene in which the "mouth of Oedipus" speaks, but with no ordinary human voice. The mistaken, substituted, interpolated, and repeated kisses that evoke the primal scene of Hardy's erotic dramas are invested with such narrative and psychological importance because they mark the moment when the amatory quest, the pursuit of the well-beloved, is both fulfilled and metamorphosed. It is at this fateful moment that the idealized figure of the beloved is replaced by the existential other, who possesses a unique history, a history which includes the body's memories of *other* kisses, other caresses, or in Tess's case, other lovers. What we witness in these scenes is startling, and here is a partial inventory of their enactments:

1. In *Desperate Remedies,* Hardy's first extant novel, the young heroine, Cytherea Graye, spends the night in the bed of her benefactress, Cytherea Aldclyffe. The repetitive play of names suggests an ingenious allegory of desire in this night where kisses and confessions are alternately solicited and bestowed. The elder woman demands, "Why can't you kiss me as I can kiss you?"[1] In asking this question, Cytherea Aldclyffe becomes the prototype of the Hardy-esque lover who demands a rapturous embrace in which what is given is received in equal measure. But this exchange, when transacted, only reveals a vexatious asymmetry. The experienced lover craves ardent caresses, but from a virginal body. When the young Cytherea Graye confesses to having been kissed, she is bitterly reproached for betraying feminine "honour": "I thought I had at last found an artless woman," Aldclyffe laments, "who had not been sullied by a man's lips, and who had not practised or been practised upon by the arts which ruin all the truth and sweetness and goodness in us" (116). The man's kiss despoils feminine truth and depredates female moral substance ("the sweetness and goodness in us"). The desirable body is likened to an unvisited paradise, "nullo cultu" (44); once the natural splendors of this idolized body are revealed to be products of human cultivation, the beloved diminishes in value and is often banished from the affections.

This desire for an Edenic body bespeaks a dream of precedence, the imperial demand to be "first" and reap the pleasures of an untutored nature. Once the experienced lover fails to possess this innocence, images and metaphors mix and merge, signaling erotic distress. So Cytherea Aldclyffe castigates her namesake, enlisting her own familiarity with the figures of the erotic tradition to express and warrant her disgust. Her misery alters her perception of the beloved's body, degraded now from a meadow *nullo cultu,* a Virgilian paradise, to a trodden thoroughfare, traveled by all comers: "But a minute ago, and you seemed to me like a fresh spring meadow—Now you seem a dusty highway" (116).

This world-transforming moment of disillusion ("But a minute ago you seemed . . .") is bitter, but not yet desperate. Desperation describes the lover's state when forced to choose between two seemingly unworthy objects, or, as in *The Return of the Native,* between two women beyond compare! The sensationalism of *Desperate Remedies* magnifies the lurid consequences of Aldclyffe's anguished decision to sacrifice her "daughter" to her illegitimate son, Aeneas Manston. So obsessive is the bond between mother and son that it deranges the "novelistic" orderings (or pretenses) of Hardy's fiction. Lawrence thought that a crude morality accounted for the generic indecisions and instabilities of Hardy's early work: "The tiresome part about Hardy is that, so often, he will write neither a morality play nor a novel" (*P.,* 435). People are not people in these novels, Lawrence observes, but types, and he classifies these as Murderer and Adulteress, Virgin and Virgin Knight. What Lawrence does not remark is that in *Desperate Remedies* the mother and son are the adulteress and murderer, while the figure of the "lawful wife" is the victim of their passions. Aeneas Manston inherits his mother's propensity for sexual errancy, which leads, in the logic of the morality play, to complete villainy. *The Return of the Native* ingeniously recasts this relation, which in both instances is a murderous one, with greater cunning and indirection. Filial piety is dramatized in more complicated registers during the rescue scene of *The Return of the Native,* where Clym is explicitly likened to Aeneas as he carries his mortally stricken mother on his back. Now the son is a more complex figure—both self-indicted "murderer" (matricide through neglect) *and* knight of deliverance.

2. In *A Pair of Blue Eyes,* the Virgin Knight is a writer, which may explain why this drama of desire takes a more Proustian turn, or, more accurately, why Proust was so interested in this novel. The writer is Henry Knight, a man proud of his refinements and ignorant of his nature, who sports a beard that shadows his mouth, "hiding the real expression of that organ under a chronic aspect of impassivity." Knight's mouth, once exposed, bespeaks a susceptible but dainty erotic palate. Knight's friend and future rival, Stephen Smith, reminds his mentor of the touchstone he proposed for detecting the true charms of female fascination—the kiss without "grace" or art:

> "You remember what you said to me once about women receiving a kiss. Don't you? Why, that instead of our being charmed by the fascination of their bearing at such a time, we should immediately doubt them if their

confusion has any *grace* in it—that awkward bungling was the true charm of the occasion, implying that we are the first who has played such a part with them." (163)

What was only a dream of precedence in *Desperate Remedies* becomes a requirement in *A Pair of Blue Eyes*.

3. The erotic plot of *Far from the Madding Crowd* proceeds along a series of unstable triangulations, beginning with that opening moment when Bathsheba smiles at her reflection in the mirror, overseen by Gabriel Oak, who falls in love with her, only to lose her to Sergeant Troy, who is envied by Boldwood. But the novel's most volatile triangulation is constructed along a female axis. The competition between Fanny and Bathsheba for Troy's affection culminates in that somewhat ghoulish scene of sexual triumph, "Fanny's Revenge." The coffin containing the bodies of Fanny and her child are brought to Bathsheba's house, where Troy discovers them: "What Troy did was to sink upon his knees with an indefinable union of remorse and reverence upon his face, and, bending over Fanny Robin, gently kissed her, as one would kiss an infant asleep to avoid awakening it." In this kiss, Troy's histrionic sexuality, symbolized by his dazzling swordplay, is sublimated into the extravagant gestures dear to Victorian sentiment. The kiss of the now prostrate Troy unites attitudes of remorse, reverence, and protectiveness, and so consecrates his love for the Victorian child-woman, Fanny Robin.

Bathsheba reacts to this private act of obeisance and belated tenderness by summoning up her reserves of womanly sublimity: "All the strong feelings which had been scattered over her existence since she knew what feeling was, seemed gathered together into one pulsation now" (326). In a kind of reverse *sparagmos,* strong feelings which had been scattered over Bathsheba's existence are now collected in one supreme moment of emotion, a cathartic and imperious pulsation that disintegrates into a cry that is both appeal and demand: "Don't—don't kiss them! O, Frank, I can't bear it—I can't! I love you better than she did: kiss me too, Frank—kiss me! *You will, Frank, kiss me too!*" (326). The commanding power of Bathsheba's demand contrasts dramatically to "the *childlike* pain and simplicity of this appeal from a woman of Bathsheba's calibre and independence" (emphasis added). Bathsheba's wail thus unexpectedly recalls the cries issuing from a child's frustrated mouth.

4. Tragic triangulation becomes the comedy of substitution in *The Hand of Ethelberta*. The most piquant scene of sexual confusion in the only urban comedy Hardy attempted occurs when the suitor for Ethelberta's hand mis-

takes—in the dark—the hand of Ethelberta's younger sister, Picotee, for Ethelberta's and plants a reverential kiss upon it. Subsequent events pardon this act of misaffection as a lawful substitution, when, in fact, this suitor later marries Picotee.

5. In *A Laodicean,* a study of sexual indecision and anomie, a kiss is an occasion of "a profanation without parallel" (255). De Stancy, the aristocratic suitor for the hand of the heroine, Paula Power, takes the role of the King of Navarre in a performance of *Love's Labors' Lost.* In the fifth act, de Stancy delivers the appointed lines, "Rebuke me not for that which you provoke / The virtue of your eye must break my oath." Paula, who acts the Princess, is about to reply when de Stancy stops her mouth by interpolating—where she should speak—the sonnet from the first act of *Romeo and Juliet,* which concludes, of course, with a literal and figurative play on *kiss.* This brazen act of interpolation becomes, for the novel's Virgin Knight and bourgeois suitor, Somerset, a scandal of public lovemaking, while the dark villain justifies the boldness of his substitution as the ingenuity of passion. De Stancy enjoys, as his reward, "a very sweet and long drawn osculation . . . followed by loud applause from the people in the cheap seats" (255). In Hardy's satirical staging of this public profanation, the kiss, as always the site of substitution, is appreciated by the spectators in the cheap seats, a class irony that is consciously played against Paula's private *prédilection d'artiste* for the decayed (but dissolute) aristocracy.

6. In *The Well-Beloved,* an "impulsive" rather than calculated kiss inaugurates Hardy's satire on the erotics of idealism. Avice Caro greets the returned native, Pierston, with a kiss that is answered by an involuntary wince. His wince initiates Avice into sexual knowledge by alerting her to those social codes of kissing that discriminate between the fond kiss, "the practice of childhood," and the "vulgar" kiss that "a young man from London and foreign cities, used now to the strictest company manners" would find offensive.[2] The usages of childhood must be renounced in the face of this profound alteration, not in Avice, but in the social perceptions of her body: "I—I didn't think about how I was altered," pleads the chagrined girl. "I used to kiss him and he used to kiss me before we went away."

Avice, "for the first time become conscious of her womanhood, as an unwonted possession which shamed and frightened her" (31), is thereby inducted into a sexual plot in which she (actually, her body) will be valued according to the fluctuations of male desire. This plot begins with a presentiment, later to be confirmed, that "the migratory, elusive idealization of what he [Pierston] called his Love . . . was going to take up her abode in the body of Avice Caro" (31). What for Avice was the shameful body becomes for Pierston the "temple" or fleshly tabernacle for the visitings of that vagrant goddess of love whose epithet, Cytherea, was a name shared by the heroines of *Desperate Remedies.* Hardy's sophisticated satire on the logic and language of idealism and his sensationalist tale of desperate passions both concern dreams of precedence that play out as dramas of restless ambition and desperate substitutions.

The original Avice, whom Pierston deserts, does appear to house the goddess he seeks, a divinity who genetically migrates across three generations of Avices. Pierston successively falls in love with Avice, her daughter, and her granddaughter. In this elaborate fantasy, Hardy presents a complicated account of the Shelleyanism he could never completely forsake, no matter how much it tormented him. Pierston's obsession with the privileged female body in which the incorporeal essence of immutable Love incarnates itself is linked to his own vocation as a sculptor who accommodates and immortalizes mortal forms, "those seedlings, grafts, and scions of beauty, waiting for a mind to grow to perfection in" (201). The fashioning of human images thus derives from the compulsions—the compulsions to repeat—of the idealizing imagination or perfecting mind. Pierston's erotic pursuits are brought to an end by an illness that brings "death to the sensuous side" of his mind, thus releasing him from his enslaving obsession but also depriving him of the motives, as well as the motifs, of his art. In the 1897 book version, this erotic fantasy concludes on a moral note. Pierston, who deserted Avice's grandmother, is deserted by her for the son of his former wife, who has herself returned after years of absence to nurse Pierston back to physical and psychological health. This amatory quartet that spans three generations is the novel's final figure of emotional and moral distributions. The narrator observes: "And so the zealous wishes of the neighbours to give a geometrical shape to their story were fulfilled almost in spite of the chief parties themselves" (204). The pursuit of ideal love finds its final sardonic expression in the zealotry that interprets an erotic fantasy as a demonstration in moral geometry.

But the 1892 version of Hardy's "Sketch of a Temperament" assumed a more sinister shape; it devolved into a recessive narrative line that culminated in a "lurid awakening" (248). In this ending, the female body reveals itself in a new—and ultimate—aspect: the grotesque. The once-beloved wife, Marcia, unveils her time-weathered face and exposes herself to Pierston's penetrating gaze:

> The face which had been stamped upon his mind-sight by the voice, the face of Marcia forty years ago, vanished utterly. In its place was a wrinkled crone, with a pointed chin, her figure bowed, her hair as white as snow. To

> this the once handsome face had been brought by the raspings, chisellings, stewings, bakings and freezings of forty years. The Juno of that day was the Witch of Endor of this. (248)

Time's revenge is wrought in the face of the beloved; the wrinkled crone that so astonishes Pierston's mind-sight contrasts horribly to his own sculptures of studied perfection. The face, rendered imperishable by idealizing memory, now becomes a "parchment-covered skull." The face as idol, stripped of its fleshly adornments, worked upon by the chiselings of Time, the sculptor, becomes the face as death's-head. Pierston, in hysterical laughter, applauds this droll ending to his "would-be romantic history" (249).

## NOTES

### PREFACE

1. Georg Simmel, "The Adventurer," in *On Individuality and Social Forms,* edited with an introduction by Donald Levine (Chicago: University of Chicago Press, 1971), 190.

2. René Girard's theory of "triangular desire" is the most subtle, yet still abstract, instance of the kind of analysis I have in mind. See his *Deceit, Desire, and the Novel,* trans. Yvonne Freccero (Baltimore: Johns Hopkins University Press, 1965), 1–52.

3. Simmel, "The Adventurer," 191–92.

4. Ibid., 195.

5. Ibid., 197.

6. Jane Austen, *Emma* (New York: W. W. Norton & Co., 1972), 285. All further citations will be to this edition and noted in the text.

7. Jane Austen, *Persuasion* (New York: Penguin Books, 1965), 37. All further citations will be to this edition and indicated in the text.

8. Simmel, "The Adventurer," 196.

### CHAPTER ONE

1. Though my interest is in First Love not primarily as a feature of popular culture, but as the myth of distinctly and highly *literary* character, I would remark the existence of "First Love" anthologies directed to an audience whose tastes are similar to those of Joyce's Gerty MacDowell. Gay Head's collection of fourteen "warm and glowing stories" of First Love, issued by Scholastic Book Services in 1963, may serve as an instructive example. Assembling stories written primarily in the mid-1950s and intended for classroom use, this anthology, which underwent six printings, may suggest, for social historians, the connection between high culture and the burgeoning of adolescent literature that occurred in the postwar years; that is, after the waning of the modernist literary movement in its grand phase.

2. Samuel Beckett, *Endgame* (New York: Grove Press, 1958), 18.

3. Samuel Beckett, *Murphy* (New York: Grove Press, 1957), 32. All further citations will be to this edition and noted in the text.

4. Walter Benjamin, "On Some Motifs in Baudelaire," *Illuminations* (New York: Schocken Books, 1977), 163.

5. Ibid.

6. Peter Brown, in his remarkable history of the body and society in early Christianity, explains the crucial place this etymology held in Origen's vision of the soul's creation. "What we now call the 'soul,' the subjective self, was merely the result of a subtle cooling off of the original ardor of the primal, deepest self: the 'spirit'. . . . Compared with the fiery spirit that flickered upward, always straining to sink back into the primal fire of God, the conscious self was a dull thing, numbed by the cold absence of love." Peter Brown, *The Body and Society: Men, Women, and Sexual Renunciation in Early Christianity* (New York: Columbia University Press, 1988), 163.

7. *Dante and His Circle,* trans. Dante Gabriel Rossetti (London: Ellis and Elvey, 1982), 30. All further citations will be to this edition.

8. Gertrude Stein, *Q.E.D.,* in *Fernhurst, Q.E.D., and Other Early Writings* (New York: Liveright, 1971), 69.

9. Friedrich Nietzsche, *Twilight of the Idols* and *The Anti-Christ,* trans. R. J. Hollingdale (New York: Penguin, 1968), 73. I cite Nietzsche in particular here because his assault on modern idols, which he characterized as "philosophizing with a hammer," is important, in ways both crucial and yet antagonistic, to my understanding of modern idolatry.

10. Søren Kierkegaard, *Either/Or,* vol. 2, trans. Walter Lowrie (New York: Anchor Doubleday, 1959), 43.

11. James Joyce, *A Portrait of the Artist as a Young Man* (New York: Penguin, 1986), 65. All further citations will be to this edition.

12. Kierkegaard, *Either/Or* 2:38.

13. Ibid., 41.

14. Franco Moretti, *The Way of the World* (London: Verso, 1987), 4.

15. Ibid., 9.

16. Ibid., 12.

17. Søren Kierkegaard, *Either/Or,* vol. 1, trans. David Swenson and Lillian Marvin Swenson (New York: Anchor, 1959), 231–32.

18. Kierkegaard, *Either/Or* 2:237.

19. For Moretti, too, the episode is "almost never meaningful *in itself.*" It "does not refer back to an objective necessity, but to a subjective possibility." The episode becomes meaningful "only when someone—in the *Bildungsroman* usually the protagonist—*gives it meaning*" (*Way of the World,* 45).

20. Kierkegaard, *Either/Or* 2:40.

21. Ivan Turgenev, *First Love,* trans. Isaiah Berlin (New York: Penguin, 1975), 1.

22. M. M. Bakhtin, "The Bildungsroman," *Speech Genres and Other Essays,* trans. Vern W. McGee, ed. Caryl Emerson and Michael Holquist (Austin: University of Texas Press, 1986), 19.

23. Ibid., 21.

24. Georg Lukács, *The Theory of the Novel* (Cambridge: M.I.T. Press, 1971), 56.

25. Virginia Woolf, *Mrs. Dalloway* (New York: Harcourt, Brace and World, 1925), 3. All further citations will be to this edition.

26. James Joyce, "Notes by the Author," in *Exiles* (New York: Viking, 1962), 113. All references will be to this edition.

27. In a long footnote to his general interpretation of the Wolf Man's dream, Freud comments on the dream's most peculiar and outstanding feature—that the wolves are depicted as motionless: "This contradicts the most striking feature of the observed [primal] scene, namely, its agitated movement, which, in virtue of the postures to which it led, constitutes the connection between the primal scene and the wolf story." Freud maintains that it is only through such reversals that the latent material or repressed fantasy can elude the dream-censorship and find its way into the dream. Sigmund Freud, "From the History of an Infantile Neurosis," *The Standard Edition of the Complete Psychological Works of Sigmund Freud,* vol. 17, ed. James Strachey (London: Hogarth Press, 1975), 44n.

28. James Joyce, *Ulysses* (New York: Vintage, 1986), 601. All further references will be to this corrected text.

29. Kierkegaard, *Either/Or* 1:256.

30. Theodor Adorno, *Minima Moralia: Reflections from Damaged Life,* trans. E. F. N. Jephcott (New York: Schocken Books, 1978), 78.

31. Ibid.

32. Ibid., 79.

33. Ibid.

34. *Letters of James Joyce,* vol. 2, ed. Richard Ellmann (New York: Viking Press, 1966), 191–92.

35. See George Bernard Shaw, *The Quintessence of Ibsenism,* in *Shaw and Ibsen: The Quintessence of Ibsenism and Related Writings,* ed. J. L. Wisenthal (Toronto: University of Toronto Press, 1979). Shaw, with his usual argumentative genius, proclaims that the "quintessence" of Ibsenism "is that there is no formula." Nevertheless, he reads the plays as illustrations of Ibsen's "thesis that the real slavery of to-day is slavery to ideals of virtue" (197). Shaw's introductory remarks, particularly his diatribe against the "womanly woman," are pertinent to my necessarily cavalier summary of nineteenth-century sexual idealism. One remark might serve, however, to remind us of the flavor of Shavian satire on "all the idealist abominations that make society pestiferous": "The truth is, that in real life a self-sacrificing woman, or, as Mr Stead would put it, a womanly woman, is not only taken advantage of, but disliked as well for her pains . . . Although romantic idealists generally insist on self-surrender as an indispensable element in true womanly love, its repulsiveness is well known and feared in practice by both sexes" (125–26). Mr. Stead is being derided for the views expressed in his review of "The Diary of Marie Bashkirtseff" in the *Review of Reviews* (June 1890).

36. Thomas Hardy, *A Pair of Blue Eyes* (New York: St. Martin's Press, 1975), 216. All future citations will be to this edition and so noted in the body of the text.

37. Adorno, *Minima Moralia,* 79.

38. John Ruskin, "Idolatry," from *Aratra Pentelici* in *The Complete Works of John Ruskin,* vol. 14 (New York: Society of English and French Literature, 1887), 27–28.

39. W. B. Yeats, "The Autumn of the Body," *Essays and Introductions* (New York: Macmillan, 1968), 191.

40. Ibid., 192.

41. Kierkegaard, *Either/Or* 2:43.

42. Beckett, *Murphy,* 221.

43. Ivan Turgenev, *Spring Torrents,* trans. Leonard Schapiro (New York: Penguin, 1983), 100.

44. It is this law that spiritually oppresses Sanin, the cynical, world-weary hero of *Spring Torrents.* He is initially presented to us as a man overwhelmed by a deep "disgust for life, a *taedium vitae,* which the Romans talked about in their time." But this ancient feeling is expressed in the images of a modern pessimism:

> He did not picture life's ocean, as do the poets, all astir with stormy waves. No, he saw it in his mind's eye as smooth, without a ripple, motionless and translucent right down to the dark sea bed. He saw himself sitting in a small unsteady boat, staring at the dark silt of the sea bottom, where he could just discern shapeless monsters, like enormous fish. These were life's hazards—the illnesses, the griefs, madness, poverty, blindness . . . Here he is, looking at them—and then one of the monsters begins to emerge from the murk, rising higher and higher, becoming ever more clearly, more repellently clearly, discernible . . . Another minute and its impact will overturn the boat. And then, once again, its outlines grow dimmer, it recedes into the distance, to the sea bed, and there it lies motionless, but for a slight movement of its tail . . . But the destined day will come, and then the boat will capsize. (14)

The images depicted show the influence and reflect the dreary if inspired force of Schopenhauer's pessimism. Life's ocean is figured as the monstrous and irrational will that feeds on life. Annihilation, the capsizing of one's personal boat, is not only predictable; it is foreseen as a catastrophic rather than natural end to life.

But this pessimism is neither monolithic nor uncontestable. Its hold over the imagination is disputed and muted, although never repudiated, by the world-altering, charismatic experience of First Love. Sanin, who seeks some "occupation to drive away the thoughts that were exhausting him," begins to search his desk until he uncovers a cross—a relic, as we soon discover, of his First Love. It is a retrieval that momentarily distracts, then reanimates him: "His features showed something that was neither compassion nor joy, and yet had elements of each. It was the expression of a man suddenly confronted by someone he once loved tenderly, but has long lost sight of; someone who appears unexpectedly before him, looking exactly the same—and completely changed with the passage of time" (15). Sanin is now imaginatively less resigned to the murky depths and less willing to submit to the appointed reckonings of the destined day. A new sounding of time, one that combines compassion with joy, presents the figure of the Beloved as both identical and completely altered. In reviving her image, and remembering their love, Sanin recovers the impulse for what Bakhtin calls "creative initiative"—the impulse that renews one's life even when the world appears a chaos of unintelligible change or bleak decay.

45. W. B. Yeats, "Moods," *Essays and Introductions,* 195.

46. Kierkegaard, *Either/Or* 2:234.

47. Florence L. Walzl, "Gabriel and Michael: The Conclusion of the 'The Dead,'" *James Joyce Quarterly* (Fall, 1966), reprinted in *Dubliners,* ed. Robert Scholes and A. Walton Litz (New York: Viking, 1962), 239. All further citations will be to this edition.

48. Lukács, *Theory of the Novel,* 84.

49. Lukács, of course, maintains that irony need not fill that space, being concerned with another task—"the self-correction of the world's fragility." Within the "new perspective" of irony, "inadequate relations can transform themselves into a fanciful yet well-ordered round of misunderstandings and cross-purposes, within which everything is seen as many-sided, within which things appear as isolated and yet connected, as full of value and yet totally devoid of it, as abstract fragments and as concrete autonomous life, as flowering and as decaying, as the infliction of suffering and as suffering itself" (*Theory of the Novel,* 75).

50. W. H. Auden, "A Literary Transference," in *Hardy: A Collection of Critical Essays,* ed. Albert J. Guerard (Englewood Cliffs, N.J.: Prentice-Hall, 1964), 139.

51. *The Letters of D. H. Lawrence,* vol. 1, ed. James Boulton (Cambridge: Cambridge University Press, 1979), 477.

52. D. H. Lawrence, *Lady Chatterley's Lover* (New York: Bantam, 1968), 4.

53. Kierkegaard, *Either/Or* 1:248.

## CHAPTER TWO

1. Quoted and translated by V. S. Pritchett, *Balzac* (New York: Harmony Books, 1973), 59.

2. Ruskin, "Idolatry," 20.

3. Ibid., 23.

4. Ibid., 27.

5. Ruskin, "Imagination," in *Aratra Pentelici,* 39.

6. Ruskin, "Idolatry," 37.

7. Francis Bacon, *The New Organon,* in *Francis Bacon: A Selection of His Works,* selected by Sidney Warhaft (New York: Macmillan, 1965), 336.

8. Ibid., 343.

9. Ibid., 348.

10. Nietzsche, *Twilight of the Idols,* 21.

11. Ibid., 69.

12. Ibid., 43.

13. Ibid., 37.

14. "It is a question," as Juliet Mitchell explains the infant's narcissistic fascination with the face, "of finding the self-image in the image of another, and of constituting the self in that discovered image." Juliet Mitchell, *Psychoanalysis and Feminism* (New York: Vintage, 1975), 39. Mitchell is summarizing D. G. Winnicott's theory, itself derived from Lacan's notion of the "Mirror-Phase," that the baby seeks its self-image in the mother's facial expressions, which in turn reflect the baby's behavior.

15. This psychological insight lies behind the "pure aestheticism" of Basil Hallward's paradox, in *The Picture of Dorian Gray,* that "every portrait that is painted with feeling is a portrait of the artist, not of the sitter. The sitter is merely the accident, the occasion." Wilde's idea that the face serves as an occasion for depicting the artist's inner life comports with Kierkegaard's insistence that the occasion is the accident necessary to actualize an inner determination. One might hazard to suggest that the reason the title alludes to a picture, rather than a portrait, is that Dorian Gray never progresses beyond an infantile stage of moral development, and so mistakenly seeks in his own ageless face what he ought to have sought in the harmonies of first love—the inner determinations of moral beauty. This helps explain why Wilde, the flamboyant aesthete, chose to write a novel about a morally repulsive, criminal beauty.

16. Samuel Beckett, *Molloy* (New York: Grove Press, 1955), 222.

17. Moran, who contends that even "a simple déjà vu seemed infinitely beyond my reach," nevertheless manages to recover the linguistic echo of the maternal and originary plenitude of Molloy's vagrant being when he claims to hear "in his soul perhaps" the distant soundings of the "proper" name:

> After all perhaps I knew nothing of mother Molloy, or Mollose, save in so far as such a son might bear, like a scurf of placenta, her stamp.
>
> Of these two names, Molloy and Mollose, the second seemed to me perhaps the more correct. But barely. What I heard, in my soul I suppose, where the acoustics are so bad, was a *first* syllable, Mol, very clear, followed almost at once by a second, very thick, as though gobbled by the first, and which might have been oy as it might have been ose, or one, or even oc. And if I inclined towards ose, it was doubtless that my mind had a weakness for this ending, whereas the others left it cold. (112; emphasis mine)

*Mol,* it appears, is the omnivorous first syllable that initiates the linguistic, hence narrative, sequence. Eventually it will reabsorb all differentiating and classificatory "suffixes" into itself. Moran, interestingly, confesses to a mental weakness for the *-ose* ending, indicating plenitude ("full of"), as against *-one* (indicating "derived from") or *-oc* (indicating "reverse of"). The plenitude of the maternal semiosis, rather than the displacements of the paternal symbolic, is, for Beckett, the preferred linguistic and onto-logical closure.

18. Thomas Hardy, *The Return of the Native* (London: Macmillan, 1969), 79. All further citations will be to this edition and will appear in the text.

19. Cf. Pater's famous and astounding description of the Mona Lisa's visage as the symbol of the modern idea:

> All the thoughts and experience of the world have etched and moulded there, in that which they have of power to refine and make expressive the outward form, the animalism of Greece, the lust of Rome, the mysticism of the middle age with its spiritual ambition and imaginative loves; the return of the Pagan world, the sins of the Borgias. She is older than the rocks among which she sits; like the vampire, she has been dead many times, and learned the secrets of the grave; . . . (Walter Pater, *The Renaissance* [New York: Oxford University Press, 1986], 80)

20. Hardy's allusion to this Hamletian complexion as a sign of the "textual" first appears in his portrait of Henry Knight, the writer of *A Pair of Blue Eyes,* whose "brow and face . . . were getting sicklied o'er by the unmistakable pale cast." *A Pair of Blue Eyes,* 159.

21. D. H. Lawrence, "Study of Thomas Hardy," *Phoenix* (New York: Vintage, 1975), 416. All further citations will be noted *P.,* followed by page numbers.

22. Thomas Hardy, *Far from the Madding Crowd* (New York: St. Martin's Press, 1979), 44.

23. Roland Barthes, "The Face of Garbo," *Mythologies,* trans. Annette Lavers (New York: Hill and Wang, 1983), 57.

24. Thomas Hardy, *Tess of the D'Urbervilles* (New York: W. W. Norton, 1979), 127.

25. Ingmar Bergman, *Cahiers du cinéma,* October 1959.

26. George Orwell, *1984* (New York: New American Library, 1981), 220.

27. Kierkegaard, "Diary of the Seducer," *Either/Or* 1:424.

28. Ibid., 425.

29. Kierkegaard, "The Immediate Stages of the Erotic," *Either/Or* 1:128.

30. D. H. Lawrence, *The Virgin and the Gypsy* (New York: Vintage, 1975), 9.

31. D. H. Lawrence, "A Propos of *Lady Chatterley's Lover,"* in *Lady Chatterley's Lover,* 351.

32. Thomas Hardy, *Jude the Obscure* (London: Macmillan, 1974), 173. All further citations will be noted in the text.

33. Pater, *The Renaissance,* 6.

34. E. M. Forster, *Howards End* (New York: Vintage Books, 1962), 206. All further citations will be to this edition and noted in the text.

35. Forster's Hellenism is most evident in his nostalgia for a genuine Panic, not the panic and emptiness of the Wilcoxes, but the salutary terrors that Bacon thought to have been allegorized in the figure of Pan, whose sisters were said to be the Fates:

In the Panic terrors there is set forth a very wise doctrine; for by the nature of things all living creatures are endued with a certain fear and dread, the office of which is to preserve their life and essence, and to avoid or repel approaching mischief. But the same nature knows not how to keep just measure, but together with salutary fears ever mingles vain and empty ones; insomuch that all things (if one could see into the heart of them) are quite full of Panic terrors, human things most of all, so infinitely tossed and troubled as they are with the superstition (which is in truth nothing but a Panic terror), especially in seasons of hardship, anxiety and adversity. (Bacon, "Pan, or Nature," *Selection,* 284)

36. E. M. Forster, *Maurice* (New York: W. W. Norton, 1987), 246.

37. Gilbert Murray, *Five Stages of Greek Religion* (New York: Columbia University Press, 1925), 100–101.

## CHAPTER THREE

1. Raymond Williams, *The Country and the City* (New York: Oxford University Press, 1973), 198.

2. Sigmund Freud, "The Uncanny," *The Standard Edition of the Complete Psychological Works of Sigmund Freud,* vol. 17, ed. James Strachey (London: Hogarth Press, 1953), 245.

3. The regime of self-silencing is observed, sometimes willingly, sometimes with bitter resentment, by the women of the novel. Thomasin, as Maiden and Wife, is the ideal quiet woman, afraid to question her husband about money, about his whereabouts, and fearful that if she does speak, harshness, rebellion, or desertion might ensue—a fear confirmed on the wild night of 6 November. Mrs. Yeobright withdraws into a stony, reproachful silence when her son, against her wishes, continues his courtship of Eustacia. Eustacia's silent operations are conducted as habitual spying; her telescope and hourglass are the material props of her militant romanticism, the first symbolizing the flight of time and the transience of all human passion, the second linked to the voyeurism that, as J. Hillis Miller has shown, is such an integral part of Hardy's "drama of fascination" and its "system of looks." J. Hillis Miller, *Thomas Hardy: Distance and Desire* (Cambridge: Harvard University Press, 1970), 119 and passim. Miller argues generally that "Many poems or scenes in [Hardy's] fiction are organized as a system of looks" (119), but it is Miller's specific observations on the "motif of the fascinated spy" (121) within this "system of looks" that concern me here.

4. Sigmund Freud, "The Theme of the Three Caskets" (1913), *Standard Edition* 12:298.

5. Ibid., 299.

6. Ibid., 301.

7. Robert Graves, *The Greek Myths* (New York: George Braziller, 1957), 48–49. Graves points out earlier that the Three Fates, like the Three Hesperides, "are the Triple Moon-goddess in her death aspect" (34).

8. Eustacia's fantasies of being delivered from her torpid existence are specifically compared to the insubstantial forms imprisoned in Thomson's "Castle of Indolence." News of Clym's imminent arrival, and folk speculation on the possible "harmony between the unknown [Clym] and herself," affect her depressed mind like "the invading Bard's prelude in the 'Castle of Indolence,' at which myriads of imprisoned shapes arose where previously appeared the stillness of a void" (127). This allusion suggests the following allegory of relations: The "depressive" Eustacia is an indolent imaginer whose "inner world," populated by inert phantasms, would be animated by the arrival of Clym, who in Eustacia's fantasy assumes the guise of the Knight of Art and Industry, son of Selvaggio and Poetry and minion of those gods who love the rural. In one of Hardy's most relentless ironies, it is the very realization of Eustacia's fantasy that displeases and maddens her. Clym becomes a true (but not *her*) Knight of Industry and heir to Selvaggio when he labors as a furze and turf cutter on the heath.

9. Thomas Hardy, *A Laodicean* (New York: St. Martin's Press, 1979), 297. All further references to this novel will be to this edition and noted in the text.

10. Karen Horney, "The Problem of Female Masochism," in *Feminine Psychology* (New York: W. W. Norton, 1967), 218 and passim.

11. Early reviewers of the novel immediately detected the thematics of Bovaryism. An unsigned 1878 review in the *Athenaeum,* for example, directly remarks that "Eustacia Vye belongs essentially to the class of which Madame Bovary is the type." The reviewer expressed his regret that "this is a type which English opinion will not allow a novelist to depict in its completeness," and that Hardy had "wasted his powers in giving what after all is an imperfect and to some extent misleading view of it." *Thomas Hardy: The Critical Heritage,* ed. R. G. Cox (New York: Barnes and Noble, 1970), 47.

12. Van Ghent remarks that Tess's lament "Why am I on the wrong side of this door?" voices "all the hopelessness of her cultural impasse." She reads Tess's stabbing of Alec D'Urberville as the moment of Tess's "heroic return through the 'door' into the folk fold, the fold of nature and instinct, the anonymous community." Dorothy Van Ghent, *The English Novel* (New York: Harper and Row, 1961), 209. Van Ghent, despite her usually scrupulous memory for detail, misremembers one critical scene in *The Return of the Native* that is worth remarking. She argues that with the exception of "one instance—when Mrs. Yeobright has a far walk to Clym's cottage, and Clym, unforewarned, fails to meet her, and she turns away—the heath in *The Return* exists peripherally and gratuitously in relation to the action" (201–2). I would question the innocence of this narrative synopsis, in which "unforewarned" and "fails to meet" give us an inaccurate version of the incident. For a more elaborate and extremely suggestive discussion of thresholds and barriers in Hardy's fiction, see Elaine Scarry, "Work and the Body in Hardy and Other Nineteenth Century Novelists," *Representations* 3 (Summer 1983): 90–94.

13. Sigmund Freud, "Repression," *Standard Edition* 14:153. Freud elaborated this simile in a footnote: "I have merely to add that I must set a permanent guard over the

door which I have forbidden this guest to enter, since he would otherwise burst it open" (153n). Eustacia's face at the window takes on forbidding meaning if read as a symbolic agent (a "guard over the door") for this process of repression.

14. I am indebted to Sam Hynes for remarking the importance of this prefix, and Hardy's likely knowledge of it, in the naming of Alderworth. His helpful remarks on this issue, as on the general organization of this essay, have been inestimably valuable.

15. Quoted in Richard Little Purdy, *Thomas Hardy: A Bibliographical Study* (London, 1954, 1968), 26.

16. Michael Millgate, *Thomas Hardy* (New York: Random House, 1971), 140.

17. See the appendix for a partial, somewhat clinical description of the role the kiss plays in Hardy's dramas of erotic devastation.

18. John Paterson notes that in the early editions, Clym's mouth is described as having passed "into the phase more or less rendered in studies of Laocoön." The explicit comparison to Oedipus, which Paterson attributes to Hardy's attempt at "underlining the parenticidal theme of the novel," appears in the edition of 1895. I also take the revision as a sign that Hardy wanted to concentrate attention on the oedipal structure of his tragedy, not to confuse it by referring, in a self-consciously ornamental way, to classical figures as a generic group. See John Paterson, *The Making of the Return of the Native* (Berkeley: University of California Press, 1960), 104–5. The reference to Laocoön reappears in similar configurations in Hardy's last fiction, *Jude the Obscure,* where the allusion is more apposite to Jude's quite different tragedy of virility. When Jude must abandon his hope for the "intellectual and emulative life," he awakens into the "hell of conscious failure," a realization of diminished being that is visible on his face: "If he had been a woman he must have screamed under the nervous tension which he was now undergoing. But that relief being denied to his virility, he clenched his teeth in misery, bringing lines about his mouth like those in the Laocoön, and corrugations between his brows."

19. Melanie Klein, "The Oedipus Complex in the Light of Early Anxieties" (1945), in *Love, Guilt, and Reparation* (New York: Delacorte Press, 1975), 266.

20. Melanie Klein, "Psychogenesis of Manic-Depressive States" (1935), *Love, Guilt, and Reparation,* 266.

21. Paterson's research shows that the "mother-son motif was not contemplated in the original program of the novel," and that the details "which ultimately justified her heart-broken incrimination of her son—the presence of his furze-hook and brambles on the doorstep—were not initially incorporated in the text." See Paterson, *The Making of the Return of the Native,* 67–68.

22. Melanie Klein, "Love, Guilt, and Reparation" (1937), in *Love, Guilt, and Reparation,* 308.

23. Thomas Hardy, *The Life and Work of Thomas Hardy,* ed. Michael Millgate (Athens: University of Georgia Press, 1985), 20.

24. Robert Gittings, *Young Thomas Hardy* (New York: Penguin, 1980), 245 and

passim. One further observation on Hardy's imaginative orderings of his recollected past: Gittings speculates on "the tremendous impact" of Hardy's Christmas visit and return home in 1896, which marked the first meeting of his wife and his mother. Gittings remarks that "to the end of his life he [Hardy] never commented on the relationship between the two women." But Gittings comments on it in the following suggestive terms: "Family tradition has it that Emma was not well received, and with Jemima Hardy's strong character and possessive attitude this seems likely enough. . . . The real importance of the visit was that he once more renewed acquaintance with his greatest creative inspiration, the homestead and the Heath beyond it." The product of this renewed acquaintance was, of course, the novel, which, as Gittings notes, bears little family resemblance in its tone or setting to the "Sturminster Idyll" of the Hardys' first years of marriage. Gittings proposes a "simple reason" for the surprising absence of "brooding menace" that visitors to Dorset discover when viewing the original of Hardy's "haggard Egdon": "The simple reason is that Hardy, returning to it this Christmas after an interval of very different experience and in the company once more of his powerful mother, saw the place, in his novelist's imagination, as it appeared to him as a child." See Robert Gittings, *The Older Hardy* (New York: Penguin, 1980), 23–24.

25. Thomas Hardy, *Under the Greenwood Tree* (New York: St. Martin's Press, 1975), 169.

26. Images as well as fears of impaling and mutilation so characteristic of the "femininity phase" recur later on that wild night of 6 November as Thomasin crosses the heath, her babe in arms. But in this depiction of the "good mother," whose name echoes Hardy's own, the paranoid fantasy of an aggressive and persecutory Mother Nature is revealed as just that—a fantasy—in the appropriate form of the pathetic fallacy. Thomasin endures the storm-lashings whose "individual drops stuck into her like the arrows into Saint Sebastian" (433). This baffling comparison, which is soon repudiated as psychologically inappropriate to her particular character, is pertinent only to Hardy's allegory of women; it assigns Thomasin a typological niche in a hagiographic order symmetrically opposite to that of Eustacia's infidel Turk, felled by St. George. But Thomasin, who lacks the Promethean imagination of victimization, never mythologizes her afflictions: "To her there were not, as to Eustacia, demons in the air, and malice in every bush and bough. The drops which lashed her face were not scorpions, but prosy rain; Egdon in the mass was no monster whatever, but impersonal open ground."

27. Melanie Klein, "Love, Guilt, and Reparation," 311.

28. Ibid., 313.

29. Melanie Klein, "Early Stages of the Oedipus Conflict" (1928), in *Love, Guilt, and Reparation,* 194.

30. Thomas Hardy, "For Conscience's Sake," in *Life's Little Ironies and A Changed Man* (London: Macmillan, 1977), 47.

31. The novel's final gesture also aspires to atone, but with more ambivalent results. A blinded Clym, newly apprised of his prophetic vocation, preaches on a morally unimpeachable subject: honor thy mother. This text, as A. Walton Litz remarks, is taken from the passage in Kings in which Solomon apparently accedes to, while actually countermanding, Bathsheba's desire that Adonijah be given Abishag the Shunammite as bride. Solomon responds to his mother's "small petition": "Ask on, my mother; for I will not say thee nay" (1 Kings 2:19–20). Litz observes the irony that Solomon puts his brother to death. See A. Walton Litz, "Introduction," *The Return of the Native* (Boston: Houghton Mifflin, 1967), xiii.

### CHAPTER FOUR

1. Hardy's stubborn literalism made this female hegemony quite personal in the initial version of the novel. Jude was originally given the surname "Head," the name of Hardy's paternal grandmother, who as a girl lived in a village called Fawley in Berkshire. In the completed version a place-name replaces a family name, yet the matriarchal nomenclature is preserved and lingers in the surname of Hardy's beleaguered heroine, Sue Bridehead.

2. Quoted in Florence Emily Hardy, *The Later Years of Thomas Hardy* (London: Macmillan, 1930), 43.

3. *The Woodlanders* is perhaps Hardy's most complicated allegorical narrative of the ill-fated yearning of natural man (represented historically in his declining phase by the deliquescent Winterbourne) for the transcendent character of Grace. Grace Melbury is a heroine who is explicitly linked to Shelley's Cythna, radiant figure for that "power, that from its object scarcely drew / One impulse of her being." But Grace, "the bright shade of some immortal dream," is a divine idea with a local habitation. As an embodied character she is concerned with more parochial issues—as, for example, whether to submit to her fascination for the cosmopolitan "stranger," Fitzpiers, or be faithful to her first—and provincial—love for Winterbourne. It is easy to see even from this crude statement of her dilemma that the figure of Grace, however divinely inspired, is naturalized by Hardy as a figure for the gratuitousness of human passion. Thus the cynical pertinence of the scene in which Fitzpiers first sees Grace and, admiring her literally from afar, begins quoting "The Revolt of Islam." Fitzpiers, somewhat clinically, remarks that the woman he poetically praises is an arbitrary figure for his own projection, and that in loving her he is "in love with something in my own head, and no thing-in-itself outside it at all." Fitzpiers is paraphrasing Spinoza on the inescapable subjectivity of human love, but this pedantry, although ironized by Winterbourne, does not come amiss. Spinoza's claim that it is man's *essence (ipsa hominis essentia)* to feel joy in his own self-projections, however indifferently the object of his projection is chosen, diminishes neither love's joy nor its power. Thus Winterbourne, who withholds the woman's name from Fitzpiers "to hinder his knowledge of Grace," could not hinder, the narrator prophetically advises, "what was doomed to arrive and

might just as well have been outspoken." An underlying theological wit animates this scene, which takes the religious formula proposing the "natural occasions" of grace (and sin) and literalizes it. The natural presence of Grace is confirmed when, in the cryptic allegorical manner of this episode, Fitzpiers asks, "How in the name of Heaven does she come there?" and Winterbourne responds, "In the most natural way in the world. It is her home." In Hardy's allegory, Winterbourne's love for an embodied and indwelling Grace involves him in the language and contradictions of an Omnipresent Irony (foremost an irony associated with a woman's promising name). All quotations are from *The Woodlanders* (Harmondsworth: Penguin, 1983), 165–67.

4. F. E. Hardy, *The Later Years of Thomas Hardy*, 41.

5. One early allusion works to identify Jude as a student as yet *uninitiated* into the higher calling of the classical disciplines. Jude openly quotes the invocation to Horace's Centennial Hymn: "Phoebe silvarumque potens Diana!" Horace's hymn addresses the unmarried and was performed before the library-temple of Apollo, one of the immanent divinities of Sue's pantheon. Its citation here ironically observes the promise of a union, in Hardy's apt and compressed phrase, of conjunctive with holy orders. The allusion thus anticipates Hardy's bitter joke on the compatibility of two sacred callings—of marriage and of divine letters—and also reminds us of the Apollonian vocation, conspicuous in its misuse or absence in this novel, of spiritual as well as bodily healing.

6. Stendhal, *Love,* trans. Gilbert Sale and Suzanne Sale (New York: Penguin, 1975), 49n.

7. F. E. Hardy, *Later Years of Thomas Hardy,* 37.

8. Those interested in the personal aspects of this collaboration and in Hardy's talent for cultivating spiritual affinities will be interested in Gittings's account of the Hardy-Henniker alliance, and in the volume of their correspondence, *One Rare Fair Woman: Thomas Hardy's Letters to Florence Henniker, 1893–1922,* ed. Evelyn Hardy and F. B. Pinion (London: Macmillan, 1972).

9. Thomas Hardy and Florence Henniker, "The Spectre of the Real," in *In Scarlet and Grey* (New York: Garland, 1977), 209–10.

10. *One Rare Fair Woman,* 33.

11. Jacques Derrida, *Dissemination,* trans. Barbara Johnson (Chicago: University of Chicago Press, 1981), 212.

12. Derrida contends that *entre/antre* participates in as it recapitulates the double logic that governs the very edge of being:

> At the edge of being, the medium of the hymen never becomes a mere mediation or work of the negative; it outwits and undoes all ontologies, all philosophemes, all manner of dialectics. It outwits them and—as a cloth, a tissue, a medium again—it envelops them, turns them over, and inscribes them. This nonpenetration, this nonperpetration (which is not simply negative but stands between the

two), this suspense in the antre of per-penetration is, says Mallarmé, *perpetual:*
*"This is how the Mime operates, whose act is confined to perpetual allusion without*
*breaking the ice or the mirror: he thus sets up a medium, a pure medium, of fiction."*
(215)

The mime besotted with Hymen, who outwits all manner of ontologies and dialectics,
is Pierrot, the eroteleptic clown whose mimes rehearse, as in Gautier's *Pierrot Post-*
*hume,* "the supreme spasm of infinite masturbation." The "folly" of Jude's idealizing
love bears an uncomfortable, if poignant, resemblance to Pierrot's aspiration to a
union with Colombine.

13. Millgate, *Thomas Hardy,* 410.

14. Ibid., 320.

15. Sigmund Freud, "The Taboo of Virginity," *Standard Edition* 11:197.

16. Ibid., 204.

17. Ibid., 205.

18. Nietzsche, *Twilight of the Idols,* 69.

### CHAPTER FIVE

1. D. H. Lawrence, *The Rainbow* (New York: Penguin, 1981), 487. All further
citations will be to this edition, which I recommend for the excellent notes provided
by the editor, John Worthen.

2. D. H. Lawrence, *St. Mawr* (New York: Vintage, 1953), 3.

3. Nietzsche, *Twilight of the Idols,* 34.

4. *The Letters of D. H. Lawrence,* vol. 2, ed. George J. Zyaturk and James T. Boulton (Cambridge: Cambridge University Press, 1981), 165.

5. Daleski advises that "it is desirable to read *The Rainbow* with the Hardy essay
in mind." See H. M. Daleski, *The Forked Flame* (London: Faber and Faber, 1965), 85.
Mark Kinkead-Weekes has written the definitive essay on the genesis of the novel and
the importance of the Hardy essay to Lawrence's innovative experiments with novelistic form. See Kinkead-Weekes, "The Marble and the Statue: The Exploratory Imagination of D. H. Lawrence," in *Imagined Worlds,* ed. Maynard Mack and Ian Gregor (London: Methuen, 1968), 371–413.

6. Lawrence, *Lady Chatterley's Lover,* 14.

7. Foucault attributed the desperate transgressions of modern man to his inhabit-
ing "a world now emptied of objects, beings, and spaces to desecrate." Sexuality thus
becomes the last frontier in which to enforce a doctrine of limits. Since Foucault's
*kerygma* is currently more fashionable than Lawrence's, let me invoke Foucault here, if
for no other reason than to emphasize his reactionary contention that "never did sexuality enjoy a more immediately natural understanding and never did it know a greater
'felicity of expression' than in the Christian world of fallen bodies and of sin":

We have not in the least liberated sexuality, though we have, to be exact, carried
it to its limits: the limit of consciousness, because it ultimately dictates the only

possible reading of our unconscious; the limit of the law, since it seems the sole substance of universal taboos; the limit of language, since it traces that line of foam showing just how far speech may advance upon the sands of silence. Thus, it is not through sexuality that we communicate with the orderly and pleasingly profane world of animals; rather, sexuality is a fissure—not one which surrounds us as the basis of our isolation or individuality, but one which marks the limit within us and designates us as a limit. (Michel Foucault, *Language, Counter-Memory, Practice* [Ithaca: Cornell University Press, 1977], 30)

The limits Foucault delineates, Lawrence, with less precision but more resistance, also draws. Foucault's terms of argument appear, in a more colloquial, even jolly, register, in Lawrence's diatribe against Freudianism, *Psychoanalysis and the Unconscious.* Lawrence satirizes Freud as the explorer who ventures into "the hinterland of human consciousness" only to return laden with strange booty: "gagged, bound maniacal repressions, sexual complexes, faecal inhibitions, dream-monsters." These *lusus naturae* of the unconscious are, Lawrence claims, the bastard spawn of mental consciousness. See D. H. Lawrence, *Psychoanalysis and the Unconscious* (New York: Vintage, 1970), 4–5 and passim.

8. Lawrence, *The Rainbow.*

9. Boulton, ed., *Letters of D. H. Lawrence* 1:45.

10. *The Rainbow* is more antinomian than Joyce's *Ulysses* in sublimating and internalizing the epos of wandering. There is little actual travel in this novel, and when the Brangwens venture beyond the immediate vicinity of the marsh, they are traveling *away* from the realm of natural or civic wonders and toward the dreary precincts of "Zolaesque tragedy."

11. Kinkead-Weekes, "The Marble and the Statue," 384.

12. Northrop Frye, *The Great Code* (New York: Harcourt Brace Jovanovich, 1982), 5.

13. Graham Hough, who notes that the romantic theme of unfulfilled aspirations initially concerns the Brangwen women, wonders why the theme "disappears" and "we are concerned with Tom Brangwen's marriage to a Polish lady." This formal discrepancy can be explained only if we see the Brangwen women as prehistorical beings, and Lydia as the woman who, precisely because she has been deeply scarred by history, marks the point at which history in the novel can be said to begin. She nevertheless represents those vital transfusions of outside forces into the Brangwen blood that will save them until they fulfill their destiny—to create the individual, self-responsible woman, Ursula. See Graham Hough, *The Dark Sun: A Study of D. H. Lawrence* (New York: Octagon, 1973), 60.

14. In the famous foreword to his *Collected Poems,* Lawrence identifies "the actuality, the body of feeling" of his early poetry with the voice of the demon, a voice distinct from the voice of the "commonplace me." "The demon of poetry is not easily loved: whereas the ordinary me is." My claim is that Lawrence, as a novelist, realized

that the demon is legion. He is everywhere, even in the likable, complacent world and speech of the commonplace. See *D. H. Lawrence: The Complete Poems,* collected and edited by Vivian de Sola Pinto and F. Warren Roberts (New York: Penguin, 1982), 28.

15. See particularly Daleski, *The Forked Flame,* 85–106, for an orgiastic reading of the visit to Lincoln Cathedral that takes into account the counterclaims of Leavis and John Middleton Murry. Kate Millett is the most prominent exponent of the theory that Lawrence suffered from womb envy. See Kate Millett, *Sexual Politics* (New York: Avon, 1971), 258–59.

16. D. H. Lawrence, *Sons and Lovers* (New York: Penguin, 1982), 175.

17. Anaïs Nin, *D. H. Lawrence: An Unprofessional Study* (Chicago: Swallow Press, 1964), 26–27.

18. Thomas Mann, "Freud and the Future," *Essays* (New York: Vintage, 1957), 320. Mann tries to salvage a future for the modern world by appealing to the example of the ancients, for whom "Life, at any rate significant life—was . . . the reconstitution of the myth in flesh and blood."

19. John Worthen points out in his notes that this chapter "was singled out in the Court Proceedings against *The Rainbow* as particularly objectionable." *The Rainbow,* 566.

### CHAPTER SIX

1. Zyaturk and Boulton, eds., *The Letters of D. H. Lawrence* 2:670.

2. D. H. Lawrence, *Women in Love* (New York: Penguin, 1983), vii.

3. D. H. Lawrence, "Foreword to Collected Poems," *The Complete Poems,* 850.

4. Lawrence, *Psychoanalysis and the Unconscious,* 15.

5. Matthew Arnold, *Culture and Anarchy,* ed. J. Dover Wilson (Cambridge: Cambridge University Press, 1961), 82.

6. In one of his last poems, Lawrence insisted on a distinction between killing and murder that he blurs here.

> Killing is not evil.
> A man may be my enemy to the death,
> and that is passion and communion.
> But murder is always evil
> being an act of one
> perpetrated upon the other
> without cognisance or communion.
> (*Collected Poems,* 715)

Yet the determination of fatefulness remains consistent throughout Lawrence's thought; the fateful act, whether in creating or in destroying life, whether in loving or in killing, involves the element of passionate communion. Nothing fateful ever takes place "without cognisance or communion."

7. The chapter headings were not added until the 1921 edition by Martin Secker. But I have interpreted them, and I believe Lawrence intended them, as a kind of shorthand denoting the generic and thematic codes of the realist novel. "Sisters" was, of course, also the original working title of the narrative that grew into Lawrence's double novel. See Boulton, ed., *The Letters of D. H. Lawrence* 1:550.

8. Lawrence, "Prologue to *Women in Love,*" *Phoenix II: Uncollected, Unpublished, and Other Prose Works by D. H. Lawrence,* ed. Warren Roberts and Harry T. Moore (New York: Viking, 1968), 104.

9. Zyaturk and Boulton, eds., *Letters of D. H. Lawrence* 2:90.

10. Nietzsche, *Twilight of the Idols* and *The Anti-Christ,* 94.

11. See M. M. Bakhtin's account of the novel's indebtedness to "judicial-rhetorical" categories of judgment and vindication in his essay "The Bildungsroman." This issue is treated, briefly, in my preface. See also Bakhtin's "Forms of Time and of the Chronotope in the Novel" in *The Dialogic Imagination,* trans. Caryl Emerson and Michael Holquist (Austin: University of Texas Press, 1981), 64–258.

12. Lawrence wrote Lady Ottoline Morrell, the model for Hermione, that she belonged to a "special race of women: like Cassandra in Greece, and some of the great women saints. They were the great *media* of truth, of the deepest truth: through them, as through Cassandra, the truth came as through a fissure from the depths and the burning darkness that lies out of the depth of time." See Zyaturk and Boulton, eds., *Letters of D. H. Lawrence* 2:297.

13. Ibid., 183.

14. Margot Norris's fine reading of Lawrence's *St. Mawr* is more suspicious of the atavistic nature of Lawrence's totemism, and more skeptical of his ontology generally. See Margot Norris, "The Ontology of D. H. Lawrence's *St. Mawr,*" in *The Beasts of Modern Imagination* (Baltimore: Johns Hopkins University Press, 1985), 170–95.

15. Lawrence's language has been the focus of many recent studies. Among the most notable are Michael Ragussis, *The Subterfuge of Art* (Baltimore: Johns Hopkins University Press, 1978), 178–225, and Garrett Stewart, "Lawrence, 'Being' and the Allotropic Style," *Novel* 9 (1976): 217–42.

16. J. G. Frazer, *Totemism and Exogamy,* vol. 4 (London: Macmillan, 1910), 6.

17. Ibid., 18.

18. Claude Lévi-Strauss, who dismisses the "totemic illusion" as a false category of cultural description, attempts to "get to the bottom of the alleged problem of totemism" through the structure of "so-called totemic representations." In totemic representations, "*it is not the resemblances, but the differences, which resemble each other.*" See Claude Lévi-Strauss, *Totemism,* trans. Rodney Needham (Boston: Beacon, 1963), 77.

19. Emile Delavenay's *D. H. Lawrence and Edward Carpenter: A Study in Edwardian Transition* (New York: Taplinger, 1971), 190–235, assesses the influential presence of Carpenter's ideas on sexuality and society in Lawrence's concept of "bloodbrother-

hood." See also Samuel Hynes's "Science, Seers, and Sex," in *The Edwardian Turn of Mind* (Princeton: Princeton University Press, 1968), 132–71, for a more comprehensive account of the new attitude toward sexuality fostered by the work of Carpenter and Havelock Ellis.

20. Frank Kermode, *The Sense of an Ending: Studies in the Theory of Fiction* (London: Oxford University Press, 1967), 25.

21. Lawrence's choice of the name *Gudrun* for his demonized heroine illustrates how the symbolic import of his chosen names actually interferes with his visionary project. Gudrun is the daughter of the Niebelung king who lures Sigurd from Brynhild through the necromantic powers of her magic drink. She enters *Women in Love,* that is, as a *known* type of the husband-slayer. She is committed, it seems to me, to the unfolding of this murderous plot. Her name itself suggests the deep duplicity of her nature, which Lawrence identifies with the deep duplicity of the modern, ironic consciousness. *Gudrun* is a deadly linguistic compound; the name combines the Old Norse *guthr,* 'war', with *runa,* 'close friend'. She thus linguistically stands for the double treachery of war and personal betrayal.

22. Zyaturk and Boulton, eds., *Letters of D. H. Lawrence* 2:662.

23. Ibid., 544.

24. Ibid.

25. Kermode, *The Sense of an Ending,* 63.

26. See Søren Kierkegaard, *The Concept of Irony,* trans. Lee M. Capel (Bloomington: Indiana University Press, 1968), 337.

27. Ragussis first commented on the importance of this passage to the novel's "open-ended" ending; see *The Subterfuge of Art,* 224.

CHAPTER SEVEN

1. Marcel Proust, *Remembrance of Things Past,* vol. 1, trans. C. K. Scott Moncrieff and Terence Kilmartin (New York: Vintage, 1982), 447.

2. *Letters of James Joyce,* vol. 1, ed. Stuart Gilbert (New York: Viking, 1966), 129.

3. As moody as Lawrence's fiction is, it retains a remarkable emotional consistency throughout. Though I believe Lawrence to be a true novelist, in some ways incomparable in his depictions of human behavior and the comedy of social manners (his portraits of Gertrude Morel, Hermione, and Gudrun guarantee his stature as a subtle delineator of the social character of the modern self), he never relaxes his narrative voice long enough to let go with something like resigned laughter. Angelic Lawrence is much too urgent in his satire to admit of the refreshing and debunking force of laughter, which for Bakhtin is one of the main reflexes of the novelistic reworking of the world. To understand how his satire can be so free of low comedy, one probably should invoke Baudelaire, who, in examining the essence of laughter, advances "this curious proposition":

The Sage, that is to say he who is quickened with the spirit of Our Lord, he who has the divine formulary at his finger tips, does not abandon himself to laughter save in fear and trembling. The Sage trembles at the thought of having laughed; the Sage fears laughter, just as he fears the lustful shows of this world. He stops short on the brink of laughter, as on the brink of temptation. There is, then, according to the Sage, a certain secret contradiction between his special nature as Sage and the primordial nature of laughter. (Baudelaire, *On the Essence of Laughter,* reprinted in *Comedy: Meaning and Form,* ed. Robert Corrigan [New York: Chandler and Co., 1955], 450)

Angelic Lawrence, "quickened with the spirit of Our Lord," must have felt the full force of this contradiction between his gospel of blood consciousness and his fear of the primordial nature of laughter as a reminder of the body's fallen and degraded state. The regaining of paradise is not through laughter, a sign of misery and the child of woe, but through the peace of an undivided consciousness.

4. Richard Ellmann, *James Joyce* (London: Oxford University Press, 1982), 156.

5. Brenda Maddox, *Nora: A Biography of Nora Joyce* (London: Hamish Hamilton, 1988), 42.

6. Frederic Jameson, *The Political Unconscious* (Ithaca: Cornell University Press, 1981), 26.

7. Ellmann, ed., *Letters of James Joyce* 2:237.

8. Joyce, *Portrait of the Artist as a Young Man,* 252.

9. Ellmann, ed., *Letters of James Joyce* 2:237.

10. Ibid., 49.

11. James Joyce, *Stephen Hero,* edited with an introduction by Theodore Spencer (London: Jonathan Cape, 1944), 33.

12. Harold Bloom, Introduction to *James Joyce's Ulysses,* ed. Harold Bloom (New York: Chelsea House, 1987), 6.

13. This is Harold Bloom's incomparable description.

14. T. S. Eliot, " 'Ulysses,' Order, and Myth," *Dial,* 1923, reprinted in *Selected Prose of T. S. Eliot,* ed. Frank Kermode (New York: Harcourt Brace Jovanovich, 1975), 177.

15. D. H. Lawrence, "Surgery for the Novel—or a Bomb," in *Phoenix,* 217.

16. Cynthia Ozick, "The Riddle of the Ordinary," in *Art and Ardor* (New York: Knopf, 1983), 201.

17. Lukács, *Theory of the Novel,* 58.

18. Bakhtin, *The Dialogic Imagination,* 13.

19. Eliot, " 'Ulysses,' Order, and Myth," 177.

20. Gilbert, ed., *Letters of James Joyce,* 170.

21. Philippe Sollers, *Théorie des exceptions* (Paris: Gallimard, 1986), 89 (my translation).

22. Fritz Zenn, "Righting *Ulysses,*" in *James Joyce's Ulysses,* 120–21.

23. *The New Science of Giambattista Vico,* ed. and trans. Thomas Bergin and Max Fisch (Ithaca: Cornell University Press, 1970), 124.

24. Gilbert, ed., *Letters of James Joyce,* 147.

25. Ezra Pound, "James Joyce and Pecuchet," reprinted in *Shenandoah* 3 (Autumn 1952): 14.

26. Roland Barthes, *S/Z,* trans. Richard Miller (New York: Noonday Press, 1974), 29.

27. *Harper's Dictionary of Music,* ed. C. Ammer (New York: Harper and Row, 1972), 128.

28. Sollers, "Joyce et Cie," *Théorie des exceptions,* 93 (my translation).

29. Roland Barthes, *A Lover's Discourse* (New York: Hill and Wang, 1978), 168.

30. Gilbert, ed., *Letters of James Joyce* 1:170.

31. Barthes, *A Lover's Discourse,* 159.

32. Diane Tolomeo, "The Final Octagon of *Ulysses,*" *James Joyce Quarterly* 10 (1973): 448.

33. *New Science of Giambattista Vico,* 90.

34. Gilbert, ed., *Letters of James Joyce* 1:170.

35. Samuel Butler, *The Authoress of the Odyssey* (Chicago: University of Chicago Press, 1967), 115.

36. Ibid., 125.

37. Austen, *Emma,* 297.

38. Barthes, *A Lover's Discourse,* 21.

## CHAPTER EIGHT

1. *Film* establishes this principle as a matter of comic argument.

*Esse est percipi.*

> All extraneous perception suppressed, animal, human, divine, self-perception maintains in being.
>
> Search of non-being in flight from extraneous perception breaking down in inescapability of self-perception.
>
> No truth value attaches to above, regarded as of merely structural and dramatic convenience.
>
> In order to be figured in this situation the protagonist is sundered into object (O) and eye (E), the former in flight, the latter in pursuit.
>
> It will not be clear until the end of film that pursuing perceiver is not extraneous, but self. (Samuel Beckett, *Film* [New York: Grove Press, 1969], 11)

We know from Beckett's vagrant fictions that the quest for "non-being" is fated to "break down in inescapability of self-perception," but here the specific filmic nature of this collapse is dramatized in a way to give a peculiar and forceful resonance to Beckett's representation of the "anguish of perceivedness." The final scene of "investment" that constitutes *Film*'s piercing denouement illustrates the dynamic nature of this encounter. The camera (E) circles O's sanctuary, then cautiously approaches his sleeping visage until it pierces his sleep and disturbs his repose. The final series of shots gives us O's (Keaton's) face captured in a look of intense and escalating horror. The anguish of this perceivedness proves unbearable. O covers his eyes and rocks himself back into quiescence. But the last shot is of Keaton's isolated eye, open, dilated, in unblinking perception. This last sustained image asserts the dominance of Eye over Self-as-Object. By so implicating the voyeuristic camera in a repressed or displaced exhibitionism of the player (E after all is part of the same "nuclear complex" as O), Beckett exposes the exhibitionism that motivates all representational and self-representational gestures. This idea is implied, although not elaborated, in his remarking that the relation depicted between E and O is a matter of dramatic convenience and has no "truth value." This dialectical reversal, which installs the dramatic in the place of the ontological, marks the Beckettian character's emergence into the Berkeleyan world where existence is a function of perception.

  2. Heinz Kohut, "Forms and Transformations of Narcissism," in *Self Psychology and the Humanities* (New York: W. W. Norton, 1985), 107.

  3. These four novellas have a publishing history worth reviewing. "First Love" was originally published in French as *Premier Amour* in 1970, at a time when Beckett's status as Nobel laureate increased the public demand for his work. The story, however, was composed in 1943 under circumstances briefly related in Dierdre Bair's biography. The other three novellas were orginally published in *Nouvelles et textes pour rien* in 1954. "The Expelled" and "The End" were translated by Richard Seaver in collaboration with Samuel Beckett, and "The Calmative" by Beckett himself. I use as my text *Samuel Beckett's Four Novellas* (London: John Calder, 1977). Individual titles are indicated in the text.

  4. Samuel Beckett, *Proust* (New York: Grove Press, 1931), 8.

  5. The phrase concludes a rather Joycean description of Belacqua's "Bollocky" masturbations, said to exemplify the "livid rapture of a Zurburban St. Onan." All these to-dos appear in Samuel Beckett, "Sedendo and Quiescendo," in *transition* 21 (March 1932): 19.

  6. Samuel Beckett, *Watt* (New York: Grove Press, 1959), 114–15.

  7. Kierkegaard, *Either/Or* 1:21.

  8. Samuel Beckett, *Malone Dies* (New York: Grove Press, 1956), 48–49.

  9. Sigmund Freud, "Inhibitions, Symptoms and Anxiety," in *Standard Edition* 20:138.

  10. "Anxiety," Freud writes in a moment of reflective pause and consideration, "is in the first place something that is felt. We call it an affective state, although we are also ignorant of what an affect is. As a feeling, anxiety has a very marked character of unpleasure. But that is not the whole of its quality." Ibid., 132.

11. Beckett, *Proust,* 49.

12. Samuel Beckett, *Premier Amour* (Paris: Minuit, 1970), 21.

13. Hugh Kenner, *Samuel Beckett: Critical Study* (Berkeley and Los Angeles: University of California Press, 1968), 25.

14. Dierdre Bair, *Samuel Beckett* (New York: Harcourt Brace Jovanovich, 1978), 257.

15. Cited by Dierdre Bair, ibid., 254.

16. Heinz Kohut, *The Restoration of the Self* (New York: International Universities Press, 1977), 291.

17. See Bair, *Samuel Beckett,* 209–10.

18. Kohut, "On Courage," in *Self Psychology and the Humanities,* 10–11.

19. Kohut, *Restoration of the Self,* 85.

20. Ibid., 76.

21. Kristeva was the first to note how Beckett's chamber pot is the profane receptacle for this "sublimated obscenity." She remarked, however, that its sacred function was linguistically signaled by Beckett's choice of the more "elegant" *vase de nuit,* with its poetic luster and its invocation of romantic night, rather than the more mundane *pot de chambre,* which clearly confines him to the chamber of his necessary but dirty doings. See Julia Kristeva, "The Father, Love, and Banishment," in *Desire and Language* (New York: Columbia University Press, 1980), 149.

22. Kohut, *Restoration of the Self,* 116.

23. Samuel Beckett, *Mercier and Camier* (New York: Grove Press, 1978), 26.

24. The *New York Times* for Tuesday 2 February 1988 reports that new research shows "direct and crucial effects on the growth of the body as well as the mind": "Touch is a means of communication so critical that its absence retards growth in infants . . . The new work focuses on the importance of touch itself, not merely as part of, say, a parent's loving presence. The findings may help explain the long-noted syndrome in which infants deprived of direct human contact grow slowly and even die." Perhaps the syndrome known as life does admit of palliation, at least for those newly born.

25. Samuel Beckett, "Assumption," in *transition* 16–17 ( June 1929): 269.

26. Given that we are contrasting empirical with imaginative precisions, let Beckett's fuller statement be recorded. "But when the object is perceived as particular and unique and not merely the member of a family, when it appears independent of any general notion and detached from the sanity of a cause, isolated and inexplicable in the light of ignorance, then and then only may it be a source of enchantment" (*Proust,* 11).

27. Ibid. Cf. Beckett's discussion of Proustian subjectivist poetics:

> Because instinct, when not vitiated by Habit, is also a reflex, from the Proustian point of view ideally remote and indirect, a chain-reflex. Now he sees his regretted failure to observe artistically as a series of "inspired omissions" and the work

of art as neither created nor chosen, but discovered, uncovered, excavated, pre-existing within the artist, a law of his nature. The only reality is provided by the hieroglyphics traced by inspired perception (identification of subject and object). The conclusions of the intelligence are merely of arbitrary value, potentially valid. "An impression is for the writer what an experiment is for the scientist—with this difference, that in the case of the scientist the action of the intelligence precedes the event and in the case of the writer follows it." Consequently for the artist, the only possible hierarchy in the world of objective phenomena is represented by a table of their respective coefficients of penetration, that is to say, in terms of the subject. (Another sneer at the realists.) The artist has acquired his text: the artisan translates it. (Ibid., 64)

28. Samuel Beckett, *Stories and Texts for Nothing* (New York: Grove Press, 1967), 119.

29. See Beatrice Marie, "Beckett's Fathers," *MLN* 5(1985):1106. Marie argues that "First Love," together with *Watt,* constitutes the "linguistic and subjective break" with Beckett's paternal heritage, which she identifies as "the patriarchal Irish family whose conflicts blocked the early narratives, Beckett and Medcalf and the Irish Protestant middle class, contemporary Irish society, which the early novels caricature through autobiographical references" (1106). She thus maintains, taking her cue from Kristeva, that "First Love" enacts a "specific linguistic and psychic murder" in which the paternal symbolic order is ritually executed. But she faults Kristeva for failing to account for this break and to expose its oedipal determinants—for failing, specifically, to account for the silent presence of Anne/Lulu, the wife-mother figure of the tale. Both Kristeva and Marie attribute to the Beckettian mother-muse a *jouissance* of which Beckett seems to have little direct experience. I will return to this point later in the essay, when I describe what precisely the mother's silence denotes. But to give my reader a clue, let me announce here that the mother's silence is decidedly not associated with an exuberant, if effaced or suppressed, *jouissance.* To hold that view is to know nothing of Beckett's own mother and to fail to appreciate the disciplined repressions of his art.

30. Samuel Beckett, "Dream of Fair to Middling Women," in *Disjecta: Miscellaneous Writings and a Dramatic Fragment* (London: John Calder, 1983), 47.

31. Kristeva, "The Father, Love, and Banishment," 149.

## CHAPTER NINE

1. Georg Simmel, "Eros, Platonic and Modern," in *On Individuality and Social Forms,* edited and with an introduction by Donald N. Levine (Chicago: University of Chicago Press, 1971), 235.

2. Ibid., 236.

3. Vladimir Nabokov, *Transparent Things* (New York: Vintage, 1989), 1.

4. Vladimir Nabokov, *Mary* (New York: McGraw Hill, 1970), 27. My thanks to Jane Miller for calling my attention to this novel and its rich relevance to my theme.

5. Gilbert Murray, *Five Stages of Greek Religion,* 100–101n.

## APPENDIX

1. Thomas Hardy, *Desperate Remedies* (New York: St. Martin's Press, 1979), 113. All further citations noted will be to this edition.

2. Thomas Hardy, *The Well-Beloved* (New York: St. Martin's Press, 1975), 30. All further citations noted will be to this edition.